EAT WHAT YOU WANT AND DIE LIKE A MAN

EAT WHAT YOU WANT AND DIE LIKE A MAN

THE WORLD'S UNHEALTHIEST COOKBOOK

STEVE GRAHAM

CITADEL PRESS
Kensington Publishing Corp.
www.kensingtonbooks.com

CITADEL PRESS BOOKS are published by
Kensington Publishing Corp.
850 Third Avenue
New York, NY 10022

Copyright © 2008 Steven H. Graham

All Kensington titles, imprints, and distributed lines are available at
special quantity discounts for bulk purchases for sales promotions, premi-
ums, fund-raising, educational, or institutional use. Special book excerpts
or customized printings can also be created to fit specific needs.
For details, write or phone the office of the Kensington special sales
manager: Kensington Publishing Corp., 850 Third Avenue,
New York, NY 10022, attn: Special Sales Department;
phone 1-800-221-2647

CITADEL PRESS and the Citadel logo are Reg. U.S. Pat. & TM Off.

First printing: July 2008

10 9 8 7 6 5 4 3 2

Printed in the United States of America

Library of Congress Control Number: 2008922838

ISBN-13: 978-0-8065-2868-7
ISBN-10: 0-8065-2868-0

This book is dedicated to my dad.
Who never gets to eat any of this stuff because
I am positive it will kill him.

CONTENTS

ACKNOWLEDGMENTS

Thanks to all the people who bought my other books, especially the first one, *The Good, the Spam, and the Ugly*. You made it much easier and cheaper and less stressful selling this one. I also wish to thank the many individuals who kept me going before I got published, reading my ridiculous websites while I moaned and bitched about how I was never going to make it. I wanted to thank all the friends who helped and encouraged me, but the list would be long and I would surely forget someone.

Doesn't matter. You know who you are.

EAT WHAT YOU WANT AND DIE LIKE A MAN

INTRODUCTION

What ever happened to real food? Does anyone remember? Can anyone remember a time when "light" wasn't spelled L-I-T-E, and we put cream in our coffee instead of "creamer," and anyone who suggested putting dyed vegetable grease on our toast would have been wrapped in duct tape and thrown off a bridge? Can anyone remember kitchen canister sets proudly featuring containers labeled not just Flour and Sugar but Grease? Does anyone remember saying the word "lard" and not trying to be funny?

I don't. I was born at around the time of the Cuban Missile Crisis, and by the time I realized I was on the planet, the insidious program of food censorship had already begun. Although oddly, not in Cuba, where people blithely sit down and eat potatoes with beef-fat gravy on top of rice. Actually, the only Cubans who eat like that are Fidel Castro and the ones living in Florida. Cuban Cubans only get food on Stalin's birthday.

By the time my parents inflicted me on the gene pool, the American public had already contracted margarine, and there was no cure in sight. Later on, we decided that eggs were evil. Oh, they looked harmless enough, but within those innocent white shells lurked a killer as deadly as nicotine; only unlike nicotine, it didn't make you look grown up or help you pick up girls. It just sat in your arteries like Helen Thomas at a White House press conference, serving no apparent purpose but to take up space and slow things down.

Doctors told us we were allowed to consume one egg per

week. I decided doctors were allowed one visit per decade. I cut back even more when I reached the age where they start sticking items up your rear end. The first time it happened, I thought it was a practical joke. But I eventually realized it was a normal part of an adult physical. Either that or my doctor was a persistent sexual predator.

I ignored the egg rule. What are you supposed to make with one egg? Egg Benedict? Scrambled egg? One egg is a tease. It's just enough egg to get your tongue aroused and ready to play. Having one egg is like lifting the hem of your girlfriend's blouse just high enough to see the hook on her bra strap and then having her father walk in in his boxers and threaten to ram his foot (with its inch-long yellow toenails) about a yard up your monkey behind.

When it comes to eggs, I like to deal in nice, round, ripe, firm yet soft and pendulous numbers. Like *six.* Pile 'em high and stick Velveeta between them.

I'll tell you what empty calories are. Licking chocolate syrup off a cocktail waitress at Motel 6.

Hmm . . . am I talking about breakfast . . . or Abu Ghraib?

For a while in the seventies, we weren't allowed to eat sugar. It would make you diabetic, and it was "empty calories." I'll tell you what empty calories are. Licking chocolate syrup off a cocktail waitress at Motel 6. *That's* empty calories. Other than that, any calorie that brings pleasure is a full calorie—a calorie to be held and embraced and loved. A calorie to be worshipped and adored. People think all calories are alike, but to me, every calorie is special. If I had time, I'd give mine names.

In the seventies we weren't allowed to eat sugar partly because it was refined. It was "unnatural." But you could eat anything that was natural. So instead of sugar, you could eat honey. Which contains—let's see—water and . . . *sugar.* And bee spit, I assume.

You were also expected to eat granola. Which is okay if you work alone or under a fume hood.

I'm pretty sure that when you ate granola, you were required to listen to John Denver, who was a big ol' nature boy named after a town in the mountains. His real name was something like Dieffenderfer, and he chain-smoked and drank and smoked dope like he was getting paid by the joint. So instead of a nice old-fashioned mountain boy, he was more like a dope-crazed, hard-drinking, ashtray-smelling city-slicker with a name straight out of an SS duty roster. But we were not concerned with details. Just the big, organic picture.

That was before we discovered Carol Brady's private tragedy, which was that she had pulled a Liza Minnelli and married a gay man. Mike Brady liked Wesson Oil, too, but he liked it on other guys.

When that insanity passed, we were told to stay away from fat. Period. Except for polyunsaturated fat, which we were supposed to suck down night and day. Of course, none of us actually knew what it was. I still don't. But Wesson Oil was loaded with it, and Florence Henderson hawked Wesson Oil. And if you can't trust Ma Brady, you might as well go ahead and suck an exhaust pipe, because there is no virtue left in the world.

That was before we discovered Carol Brady's private tragedy, which was that she had pulled a Liza Minnelli and married a gay man. Mike Brady liked Wesson Oil, too, but he liked it on other guys. So Ma was left all alone at night with Alice, who was warm and sympathetic and unattached and just a bit butch, and I think her full name may have been Alice Poundstone.

Eventually, we got to the point where mentioning lard in polite company was like escorting Golda Meir to a Gestapo ball. We became Food Nazis. We're so brainwashed that when you talk about putting lard in food, people smile tolerantly and say, "I think you meant *Crisco*."

Hell no, I didn't mean Crisco! Have you ever smelled that stuff? It smells rancid straight from the factory. Like a sheep in a sauna. People weren't meant to eat that stuff. It's like frying food in Brylcreem.

We've now reached the point where people make bad food *deliberately* because they don't want the Hitler Food Youth or whoever to catch them using real ingredients. Some idiots actually use low-fat milk in *desserts*. Hello? Desserts are *supposed* to be bad for you! That's the *point*! You wade through the other crap—the healthy crap that's supposed to keep you alive so you can live long enough to end up propped up in a Craftmatic bed in a nursing home watching the fifty-seventh season of *Survivor* while trying to remember not to talk to the flowers on the wallpaper—so you can get to the food that actually *tastes* good. Dessert is supposed to be a reward, but now that dinner resembles a long, dreary beating, dessert has become a final kick in the ass.

I remember how the Black Law Students Association at my law school used to have soul food sales to raise money. If you can't trust black people to make good food, who can you trust? I paid my five bucks and I waited in line, and they had the damn *gall* to serve me collard greens made with *turkey*. What is this, Thanksgiving? If so, I don't have a hell of a lot to be thankful for. Put some hog meat in those greens. Like God and Jimmy Dean intended.

Once you marry and give up your soul and what little backbone you may have had in the first place, your wife is going to see to it that you never have any joy again in your life.

It's high time someone stood up to the Diet Police. Sure, if you have inferior genes and everyone in your family croaks at forty, you should sit in a closet eating margarine and oat bran, but the rest of us want *real food* once in a while. Real food with *real ingredients*. People, real ingredients *taste better*. Salt, butter, lard, sugar, eggs, red meat, beer that isn't "Lite" . . . these things are not evil. And you need to learn how to cook with real ingredients so that every so often, you can sit down to a plate of historically accurate food and pretend you still have a spine.

This is especially important for men, because once you marry and give up your soul and what little backbone you may have had in the first place, your wife is going to see to it that you never have any joy again in your life, and the first thing she'll take away, after the pictures of your exes who had bigger breasts, is your food.

She may try to be subtle. She'll sneak the new plastic food in on you. You'll come home from the grocery, and you'll say, "Oh, honey, you bought Hellmann's Light by mistake." And she'll say, "Snookums, I wuv you so much I didn't want you to have a bad old coronary bypass, so I bought it for you to try, and you'll never know the difference because it tastes just as good as the regular, and if you don't shut your stinking back-talking hole and eat it, *I'll take the kids and get a lawyer and gut you and you'll be work-ing six jobs and eating bread sandwiches until we show up at your funeral to sit in a circle and pour 'I Can't Believe It's Not Butter' on your grave.*"

There's no way in hell your wife is going to cook real food for you once she gets a ring on her finger. That goes out the window right after the Stairmaster, the diet, and pretending to enjoy sex. You need to master the Art of Lard on your own. Then you'll have something decent to eat while watching improving stuff like the Stooges and *The Man Show*.

You're very lucky you bought this book. Not as lucky as me, because now I have your money and all you have is a stupid book, but still, pretty lucky. Because I am going to unlock the doors to Eternal Bliss for you.

The recipes I provide in this book are dear to my plaque-encrusted heart. They *work*. I am no chef, and I don't cook many things, but the things I cook, I cook well. People beg me for treats like ribs and brownies and biscuits. And make no mistake: if you eat this stuff regularly, you *will* die young. Unless you're already old. In which case, *laissez les bontemps rouler.*

Now please pass the pork.

CHAPTER 1
RIBS

BYPASS RATING:

(QUINTUPLE)

THE BIBLE TELLS us Eve was created from Adam's rib. What it doesn't tell us is that Eve was a second draft. According to a parchment scroll found in the ruins of an ancient barbecue stand in Nineveh, before Eve came along, Adam had another wife. Petunia. She was also made from a rib, but unfortunately for her, it was a delicious pork rib. Which led to the following totally fictional exchange between Adam and Satan.

ADAM:

(sitting under a pomegranate tree, with his arm around a hog)
This is the life, eh, baby? No work, no disease, no war, and all the salad you can eat!

PETUNIA:

Oink.

ADAM:

I'm really looking forward to lunch. I'm having fruit medley. Tree of Wisdom, Tree of Good Looks, Tree of Fun, and Tree of Washboard Abs.

PETUNIA:

Oink?

ADAM:

What? Nooo you don't look fat. Why do you keep asking that?

SATAN:

(slithering up and coiling at Adam's feet) Tho. I thee you thuckers are thtill eating thalad.

ADAM:

What?

PETUNIA:

Oink?

SATAN:

I thaid . . . I thee you thuckerth are thtill eating thalad.

ADAM:

What's wrong with salad?

SATAN:

Nothing. It'th jutht that everyone in heaven eatth barbecue.

ADAM:

What'th . . . what's barbecue?

SATAN:

Oh, it'th great. You thoak it in brine and thider vinegar, and then you rub thpiceth on it and thmoke it for hourth, and you dip it in thauthe made from tomatoeth and muthtard. All the cherubim and theraphim are eating it.

ADAM:

And cherubim and seraphim are cool?

SATAN:

Abtholutely.

ADAM:
You know what? I think I want barbecue!

PETUNIA:
Oink, oink, oink, oink, oink!

SATAN:
Great! But you'll need pork.

ADAM:
What's pork?

SATAN:
Oh . . . It'th a kind of fruit. With hooveth and brithtleth. And a turned-up thnout.

ADAM:
I think I've seen that here somewhere . . . if I could just remember.

SATAN:
Think hard!

PETUNIA:
Oink!
Adam and Satan both look at Petunia. Petunia looks at Satan and Adam. Adam lunges. Petunia bolts.

PETUNIA:
Oink! oink! oink! oink! oink! oink! oink! oink!

ADAM:
She made it under the fence! Dang!

SATAN:
You'll get her next time. Meanwhile, let'th talk about Bahamian time-thares.

Ribs are one of the few items of food that come with their own religion. All over the U.S., there are nuts who belong to various rib cults. The smokers. The grillers. The dry-rubbers. The marinaters. And each faction has sub-factions. For example, some smokers use hickory, and some use mesquite. All the factions and sub-factions make fun of each other and claim they alone are the keepers of the One True Recipe, but the truth is, they are nerds. And anyone can make great ribs. Just remember, don't ever boil them, and make sure you slow-cook them with low heat. Everything else is small strokes.

When an intolerant barbecue nut blows himself up, society benefits in countless ways, but someone has to come along behind him and clean up the mess. You can't always leave it to the crows and the neighborhood cats.

Smoking is a pain in the ass, as you may already know. But it's probably the best possible way to fix ribs. And it's the orthodox way, so you don't have to worry too much about barbecue fanatics running into your yard and blowing themselves up. I realize that when an intolerant barbecue nut blows himself up, society benefits in countless ways, but someone has to come along behind him and clean up the mess. You can't always leave it to the crows and the neighborhood cats.

I can't understand why anyone would be a tightass about barbecue. Hating people for drinking bad beer? Yes, I understand that. But barbecue? No.

Smoking does not have to be expensive, you can go to a Home Depot and get a bullet smoker for maybe fifty bucks and it will work fine. That's what people with common sense do. Now let's talk about what people like me do.

I have a bullet smoker. It's an electric Char-Broil H_2O, to be precise. I got fine results with it. Purists will whine that electric smoking isn't real. But of course they are idiots. The charcoal in a smoker doesn't contribute much to the flavor (compared to the wood), and what it does contribute may be bad. The wrong charcoal, or the right charcoal used incorrectly, can produce off-flavors. As long as you have heat and smoldering wood, it's real smoking. And you get less ashes to clean up.

The Char-Broil was okay, but it was a bitch to use. The water pan is way down under the meat, so it's hard to refill without soaking the food. And to get the thing going, you have to take it apart, line the bottom with foil, put the middle section on, put in the water pan, fill it, add the first rack, add the meat, add the second rack, add more meat, and turn it on. Really, it was like work. A thing I despise.

On top of that, it was small. I turned a twenty-two-pound turkey into a turducken and smoked it, and it barely fit on the rack. That's no good. What if you want to smoke three dozen wings or three racks of ribs? You're screwed, buddy. Give up.

So I created the Hoginator.

Now, I realize there are more impressive smokers out there. The smoking world is full of twisted lunatics, and they compete to see who can build the most grandiose, expensive, and hard-to-use smoker. I promise you that somewhere in your city, there is a nut with a fifteen-foot-long, five-thousand-dollar smoker mounted on a trailer, and this person thinks that is perfectly normal and does not see himself the way you and I do. As the Ted Kaczynski of ribs. The Unasmoker. One company built a smoker around thirty feet long, in the shape of a jet. I can't compete with psychos like that. I have to think about zoning laws.

I'll tell you something else. People like that often make crappy ribs. They're like yuppie goofs who buy Ducati leathers and *then* buy motorcycles.

I went to a fishing seminar once, and the program said something like "*Lunch catered by the award-winning Florida Ribwerks™ team!*" I don't actually remember the name of the company, but it was something pretentious like that.

I sat through the morning session, salivating over the prospect of barbecue. Then they herded us into the food area, and we all lined up behind a gorgeous stainless steel trailer-mounted smoker full of pork and chicken and beef. And I bought myself a pork sandwich. And I swear to God, if I had mixed boiled pork with the juice from a can of pork and beans, it could not have been much worse. These people didn't have the slightest clue what cooking was about.

"Award-winning" is a phrase that should always scare you. If you buy a stainless smoker on a trailer and make the worst ribs in the world, and your mommy gets out a gold star and sticks it to your forehead, *technically,* you made "award-winning ribs."

Never be intimidated by a moron with fancy equipment. The only thing that matters is your skill. Or at least your ability to read a recipe. Supposedly Alton Brown did a show where he smoked ribs in a cardboard box.

My smoker may not look like a 707, and it may not be stainless steel, but it's pretty nice and it's easy to use and I'm really proud of it. I'll tell you how I did it.

I got myself a Char-Broil Santa Fe grill. This is a boxy charcoal grill with a high capacity. It has a big door in the front you can use to add wood, and it comes with a nice porcelain grid and a stainless pan that covers the bottom. I figured it was a good box to start with.

Obviously, any metal box not coated with poisonous paint will do. But I'm feeble with tools, so I didn't want to start from zero. If you're a welder, get yourself some steel and go to town.

I got myself two smoker heating elements off the Internet. They cost around forty bucks each, and they came with dial thermostats. Very nice. I got a Dremel tool with a cutting wheel, and I cut two rectangular holes in the back of the grill, for the thermostats to go through. I put them about two feet apart, at a height that would allow the elements to sit level on the stainless pan. I threw out the cheesy chrome pan supports and I put a couple of pieces of inch-thick clay tile on the bottom of the grill. I put the pan on top of them, and I added a tiny hole on each side of each thermostat opening. Then I got stainless screws and wing nuts to go in them to hold the thermostats in place. I taped off the area around the thermostat holes, sanded it, primed it, and painted it with grill paint.

I also bought a decent grill thermometer and two huge fender washers so I could mount it in the hole to replace the pathetic "cold-ideal-hot" thermometer that came with the grill.

I got a discarded broiler pan, and I made sure there were holes in the rim at each corner. I took a sturdy coat hanger and cut four pieces of wire from it, maybe seven inches long. I made loops at the ends and permanently attached them to the holes in the pan. I made hooks at the other ends to connect to the grill surface. Now I had a water pan that I could hang in the center of the grill, between the elements and the meat. I'd say it's about two inches off the stainless pan the elements sit on. You want it to cover the elements and block all the radiant heat so it doesn't burn the meat. If it's too narrow to block the heat, when you line it with foil, you can let the foil hang off past the sides.

At that point, I was done. I now had a high-capacity horizontal smoker that would go as high as 300 degrees Fahrenheit. If I wanted, I could actually roast a turkey in this thing.

I have screwed around a lot with wood, trying to figure out the best way to use it. You can use dry wood if you wrap it in foil first and poke a few oxygen holes. You set it directly on the elements, and the foil makes it smoke instead of burning. This is a lot of aggravation, but it works. The better way is to buy wood, soak it until it sinks, and then freeze it for later use. You can't keep soaked wood at room temperature because it will rot and stink. And you can't soak it the same day you use it, because the water won't penetrate. Freezing it seems silly, but it's the best solution I could come up with. Since then I've learned that other people do it, too.

Another possibility is an external box dedicated to smoke, with an electrical element in it and a tube connecting it to the main box. I finally got off my rear end and did this, and it works great. I added some related material to this chapter, below.

Since I created the Hoginator, hardcore barbecue kooks have lectured me on the folly of using soaked wood. They say it produces thick blue smoke that contains creosote, which adds a medicinal taste to food. Sometimes you can't win for losing. You can always use small amounts of dry wood and maintain a low level of clearish wispy smoke, but it's more work because you have to watch over it.

The only thing missing from the Hoginator is a hood ornament. I keep meaning to order one. I found a nice chrome pig with wings.

The one weak spot is the weatherability. The wood Char-Broil uses on these things is crap, and it will disintegrate after a month of exposure. Literally. You can replace it with plywood or strips of weather-resistant wood like cedar, which is what I used. The finish is also subject to rusting, but you can always pressure-clean the grill and apply grill paint.

This thing will run you maybe a hundred and fifty or two hundred bucks, depending on how good you are at scrounging. It works really well, however, and you can use it about a million times between ash removals. And it looks great. It also has the benefit of symmetry. Offset smokers tend to cook fast on one side and not at all on the other. With the Hoginator's dial thermostats, you can regulate the temperature to within a few degrees, especially if you spring for a digital thermometer.

If you're a real *Tool Time* kind of guy, you can put a hole in the back of the lid and mount the probe from a twenty-dollar digital with a clock and alarm on it. If you're truly sorry and spoiled, get a digital with a wireless alarm so you can smoke ribs while you're indoors watching NASCAR.

Caution: If the wood is damp enough to conduct electricity, you may get some exhilarating shocks when you touch metal parts of the grill. Try not to kill yourself. I never said I knew anything about safety.

It ought to be obvious how you use it, but I'll be nice and tell you anyway.

1. Make sure the crap from the last time you used the smoker isn't going to cause a problem. If it is, clean it out.
2. Put a fresh layer of foil on the water pan and hang it where you want it. This is kind of a pain, but it only takes a minute. Put the pan in there, even if you don't use water, to keep the heat from the elements from burning the meat.
3. Fill the pan with water or beer or whatever. If you use beer, you can refresh it with plain old water while you smoke the meat. You don't have to go through three cases. Cheap beer tastes best.
4. Crank the heat up to a little past medium on both thermostats.
5. When the smoker is hot (I like 250°F for most things), put wood on the elements and put the meat on the grill. Adjust the thermostats as needed. You're smoking. Wow.

Go-Jo is good for getting the filth off your hands after you set the smoker up.

Okay, now what do you smoke? Anything you want. But as long as we're talking about ribs, I'll give you a really easy recipe that works great. Change it if you want. I made it up in about five minutes. It's excellent. Works on chicken, too.

3 tablespoons dry mustard
2 tablespoons sugar

> 1 tablespoon ground cumin
> 1 tablespoon paprika
> 1 tablespoon black pepper
> 1 tablespoon cayenne (chipotles ground in a coffee grinder
>   are better)
> ½ tablespoon garlic powder
> 2 tablespoons salt (1 tablespoon for brined meat)
> 2 racks pork spare ribs (or beef ribs)

I'm generally too much of a snob to use garlic powder, but it works well in a dry rub. It has a sharper flavor than fresh garlic. But snob out and use fresh if you want.

Combine all the powdered ingredients but the salt. Taste. This is your chance to mess with it. Once the salt is in there, you won't be able to taste anything else.

I use white sugar instead of brown sugar on purpose, because I want a neutral flavor that won't interfere with sauce. But if you have a neurosis about white sugar, go ahead and use something else.

If you're a nut who likes to experiment, this rub makes a good place to start. It's fairly neutral. It doesn't go too far in any particular direction. So it should be easy to build on. More heat? More cayenne. Et cetera.

The sharp, crappy taste that makes American beer the beverage equivalent of horse urine also makes it great for smoking meat.

Mix the salt in and rub this stuff all over the ribs. It will go further if you apply it using a big shaker. This recipe is just barely enough for two racks. Let the seasoned racks sit overnight if you have time. This is a hell of a lot easier than marinating because you don't have to keep them immersed. You just stick them in a flat pan and cover it with foil or plastic.

The next day, smoke them with your favorite wood, at around

250°F. Do it over a pan full of cheap American beer. The sharp, crappy taste that makes American beer the beverage equivalent of horse urine also makes it great for smoking meat.

I like to smoke the ribs for maybe half an hour to get the rub "fixed" and then brush them with beef fat or lard or bacon grease. If you put the fat on right at the beginning, it tends to smear the rub around too much.

Give the ribs at least 4 hours, turning a few times. I usually go over 5. They're ready when you think they're tender enough. Add wood as needed. Try to smoke them until they get a little dark. If they get dark early, you can quit adding wood and continue cooking without smoke. It seems like the "no creosote" fanatics like ribs that aren't darkened at all. To each his own.

Some people pull the membrane off the underside of the ribs before smoking. I never do. If you smoke them right, it gets so tender you don't even know it's there. But if it bothers you, peel it off. Barbecue princess.

You are really going to like these ribs. They're smoky and spicy and delicious. And best of all, you get none of the guilt or social consequences of smoking your wife or girlfriend.

Whatever you do, don't brine the ribs. It's pointless, and it adds salt, regardless of what misguided food nerds tell you. I brined some as an experiment, and for the rest of my life, I'm going to be hearing salt complaints from the people who ate them. Ingrates. I brine big, thick things like pork shoulders but that's about it.

You are really going to like these ribs. They're smoky and spicy and delicious. And best of all, you get none of the guilt or social consequences of smoking your wife or girlfriend.

Addendum: Hoginator Improvements

If you didn't think I was nuts already, let me remove all doubt. For a long time now, I've wanted to improve the Hoginator design by installing an external smoke generator. Unfortunately, something prevented me. And by "something" I mean "extreme, pathological laziness."

The Hoginator works well, but with the wood inside the box with the heating elements, it can be a chore making the smoke thick without raising the heat too much. And it's sort of a pain, working through the door on the front. So I fixed it. This is beautiful. If you're a man, you'll love this. If you're a woman, you'll probably cluck your tongue and ask aloud whether it's really a good idea to have this much fun when you could be doing something important like feeding bums or turning your compost or throwing out your husband's favorite pants while he's at work.

Here is what I did. As mentioned above, I had an old Char-Broil H_2O electric smoker. This thing has three sections. A bowl-shaped base with a heating element, a two-foot-tall tube containing grill racks, and a dome-shaped lid.

The old Char-Broil was looking pretty sorry, so I decided to cannibalize it. I went to a Home Depot and bought four items. First, a piece of two-inch rigid electrical conduit with a ninety-degree bend. This thing is something like two feet long, measured on the curve. Second, two end pieces for connecting it to an electrical box. These things have threads on one end to screw into a hole in the box, and the other end has openings with set screws to receive the conduit. Finally, I got a 500-watt Char-Broil charcoal starter, which is just a heating element with a handle.

I drilled a 2¼-inch hole in the top of the H_2O, near the middle so it was almost level. I drilled a similar hole in the back of the Hoginator, just below the rack. I screwed the end pieces into the holes. Then I crammed the conduit in. Finally, I stuck the charcoal starter in the existing hole for the H_2O's element. Now I had a small smoke machine behind the Hoginator with a chimney running into the Hoginator's rear side.

I bought the charcoal starter because it drew less power than the H_2O element. I didn't want to blow all my breakers.

Here's how it works. You line the H_2O's bottom with foil. You put the charcoal starter in. You dump soaked chips on the element. You close the lid, attach the conduit (no screws needed), and turn on the electricity. Within a few minutes, you have tons of gorgeous smoke.

The beauty of this is that your smoke has nothing to do with the temperature in the meat area. You can smoke at 100°F or 300°F.

It draws perfectly. The Hoginator is maybe a foot and a half higher than the smoke box, so the heat of the smoke pulls it right up the conduit.

I can't say enough about how well this works. The original Hoginator was great, but this thing kicks its ass. And if you root around for cheap parts, you don't have to spend much. You can use any type of metal box that will stand up to the heat. An old miniature Weber kettle, for example. Anything that won't fall apart.

One problem I found is that a really hot fire inside will melt the paint on the smoke box as well as the hardware that fastens the tube to the box. If you're a creosote phobic, you may want an unpainted box (I've been told small Weber kettles will take the heat), and you'll need to find some fireproof way to fasten the tube to it. Weld it, maybe.

It would be even better with a flexible chimney. You could probably find something nice at a car parts store. But again, I am quite lazy.

You might be able to run the Hoginator with one heating element instead of two once you install the smoke box, because you get a little heat from the smoke element. I guess it depends on your weather. Worth an experiment or two, because even with a small smoke element, it draws a lot of juice. If power is a problem, you can always use charcoal in the smoke box, the Hoginator, or both. Give it a shot. You won't be sorry. Probably.

Unless you get a severe shock and go into fibrillation. If that happens, try not to fall on the meat.

You can put one of these on anything you cook in, as long as it's higher than the smoke box and there's a way for smoke to escape. One of these days, I'm going to put one on a caja china. Then Cubans will openly worship me. I'll explain what a caja china is later.

Give it a shot. You won't be sorry. Unless you get a severe shock and go into fibillation. If that happens, try not to fall on the meat. After all, the survivors will still need food.

More!

As mentioned above, after I built the Hoginator, I caught crap for using heavy smoke that deposits creosote on the meat. Good God. Like I need one more thing to worry about.

It turns out wood doesn't really burn. What happens is, when you heat it, it pumps out "wood gas," which *does* burn. And unburned wood gas is full of stuff that can condense on your meat and turn it dark. This is creosote. If you have thick smoke, you have creosote. Real barbecue nuts insist on smoke that is barely visible.

Personally, I think you need some creosote to make it taste like real barbecue. *But* I was mad because people had had the gall to suggest I was wrong about something. So I decided to fix it.

Here's the deal. If you burn wood gas completely, with a big enough open flame, you get rid of most of the creosote, but you still have enough smoke flavor to make the meat taste good. It's a giant pain, however. Smoking meat over an open flame takes skill and industry, and I have neither.

You can also smoke wood over red-hot embers, which also produce almost no creosote. But it's hard to manage embers.

I tried creating an open flame inside the Hoginator smoke box, but unfortunately, certain parts of it melted and the smoke box had to be euthanized. And I came up with a solution. Behold the new smoke box!

It is an ordinary propane tank, modified to suit my whims. I had to learn how to weld in order to make this damn thing. I cut it in half, welded an inner flange around the upper lip of the bottom half (for the top half to fit over), added legs, put in a door, stuck a vent pipe on the side, welded the chimney pipe on top, added tabs and a grate made of expanded metal, and put a small expanded metal grate on the bottom to keep the coals off the metal. Then I added 1,200-degree grill paint.

This thing is much, much tougher than any grill you can buy at the mall. It's very thick and will probably outlive me. And it was cheap. Unless you count the cost of the MiG welder.

Now I can have a roaring fire in there that doesn't melt. The paint will always be a problem, because there is no such thing as affordable high-temperature paint that is completely reliable, but the grill itself won't dissolve. I can have charcoal burning in the bottom, to keep the whole works alive, and I can throw chips on the grate above, and they burst into flames.

It works well if you use small chips and throw them in pretty often. Alternatively, you could have a separate grill or box and burn wood in it, to create red-hot coals. Then you could shove them in the smoke box. If you put big pieces of wood over the charcoal, without getting the wood burning first, the wood will give off creosote before it flames up.

I miss the convenience of an electric smoke box, but it's pretty much impossible to use electricity to make smoke without making creosote.

That's about all I can do for you. Unless you're a real princess, you'll be satisfied with anything you make, following my directions.

CHAPTER 2
HOW TO SMOKE YOUR BUTT

BYPASS RATING:

(TRIPLE)

AS LONG AS I'm helping you out with barbecue, I might as well give you the lowdown on pulled pork. I used to wonder what "pulled pork" meant. I did not see how pulling on a piece of pork could make it taste better. I had similar questions concerning jerk chicken. I guess I was kind of a dumbass.

Turns out the pulling thing has nothing to do with applying tension to the meat. This would be pointless and odd. The "pulled" in "pulled pork" refers to what you do to the pork after you cook it. Pulled pork is generally made from big bony gristly knots of inexpensive pork, so carving it with a knife is pretty much impossible. So what you do is, you cook it until it starts to fall off the bone, and when you want to get it ready for serving you pull it loose with a fork or tongs.

I wish they made turkeys like that. Imagine; you'd just carry the turkey in before your waiting relatives, put down the carving knife, yank the meat off, and throw it in a pile. Pulled turkey would sure beat the normal kind, which is hacked off the bones with a dull knife by an angry drunken father.

Once your pork has been pulled, you can do all sorts of things with it. You can stir sauce into it or sauté it with onions or whatever makes you happy. It's wonderful stuff. I'll tell you how I make it.

I start with a Boston butt. Don't laugh. That's what it's called. It's a big ol' piece of pork that actually comes from the pig's shoulder. You can also use a picnic ham, which isn't really a ham. It's a slightly less desirable piece of shoulder meat.

These things come with a thick layer of fat. You'll hear people moan about how it's a sin to pull the fat off because it keeps the meat moist as it cooks. That's a load of crap. You can make moist pulled pork with the fat peeled off. What you *can't* do is make smoke and seasonings sink through an inch of flubber. And if you get a gamey piece of pork, it will be tough to get the smell out of the fat. So peel it.

The fat is hard to hold on to. Some people grip it with a paper towel and use their other hand to cut the fat free from the butt with a serrated butter knife. A Normark fillet glove (try a tackle shop) works well; it makes it harder to cut your hand and you can throw it in the washing machine. A little fat here and there, like an eighth of an inch or less, is fine; what you want to avoid is a thick, leathery covering.

You got the fat off, right? Great. Now that the barrier is gone, you need to brine the meat. Mix salt and water in a 1:16 ratio. Make enough to submerge the pork. If the pork smells "off," you can kill a lot of the stench by replacing maybe 25 percent of the salt with baking soda. If you're adventurous like me, forget the salt and use 100 percent baking soda. It works.

Use any salt but rock salt, which tastes awful. Kosher salt is a scam, but use it if it makes you happy. It takes ages to dissolve and contains exactly the same thing as ordinary salt (i.e., salt).

People argue all the time about what to put in brine. You can replace some of the water with cider vinegar, or you can use white wine, or if you're a big spender, Jack Daniel's. I prefer to use plain old salt and/or baking soda and water and worry about the flavoring later. It's easier, cheaper, and more effective.

Keep the pork in chilled brine for a day or so. Now you're ready to start cooking.

You need a horse hypodermic. Yes, you do. It's for injecting flavoring into the meat, and you can also scare the kids with it.

You need a horse hypodermic. Yes, you do. It's for injecting flavoring into the meat, and you can also scare the kids with it. I know, you went to the store and they had a chrome monstrosity with something like "Super Duper Official Cajun Flavor Injector" stamped on it. Do *not* buy one of these things. I bought one, and it cost thirty bucks, and it was a complete piece of crap. The needle kept falling off, the threads galled up when I washed it, it was impossible to keep clean, and it was a gigantic waste of money.

If you go online and look for plastic horse hypodermics (60 cc or bigger), you can get a better product than the Cajun thing for about two bucks. I buy a dozen at a time, with the thickest three-inch needles I can find. You want at least 16-gauge, but 14 is better. And get stainless, because they last forever. I got a dozen syringes and ten stainless needles for something like twenty bucks. I hope some frustrated cook finds the crook who makes the other ones and uses his own product to fill his buttocks with Tabasco sauce.

You can clean a plastic hypo several times and reuse it, although it will eventually start to stick. I think the lubrication disappears and the plunger swells. Not sure. Anyway, you can extend the hypo's life by greasing the inside with lard.

So you get your hypo and your brined pork, and you shoot the pork as full of flavoring as you possibly can. Seriously, give it fifty or more doses. All over. A lot of it will run out, but a lot will stay in, too.

Now, what to inject it with? You can use anything you want, but here's something I like. Mix equal parts honey or real maple syrup, Jack Daniel's, and cider vinegar. Season with garlic and hot sauce. Take this mixture and combine it in equal parts with your favorite barbecue sauce. A teaspoon of instant coffee, if you want. Once you're sure the flavor is right, add one tablespoon of salt per cup. Stir to dissolve. If necessary, strain this stuff so it won't clog your needle.

Once you have the meat injected, let it drain until it's dry enough for a rub to stick to, and apply the rub you read about in the previous chapter. Smoke the pork just like you did the ribs, making sure to coat it with fat once it gets going. But give it a minimum of twelve hours.

If you want to use mopping sauce, feel free, but I've had a lot of "authentic" pork made with mopping sauce and I was not impressed. I just brush the pork with the marinade a couple of times during the last hour of cooking.

You'll know when it's done because the meat will come off the bone very easily. I put the pork in a big pan and get tongs and a carving fork, and I hold the pork down with the fork and pull with the tongs. I can literally strip a ten-pound piece of pork in less than two minutes. If it takes you longer than that, your pork isn't done. Or you're completely inept. Or drunk.

Now, most people will take the pork and put it on a bun with barbecue sauce and eat it. And that's fine. But you can do better. I like to throw some onions in a skillet with a little lard and cook them clear, then toss the pork in with Jack Daniel's and some fresh garlic and maybe a quarter of a teaspoon of celery seeds. Maybe some peppers. Oh God. Yes, some peppers.

You set the JD on fire (stand back) and cook it down until

most of the liquid is gone. Sometimes I do this twice. Then throw in the celery seed and a dose of your favorite barbecue sauce, and toss the meat until it's hot and completely soaked. Burn it a little, if you want. *Now* put it between two *toasted, buttered* onion buns. And chow down.

You couldn't pay me to drink Jack Daniel's, but it's fantastic for cooking. Much better than most bourbon or sour mash whiskey.

There are other things you can do with pulled pork, but they don't really fit in with the barbecue motif, so I'll mention them later.

CHAPTER 3

BBQ BEANS, TEXAS TOAST, AND THE INEVITABLE MEL BROOKS REFERENCE

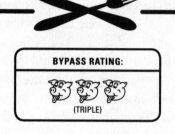

BYPASS RATING:

(TRIPLE)

WHEN YOU HAVE BARBECUE, there are certain other foods you are required by law to have with it. For example, baked beans are mandatory. Even if you don't like beans.

Of course, the law also requires the consumption of beans under other circumstances, such as when you're a cowboy. Remember *Blazing Saddles*? The amazing thing is, they filmed that scene right beside a campfire and no one got hurt. That's because the filmmaker used nonflammable stage gas. You know, like stage blood made from corn syrup and food coloring. A tank of helium was kept beside the set with a long hose and an enema nozzle. Between takes, the smaller actors kept floating away. Then of course terror would make them expel the gas, and with it the buoyancy, causing them to plummet to their deaths. Grisly, yet comical.

And the toots had to be dubbed because they came out in such a high pitch. Like hamsters sneezing.

I never particularly liked baked beans until I came up with my own recipe. My beans are so tasty, you'll almost look forward to the painful, incapacitating, houseplant-killing, wallpaper-charring, smoke detector–melting, seismograph-disturbing, Kyoto Protocol–flouting, hazmat suit–piercing, noise ordinance–violating flatulence.

I scribbled down a recipe and mixed the ingredients and chucked it in the oven, and damned if I didn't end up with the finest baked beans I had ever eaten. I figured I would just eat one serving in order to see if they were okay. It's not easy to make me go back for a second helping of baked beans; I value my sleep. But I kept going back over and over until the beans were gone and I had sauce in my hair. From licking the inside of the Pyrex.

I had to work to make it unhealthy. Beans are inherently healthy, so I screwed them up as much as possible without actually pouring rat poison on them.

This recipe is unbelievably simple to fix. Sure, you have to fry some bacon (you fat lazy piece of crap) but other than that, you just throw ingredients into a dish and turn on the oven.

I start with canned beans from the store. I think everyone does.

Bacon strips
1 large white onion (not Vidalia), diced coarsely
3 (28-ounce) cans baked beans (I like Bush's)
½ cup ketchup
1 teaspoon pepper
¼ cup molasses
3 tablespoons hot prepared mustard (Mister Mustard)
1 tablespoon brown prepared mustard (Gulden's, for example)
1 teaspoon instant coffee
1 teaspoon liquid smoke

Preheat the oven to 400°F. Fry a few strips of bacon (about 7) until they're cooked but not crisp. Dice the onion coarsely.

I know, I know, I said it was easy and then I said you had to fry bacon, and now I'm making you get off your big Jell-O behind and dice an onion. Cry me a river, butterball.

Dump everything but the bacon in a 9-inch Pyrex casserole dish. Stir. Cover the beans with the bacon. Bake for 1 hour, uncovered. You may want to pour off some excess sauce before baking. Drink it. Nobody's looking.

If you can make them even tastier and less healthy, then by all means you should.

I guessed at the bacon quantity because coverage depends on the brand and type of bacon. You want enough to cover the beans. Now you're whining because you have extra bacon and you don't know what to do with it. Yes; that's a brain-teaser all right.

You might want to reduce the pepper a little if you're not a pepper freak.

I am not kidding when I say I was stunned at how good these were. If you can make them even tastier and less healthy, then by all means you should. Get ready for the finest beans and franks ever seen outside the set of a Mel Brooks movie.

Making It Worse

1 Hillshire Farms smoked sausage (not beef)

Scared you, didn't I? You thought a big list was coming. Pansy.

I assume these things are made from pork, but I don't really know. When you start asking what's in a particular kind of sausage, you are jimmying the lid off Pandora's box. The label just says "smoked sausage," which leaves a lot of disturbing leeway. If those things are actually pork, the Hillshire Farms people should go ahead and say so. I bet I'm not the only one wondering.

Slice it. Brown it. Fry the slices in a skillet or put them in a Pyrex dish and microwave them until cooked through and browned. Serve with beans. It's best to put them in the beans before you bake. You could omit the bacon, since you now have pork in the form of sausage. But why?

That's it.

I just can't believe how well this came out. Somebody crack a window.

More: Texas Toast

Ah, Texas. How I miss her. Home of George Bush, big hair, the Alamo, and Lee Harvey Oswald. A state where it's legal to carry a semiautomatic weapon in public without a permit, *as long as you hold it in front of you where everyone can see it.* God almighty, you have to like the way those people think.

I lived in Texas for a while. I went back to college as an adult, intending to become a lawyer and serve Satan through his subsidiary, the Florida Bar. Naturally, I became a physicist instead. And then later I became a lawyer anyway. Go figure.

I don't know what drew me to physics. I mean, you'll never catch me on eBay, bidding on Brent Spiner's used underwear. And I kissed a girl once.

I went to class and sat with a lot of friendly Chinese people whose government had sent them here to get the latest tips on knocking down American missiles.

I got accepted as a graduate student at the University of Texas, so I left Florida and moved into a typical Austin apartment the size of a storage closet. Each night, I was treated to live entertainment in the form of my white-trash upstairs neighbor bouncing his live-in girlfriend off the walls. Dur-

ing the day, I went to class and sat with a lot of friendly Chinese
people whose government had sent them here to get the latest
tips on knocking down American missiles.

Things didn't work out too well. I had recently been diagnosed
with ADD, and the drugs the doctor gave me were driving me
out of my mind. In Miami, the doc had put me on Ritalin, which
is like cocaine mixed with Valium, but I had complained that
it didn't last long enough, so he put me on Cylert, an oil-based
stimulant that stays in your system for about two days.

Cylert has interesting side effects. It gives you the warm dis-
position of a sunburned badger and the sex drive of ten Charlie
Sheens plus two. It makes the contents of your pants buzz like
a palm sander, and God help anyone who tries to talk back to
you.

Sometimes I would actually up the dose if I knew I was going
to have to talk to someone difficult.

ME:

Excuse me, can I talk to you about this bill I got last week?

BLOCKBUSTER VIDEO MANAGER:

Hmm . . . seven-hundred-dollar late fee for *Ninja Midget Bond-
age Booty Fest 38.* What seems to be the problem?

ME:

Well, it was only a day late. Fee seems a little high.

BLOCKBUSTER VIDEO MANAGER:

(*tap, tap, tap, wait, look*) I'm afraid you're mistaken. You rented
that video in February, and this is November, and we still don't
have it back.

ME:

I don't mean to be argumentative, but I am certain I returned it
in February.

BLOCKBUSTER VIDEO MANAGER:

Sir, I am a highly trained video store manager and almost a high school graduate, and I believe I know how to check my own records.

ME:

Oh, you do, do you?

BLOCKBUSTER VIDEO MANAGER:

Yes, I do.

ME:

Well, that's one way of looking at it. Here's another, *You inbred, bucktoothed, cross-eyed, sister-loving mutant. I returned that video in February and for seven hundred dollars, I could have rented the midgets themselves, and I can see the tape sitting on your shelf from here, and if you don't cancel that late fee, I'm going to hold you down and pull your intestines out through your belly button. I am totally wired on prescription speed and completely capable of tearing out your carotid arteries with my teeth. You can either cancel that late fee or spend the weekend straining to pass your hard plastic name tag.*

BLOCKBUSTER VIDEO MANAGER:

Tell you what. I'll give you the benefit of the doubt.

ME:

Thanks so much.

BLOCKBUSTER VIDEO MANAGER:

What's that buzzing noise?

I had terrible problems with Cylert and all the other stimulants the doctors gave me. I developed such huge tolerances that the pharmaceutical companies changed the literature they put in the packaging for veterinary use. In the list of recommended dosages, right between "rhinoceros" and "blue whale," it now says "Steve."

I couldn't study. I couldn't eat. I couldn't sleep. I'd stay awake for three days in a row. But give me a handful of Cylert, and within hours I could have impregnated half the chicks in Austin and most of the livestock.

They put me on other things after that, none of which worked. And when the drugs affected my studies, the people in the physics department were not very understanding. Texas has a lot of people of German descent, and you can see their influence when you deal with the desk jockeys at the university.

ME:

Can I have an incomplete in Solid State I? I haven't slept since August, my last meal was a week ago, and when I close my eyes, I see reruns of *My Three Sons*.

BUREAUCRAT:

No. We can't make any exceptions for qualified students just because they have debilitating medical problems beyond their control. If we give you a break, then other students will start expecting understanding and compassion, and the first thing you know, there is panic in the streets and a total breakdown of the educational system. Plus I might have to exert my tiny pea bureaucrat brain and fill out a form.

CHIP:

Look what I found in Uncle Charlie's room!

ERNIE:

Holy cow! A nightgown! But he doesn't know any girls!

BUREAUCRAT:

What was that?

ME:

Nothing. I think I deserve a chance. As an undergrad, I got a physics degree in three years, with no background in math, and I regularly took advanced courses simultaneously with their prerequisites.

BUREAUCRAT:

Nein, mein herr. I mean, no. It makes no difference to me, you understand. This student, that student. It's just the inconvenience to the list. Now get back in your office with the rest of the Sonderkommando. I mean teaching assistants.

I gave up my dream, but I regained something few physicists will ever possess: the tiny chance that I might some day have sex with a fully conscious woman not made of vinyl.

Eventually, I left and attended law school, where I got good grades without actually doing anything. I gave up my dream, but I regained something few physicists will ever possess: the tiny chance that I might some day have sex with a fully conscious woman not made of vinyl.

I still have hopes.

I mention Texas because I'm about to tell you about a great barbecue side, Texas toast. Which, oddly, is not always on the menu at Texas barbecue joints. It's really simple, and if you have a food processor, it takes about as much effort as persuading a Frenchman not to bathe.

1 packet (1 tablespoon, more or less) yeast
1 teaspoon sugar
¾ cup water
Garlic butter (1 stick unsalted butter, with 1 clove garlic
    and ½ teaspoon salt added)
4 cups all-purpose flour (high-gluten is good)
2 teaspoons salt
2 tablespoons butter

Preheat the oven to 375°F. First, you want to activate your yeast. Do not ask me why. It always says "active" on the package, but if you don't give them a little jab in the butt, the yeast cells just lie there and you end up with a big white wheat brick. You have to wake them up. Mix a teaspoon of sugar into the water, stir until dissolved, and stir in the yeast. After 10 minutes or so, the mixture should foam up, demonstrating that the yeasts are awake and feeling romantic.

Put the garlic butter in a Pyrex container and nuke until the garlic is cooked. I like 10 minutes at the 20 per *If you have a food processor, it takes about as much effort as persuading a Frenchman not to bathe.* cent setting. Throw the dry ingredients and the 2 tablespoons of butter into a Cuisinart (you need a pretty big one) and blend until . . . blended. Use the regular blade if you can. If not, the small plastic dough blade. Pour warm water mixture in top until dough gloms into a coherent mass that sort of bounces around. Blend for 60 seconds once you hit this stage. Form into a sort of loaf shape and place in a bread pan that you have brushed with the melted butter. Brush the loaf with butter. Allow to rise until doubled in size. Punch down. Allow to rise until it comes up over the rim of the pan. Let it get really big. Bake for 25 to 30 minutes. Take it out when it looks like bread.

It's impossible to give perfect flour-to-water ratios in a cook-book, because flour's density varies due to various annoying factors. Don't worry about it. Adjust quantities as needed, until you get something wet enough to bake, but not so wet you can't handle it. Some people say to weigh the ingredients and use a 3:2 ratio of flour to water, if that helps.

You don't really have to let it rise twice, but the theory is that you get a better texture that way. You'll want to keep the bread from drying out while it rises. I usually drape a heavily buttered piece of plastic wrap over it.

If you're a big salt fan, salt the top before you bake. Speaking of salt, it's hard on yeast, so the more you use in the dough, the slower the bread will rise.

Simple, right? Now, to turn it into Texas toast, toast it on your grill. Or under a broiler set on high. Do both sides. *Then* and only then, apply the melted butter with a brush. Or if you're really sick, put the butter in a shallow dish and *dip* the bread. Jesus, did I really write that? If you want you can toast it a little more, to brown the butter slightly.

You don't have to broil or grill it. You can fry it in the garlic butter. I'd strain the garlic out first. The flavor will stay behind, and you won't end up with horrifying bits of blackened garlic on the toast.

If you're not an uptight foodie purist, you can eat this with Italian food. Dump grated cheese on the toast along with the butter, and put it back in the oven for a minute or two to melt the butter.

If you leave out the garlic, you can eat the toast with butter and jelly or whatever you want, because then it's just bread. But I guess you could have figured that out yourself.

I hate to say it, but fresh-baked garlic bread is actually better than ribs. And thanks to me and my Cuisinart, it's easier, too.

There is one more essential side to good barbecue—roasted corn. It's so simple, even a Yankee can do it. With proper training. And of course, gratuitous electric shocks.

A lot of people insist on roasting corn in the shuck. These are the same folks who put frilly covers on toilet seats and demand chopsticks at Chinese restaurants. I use foil. You can seal butter inside foil. Try that with a corn shuck. And when you use foil, you can get rid of all the silk before you cook so your guests don't have to do it at the table.

Some cookbooks say to roast corn for maybe twenty minutes, until it's barely cooked. The people who wrote these books should, themselves, be roasted in foil. And don't even get me started on boiled corn. You haven't had real roasted corn until you've had corn that is slightly browned, so it gets kind of a caramel taste.

Fresh whole ears of corn, with the shucks and silk removed
Salt
Butter and/or bacon grease

Preheat the oven to 450°F. For each piece of corn, you need a piece of foil at least four inches wider than the ear is long, and long enough to go around the ear at least one and a half times. Cut the foil out in advance with scissors; it saves time.

Place an ear of corn on a sheet of foil, at one end. Sprinkle with salt. Add at least a teaspoon-size slice of butter. You can use more if you want. You can use bacon grease in addition to or instead of butter. Truthfully, you should use a little of both.

Roll the corn up in the foil and twist the ends shut.

Place the ears of corn on the oven rack, at least half an inch apart. You should probably put a pan on the next rack down, to block radiant heat and catch leaking butter. Roast until you get a little browning on one side of each ear. I give it around 1 hour and 20 minutes.

I always take the corn out and put it all in a big bowl, with the foil still on. It will stay hot for at least 45 minutes.

Now you're pretty well set for sides. And corn is almost healthy, because of the fiber. Like my friend Tommy says, "Corn is the ball bearings of food."

Sorry I mentioned that.

CHAPTER 4
BREAKFAST AS A MIND-ALTERING DRUG

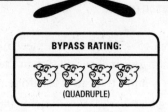

BYPASS RATING:

(QUADRUPLE)

TODAY'S LESSON: BREAKFAST. I just had a hum-dinger. I conservatively guess I took in nine thousand calories.

They say breakfast is the most important meal of the day. I don't know about all that, but it's definitely the earliest, which is a big plus. Here's what I always say: gratification delayed is gratification denied.

To make a decent breakfast, you need ham. I mean *real* ham, which means country ham. Oh, I know, you think you've had country ham because once when you were at your local diner in Bensonhurst, you had a piece of something called Virginia ham, and it was real salty, and it made you cry, and you made Mommy promise never to make you eat it again. Let me explain something to you. If you bought a piece of mass-market ham made in Virginia, odds are you bought a piece of crap not fit to be force-fed to Mullah Omar in the rec room at Club Gitmo.

A real country ham takes over a year to create. You whack off the pig's leg, rub it down really good with a thick mixture of salt and sugar and maybe a couple of other things, and you hang it in a barn while the mold and bacteria have their way with it. A year or so later, after the pig has been fitted with a prosthesis and put through physical therapy, the ham practically stinks. I wouldn't call it cured. I'd say "diseased," in a way that's *better* than cured.

By the time your ham has essentially rotted for a year, it will have developed a wonderful aroma sort of like prosciutto, only a thousand times better. When you cook it, the smell will waft through your house permeating everything with a reassuring stench that shouts "*gluttony.*" Try that with a crappy Virginia ham. Your house will smell like Slim Jims and old athletic supporters.

The mass-market hams gullible Yankees buy are typically aged only a few weeks. If you want something more like the real thing, try the website www.newsomscountryham.com. These people hang their hams over a year. I don't get a dime if you buy from them, but I'm mentioning the link anyway because Uncle Steve loves you. These hams are a lot like the ones my grandma used to cure back in Kentucky, which is to say, they're damned good.

I guess there is no reason you can't buy a young ham and hang it a few months.

Here's a sad sidelight. The Food Nazis have even put pigs on diets. Pigs used to be loaded with fat, and it made for excellent hams that made tons of gravy. But the Food Nazis genocided the good pigs and put the remaining lame pigs on diets, so now the only really good hams are made by people who raise their own hogs. Sorry about that. Find the best ham you can.

Okay, you have your ham. What do you do with it? You cut it in quarter-inch slices and fry it on medium heat. The fat around the ham will shrink and make the slices twist up; I like to cut it off and fry it beside the slices. Or I nuke it in a covered Pyrex cup for three to four minutes and use the melted fat to fry the ham. You can also reduce the warping by making little cuts across the fat.

If the salt is too much for you, put like an eighth of an inch of water in the pan and boil the ham in it for thirty seconds per side. Then toss the water.

Here's a horrid confession. Sometimes after I nuke and drain the fat, I can't resist eating the crunchy pork-rindy sort of things that remain in the Pyrex. I know it's disgusting, but that doesn't mean it isn't good.

And by the way . . . a Virginia factory ham won't make much gravy. Those hams are made from anorexic pigs. It's like trying to make gravy from an Olsen twin.

When you're done, in addition to ham, you should have something called "red-eye gravy." A lot of people mistakenly use that term to refer to cream gravy (see recipe at end of chapter), which has milk and flour in it, but in my granny's kitchen, "redeye gravy" always meant "frying grease." You add a couple of tablespoons of water to the grease, scrape the bottom of the skillet with a spatula, stir it all up, and pour it into a bowl. Use sweet coffee instead of water if you want. And by the way, as you might guess from the information provided above, a Virginia factory ham won't make much gravy. Those hams are made from anorexic pigs. It's like trying to make gravy from an Olsen twin.

Redeye gravy generally has some sort of red material sloshing around in the bottom of it. I think this is stuff that oozes out of the ham bone when you cook it. The gravy is good with or without it.

I know you're totally disgusted by now. A rotten ham, and gravy made from grease? Stifle it. This isn't a democracy. Do what I tell you.

You will now need some biscuits. But before you can have biscuits, you'll need another variety of grease. Bacon grease.

One of the bizarre beliefs held by many modern Americans is the one that says pork grease makes things taste heavy. Funny thing; the exact opposite is true. *Vegetable* grease makes things taste heavy. And bad. It doesn't blend the food's flavors the way animal fat does. The reason we switched over to vegetable grease (like Crisco) isn't that it tastes better. In fact, it's inferior. We switched over because Crisco is cheap and it allows greedy companies to save a penny or two on each pallet of cookies. Lard and other kinds of pork fat actually make baked goods lighter and fluffier. The flakiest piecrusts are made with lard. And you need pork fat to make good biscuits.

The real name is rape oil, because it's made from something called rapeseed. I guess you plant this stuff in your backyard, and a month later, in the middle of the night, a bunch of drunken Kennedys come clawing at your screen door.

A lot of people eat grease made from canola oil. Apart from sounding foreign and therefore suspicious and wrong, "canola oil" is an alias. The real name is rape oil, because it's made from something called rapeseed. I guess you plant this stuff in your backyard, and a month later, in the middle of the night, a bunch of drunken Kennedys come clawing at your screen door.

Obvious conclusion? When you buy Crisco, you're endorsing rape. That's why I use bacon grease.

To make good biscuits you need good bacon grease, and to get that you need good bacon. Some brands are no good at all. I can recommend a couple of brands that taste great. One is Roegelein's, which you can find in Texas. When I moved from Texas to Miami, I brought six pounds in a cooler I bought just for that purpose, and I also balanced a quart cup of grease on the dash of my U-Haul. For fourteen hundred miles.

If you live in the South, you could also use Hickory Sweet, which they sell in Winn-Dixie stores. Or West Virginia brand. Both very nice. Don't use country ham grease unless you cut it with lard, because it can be bitter.

Whenever you fix bacon, pour the grease into a cup or bowl

and shove it in the fridge. Eventually, you'll have a nice strategic grease reserve you can call on. When you get in a grease bind, you can always throw some bacon in a covered Pyrex dish and microwave it to get more grease.

Okay, you measure 2 cups of self-rising biscuit flour into a bowl. My favorite brand is Martha White, because it's the only brand scientifically proven to be "pea-pickin' good." Then you take a quarter cup of bacon grease, dump it in the flour, and mash it around until it's mixed in good. You want to end up with a bowl full of tiny grease-laden crumbs of flour. You can use all-purpose flour and add baking powder, baking soda, and salt, but it's a pain.

Add half a cup of milk. *Whole* milk, you wuss. Don't get me started on that gray water they call "skim." It makes horrible biscuits. If you want to use skim milk, put down my damn book, Karl Marx. I'm going to eat saturated fat and wear fur (even though I'm not gay or a professional athlete), and you can kiss my fat non-progressive ass.

God, I love beer. Beer is the humorist's friend.

Mix the milk in until you have a rollable dough.

Dump the dough onto a flat surface, roll it out until it's half an inch high, and use a glass or biscuit cutter to cut biscuits out of it. Eventually, you'll end up with a bunch of mangled dough you can't cut any more biscuits out of, so mush that up and roll it out again.

Put the biscuits on a cookie sheet. I like the two-layer ones that don't burn the bottoms of the biscuits. Smear a tiny bit of bacon grease on the top of each biscuit. Bake the whole bunch at 400°F for about 13 minutes. You should be able to tell when biscuits are done, unless you're an utter simpleton. If you're the kind of person who thinks reality TV is pretty good entertainment, hire a chimp to help with the judgment calls.

Okay, you have biscuits. You have ham. You have redeye gravy. If you really want to go nuts, make cream gravy, too. This takes some skill. I put detailed instructions at the end of the chapter. When you've done all this, you can finish up by scrambling some eggs. Or not. Do you really need them, with all this stuff on the table? Hell yes, go ahead. I'll wait. Scramble them dry, okay? Wet scrambled eggs always look like someone just blew their nose on them. I mean, hey, if you *like* a big ol' plate full of warm snot, be my guest, Karl.

Here's what you need to go with this stuff: sorghum, butter, orange blossom honey, and blackberry jam. Again, even though I'm not getting paid, let me refer you to a site: www.fatherscountryhams.com. These people just happen to sell the finest sorghum on the planet, and their jam is great, too.

I know you think you've had molasses. You thought you had had country ham, too, but now you know better, don't you? The great bulk of molasses sold in this country is garbage. I happen to know this because I come from the molasses capital of the world, which is also the ham capital of the world, which is Kentucky. People from Kentucky don't do many things right, so you better pay attention when we finally get something figured out.

If you wander into your local grocery right now, they'll probably sell you something called molasses, which actually contains blackstrap and corn syrup. Blackstrap is some sort of bitter crud that accumulates when real molasses is made. I think. Real molasses has no bitterness at all, and it certainly doesn't taste like corn syrup. If you get real Kentucky molasses, you'll slap yourself for eating crappy blackstrap all your life.

All right, you're all set. You can put the biscuits on your plate and bury them in bread gravy and eat them with a fork. You can tear them in half, put redeye gravy on the halves, put a slice of ham in the middle, and have tiny little sandwiches. You can butter the biscuits and take turns eating them with honey, sorghum, and ham. Or you can do all these things at once, which is what I just did. But unlike me, make yourself some nice coffee or iced tea; don't chase the food with three canned Dr Peppers.

The biscuits were beyond description. Because I shun all forms of vegetable grease—except in a sexual context—my biscuits are so light and fluffy they practically fly.

I didn't make eggs or cream gravy this morning, but I made all that other stuff, and now I am totally useless. I can't even get up to move the dishes. It was all I could do to stagger to the fridge, open the door, get out a bottle of homebrewed beer, carefully hand-wash a crystal Pilsner glass, pour it in, make my way back to the couch, and turn on the laptop.

The biscuits were beyond description. Because I shun all forms of vegetable grease—except in a sexual context—my biscuits are so light and fluffy they practically fly. Filled with melting butter and blackberry jam, they were lighter and flakier and more delicate and flavorful than fine French pastries. And with ham in the middle and a few drops of hot redeye gravy . . . I want to describe it, but sometimes words are such awkward tools. It would be like reattaching a finger using a backhoe.

More: Cream Gravy

Gravy. From the Latin *gravitas*, meaning "weight" or "the ability to convince swing voters to back a presidential candidate who can't pronounce 'subliminal.' " What is food without gravy? Naked. In a world ruled by reason, *all* food would be clothed with gravy. That includes doughnuts, watermelon, fruit salad, and snow cones.

When I was a kid, "gravy" meant "cream gravy," which, oddly, is made from milk, not cream. On the weekends, my dear departed mother got up, ran out to the car in her fuzzy blue housecoat, rummaged through the ashtray for viable butts because she had run out of cigarettes, and dashed back into the house to make gravy, along with eggs, sausage, and biscuits. Now that she's gone, I make my own gravy. Only I make it better, God forgive me. In fact, let's just put that remark on page 2003 of Volume XXVIII of *Things for Which Steve Will Do a Turn on Hell's Giant Rotisserie.* Right after the times I've watched female gymnasts for all the wrong reasons and then found out they were younger than most of my socks.

Mom always used to make gravy with sausage grease, which was nice, because it already had sage and pepper and salt in it from the sausage. But the truth is, you can make gravy from *any* kind of grease. If the seasonings aren't there to start with, you just throw them in as you cook. The best gravy I've made came from plain old bacon grease, which is flavored only by smoke and carcinogens.

Now I *know* some Food Nazi idiot out there is going to snatch this book from the trembling hands of her prime-candidate-for-euthanasia husband and chirp, "I can make it just as good with canola oil and skim milk." *Wrong,* you fun-killing, preorgasmic, tofu-sucking Oprah minion. Hike up your Banana Republic muumuu and go sacrifice an emaciated free-range chicken to Dr. Phil; your husband and I are talking Man Stuff.

I realize that if you're reading this book, you're probably a man, and you therefore think the stove has two settings: (1) Off and (2) Hiroshima.

Use good bacon. It pays. And cook it on low heat. High heat will make it bitter.

I realize that if you're reading this book, you're probably a man, and you therefore think the stove has two settings: (1) Off and (2) Hiroshima. I know heat modulation is one of the hardest lessons for men to learn in the kitchen. In the bedroom it's, "Don't let her catch you watching the game during sex," but in the kitchen it's, *"Turn the damn heat down."*

Higher heat does *not* equal the same food in less time. It equals crap and a new smoke detector battery.

So, let's say you succeeded in frying bacon without turning it into sticks of charcoal. Now you should have two or three tablespoons of prime grease leering seductively from the bottom of your skillet.

2–3 tablespoons grease
3 tablespoons flour (all-purpose is fine, so is self-rising)
1 teaspoon pepper—some guys use fresh pepper; I like *real*
** pepper. The kind that comes in a *can.* No, not really, but**
** I'm usually too lazy to grind it.**
¼ teaspoon ground sage
2 cups whole milk

In a skillet, get the grease hot and throw in the flour, pepper, sage, and salt. If you started with sausage grease, you probably won't need sage, and you'll need less pepper. Fry the flour for a few minutes; this will keep it from tasting like dough. If it starts to turn brown, you're going too far; you've blown it, cupcake. Put on your tutu and mince on over to the day spa for some bean curd with estrogen sauce.

Once the flour is no longer raw, pour in the milk. At first the flour will lump up, but soon it will relax, recline, and spread itself out expectantly. If you listen closely, you'll hear it purring. Keep scraping the flour off the bottom of the skillet with the spatula. Your biggest problem will be keeping it from sticking.

The worst thing you can do to gravy, other than reducing the fat, is scorching it. You want to keep the heat at medium or below.

After a few minutes, it'll thicken right up. What you want is something thicker than water but thinner than a milk shake. You should be able to pour it, but it shouldn't be much thinner than that. If it's too thick, add milk carefully, stir for a while, and check again.

The taste you're shooting for is peppery, not milky. If it's not spicy, you need to add more pepper.

Now, here's where it gets fun. You can make this gravy with any kind of meat, including chicken-fried steak. If you make it with pork or chicken, you can really soup it up by adding a little bit of dry white wine. About a quarter cup is right. Just reduce the milk accordingly, and don't add the wine until after the gravy has started to thicken. If you try this with beef, however, you're on your own. It doesn't work all that well with red wine.

If you want to get weird—who doesn't?—sherry or marsala. I don't know what you would eat with sherry gravy, but damn it's tasty. I think it would go great with fried alligator tail. But I don't have any alligators since having the yard sprayed.

If you make it for biscuits, you want it thick so it will cling. If you make it for potatoes, you want it thinner and browner.

I know that if you haven't had this stuff, it sounds a little gross, but believe me, there's something magical in the interaction of the fat and the wine and the sage. It's as if the wine carries the pork and sage and pepper flavors up your nose on tiny, flittering wings and stomps them into nerve endings leading straight to your brain.

Pour this stuff over bacon-grease biscuits, and you may well levitate. Later on, you may feel like you swallowed a truck. But that's just the price of true manhood, and frankly, I'm willing to pay it.

CHAPTER 5
CHICKEN-FRIED RIB EYE ON A HUGE BISCUIT

BYPASS RATING:

(QUADRUPLE)

HERE'S AN EXPERIENCE I have all the time, and I'll bet you can relate. I find myself looking at fried chicken, and a tear comes to my eye and I think, Why couldn't it be something a little more realistically scaled. Like a fried cow.

You can't actually fry an entire cow with the pathetic cooking vessels they make these days, and it's a crying shame, but you can definitely fry a big *piece* of a cow. And it has advantages other than size. For one thing, it doesn't take nearly as long as chicken.

I've never been able to figure out why some meats seem to take longer to cook than others. Maybe it's my imagination, but it's like deep inside the meat, there are varying levels of asbestos or something.

Think of pork chops. I often do. Your average pork chop is half an inch thick. But it takes like twenty minutes to cook. What's up with that? Chicken is possibly even worse. Fried chicken is a half-hour ordeal. It's like pork and chicken have been through those yuppie fire-walking seminars where bead-wearing kooks convince middle-management simpletons that having a positive outlook will make their feet fireproof.

If I went to one of those classes, I would raise my hand and say, "Yo, Swami, if you want to impress *me*, don't prance across the coals like you're running to the john after a big bowl of curry. Walk out in the middle and lie down." But you know what would happen. I would get an earful of new age crap about dealing with my rage and being a vegan, and they might even try to rebirth me without the proper grease. Never put yourself between a mystic and a moron's wallet.

Picture it.

STEVE:
Hey, Swami! Yo, Bhagwan! What's the hurry? Slow down; we're paying good money for this show!

SWAMI:
(*mincing across the coals like Michael Flatley riverdancing on a hotplate*) Who said that?

STEVE:
Is that all you got, chief? Let's see some break dancing.

SWAMI:
You're blocking the flow of my chi.

STEVE:
Try Grape Nuts. Hey, get down and roll for us. What are you scared of? Is that dress polyester?

Chickens and pigs would kick ass at those seminars. They would wander out onto the coals and stand around blinking, wondering what all the fuss was about. Because they take forever to cook.

A cow, on the other hand, would be nicely done after about

two minutes. Because for some reason, cows cook fast. Or maybe we just eat them rare. Whatever.

That brings me to today's lesson.

Say you want a nice, greasy fried treat, and a chicken just isn't big enough to satisfy the black, yawning, steaming abyss that is the hole in the center of your face. And besides, you lack the character to wait half an hour. If there's one thing I can relate to, it's having no character. I have the answer to your problem: chicken-fried steak. It has all the crunchy goodness of fried chicken, it goes just as well with biscuits, and it takes ten minutes to fix. Plus, it's way bigger than chicken. Therefore, superior.

I don't know where chicken-fried steak comes from. Some say Texas. That would make sense, because in Texas, cows and chickens are common and food is quite large.

Now, as you might have guessed, I was not content merely to take someone else's sad, sorry traditional recipe and repeat it. Oh, no, peoples. Stevie don't play dat. Steve is all about occluded arteries and having your pants let out. I took the concept of chicken-fried steak and amplified it.

The main thing I fixed was the pathetic main ingredient of the traditional chicken-fried steak. It's not really steak at all; it's cube "steak." Have you ever eaten this stuff? It's like a pot holder with big gray veins hanging out of it. It could be beef; on the other hand, it could be horse uterus.

Recipes often say "have the meat tenderized by your butcher." In other words, this "meat" is so crappy you have to pay a fat sweaty guy in an apron to beat it with a hammer. Isn't that a clue that maybe it's okay for the packers to put this stuff in the "by-products" bin and give up trying to feed it to humans? Couldn't they at least grind it up in the hamburger, the way they do all the other stuff that's too scary to eat whole?

So anyway, screw cube steak. What you want is a boneless rib eye.

Let me take a moment to praise rib eyes in general. In my opinion, this is the finest piece of meat on the cow. With the bone in, it makes a huge, tender, flavorful steak, or a thick, tasty slab of prime rib. With the bone out, it makes a wonderful miniature steak. Even the fat on a rib eye tastes good. And it doesn't have to be prime. A choice T-bone is like a shoe with bones. A choice rib eye is tender and delicious.

What else did I change? Don't be stupid. This is a fried dish. You know perfectly well what I did. I changed the frying oil to lard. You get a lighter, better-tasting crust, and you end up with better grease for gravy. But corn oil is also fine, and it's less likely to smell (good odorless lard is hard to find).

I haven't tried beef fat or duck or goose fat. But I should have. I think beef fat would be better than lard, but I haven't been able to find anyone who will sell it to me pre-rendered. It's like trying to buy a suitcase nuke. You can render your own, however. See the French fry chapter.

Lard or bacon grease
Salt and pepper
2 small boneless rib eye steaks—aged would probably be
   best
1 egg
¼ cup milk
All-purpose flour

You need at least ¼ inch of lard in your skillet. When frying, deeper is usually better.

The first time I made this, I used lard that had already been used for frying chicken, and I think that helped a lot.

Salt and pepper the steaks—which should be at room temperature—pretty heavily. Let them sit a few minutes so the salt dissolves and works in. Mix the egg and milk. Heat the fat on medium. Dip the steaks in the egg mix, including the edges. Coat them with flour. Then do it all again.

Chuck them in the skillet and fry for 5 minutes on a side. I don't believe in frying beef through. Five minutes on a side should leave it medium-well. It'll be hot and juicy and really tender, with just a tiny bit of pink. For this purpose, prime beef would not be much better. Although I see no reason not to use it if you want.

Drain (or not) on paper towels. Save two tablespoons of lard and use it to make cream gravy with salt, pepper, and milk.

There you go.

Hardcore Version

That recipe was for the wussies. If you're a wussy and still reading, close the book and sashay off to tai chi class. This part is not for you.

I take it only the real men are still with me. Check this out. It's not enough to eat corn-fed beef bursting with fat and cholesterol. It's not enough to coat it with pure carbohydrate and fry it in lard. It's not enough to submerge it in gravy so greasy that if allowed to cool, it could be used as a candle. Oh, no. You

If you eat this, you are almost certain to die before leaving the table.

have to finish the job. You have to drive the last nail in the coffin. And that nail . . . is a super-giant *biscuit.*

Yes, it sounds disgusting. It's too much. Too rich. Too big. Almost sordid. That's the whole idea. Any idiot can fry a steak. Only a True Believer will combine it with a biscuit the size of a Frisbee.

It's simple. You flip back to my biscuit recipe. Make the dough. Roll it out into one mammoth disc big enough to cover the steak. Then bake.

If you're highly skilled with sharp instruments, take a long knife and split the biscuit. Then shove the steak in the middle.

If you're a clumsy oaf who holds a spoon like a tennis racquet, put the steak on top of the biscuit. Doesn't matter. Now, pour at *least* twelve ounces of gravy on top. I recommend putting about a quarter teaspoon of sage in the gravy, just like you did when you were cooking breakfast.

If you eat this, you are almost certain to die before leaving the table. I only survived because for years I have been building an immunity by systematically putting lard in syringes and shooting up. This dish is almost poisonous. But damn, is it good.

Eat it before they pass a law against it.

CHAPTER 6
GREASE BURGERS

BYPASS RATING:

(QUADRUPLE)

YOU HAVE TO love cheeseburgers. They have it all. Red meat, cholesterol, saturated fat, carbohydrates, bleached flour, and salt. And onions, so when you finally have the Big One, the gutless EMTs refuse to give you mouth-to-mouth.

There are lots of ways to make cheeseburgers. You can grill them, broil them . . . you can buy boxes of prefab White Castle cheese sliders and heat them in the microwave. My personal favorite is frying. It conserves valuable grease and enhances my chances of blowing out a ventricle before I have to make my next Visa payment.

When I was a kid, McDonald's had commercials saying you could order two cheeseburgers, fries, and a Coke and still get change for a dollar. These days the Coke alone is $1.49. And no wonder. It's the size of a kiddie pool. Without the pee. Usually.

Yes, I know George Foreman says frying is bad for you. He says you have to use his patented grill, which collects all that lovely grease so you can pour it in the trash. Let me ask you a question. Have you seen George Foreman's behind?

There's a reason why a fifty-year-old man survived fights with young heavyweights. He was hiding behind a nine-inch-thick layer of man-meat. Hell, I could fight Evander Holyfield too, if you made him punch through a curtain of bacon.

Taking diet advice from George Foreman is like taking driving lessons from Ted Kennedy.

I always think of cheeseburgers as fifties food. Seems like that's when the great American cheeseburger industry really started cranking. Have you ever seen a fifties movie where somebody didn't have a cheeseburger? I'm pretty sure they did it even in stag films. Not that I would know. Seriously. All right, shut up.

> WICKED WANDA:
> So, Doctor Rex, do I put my feet in the stirrups now?

> DR. REX:
> Yes, Wicked Wanda. What are you waiting for?

> WICKED WANDA:
> I've never seen stirrups in a dentist's office before.

> DR. REX:
> I'll explain. But first let's go to a crappy diner run by a fat guy in a white undershirt who sweats into the food, calls everyone "Mac," and always has a half-smoked Lucky hanging off his lower lip. I could really go for some ash-flavored burgers and a cup of Joe.

> WICKED WANDA:
> Can we smoke while we eat?

> DR. REX:
> You damn betcha.

I have to stop. My head is bursting with "cavity" jokes.

When I was a kid, McDonald's had commercials saying you

could order two cheeseburgers, fries, and a Coke and still get change for a dollar. These days the Coke alone is $1.49. And no wonder. It's the size of a kiddie pool. Without the pee. Usually.

However, the cheeseburgers are still the same tiny meatless marvels they always were. A McDonald's cheeseburger is a piece of ketchup-flavored bread with a tiny sliver of meat hidden inside like a Cracker Jack prize. And what did McDonald's do when customers complained? They rolled out the mighty *Quarter Pounder,* a massive four ounces, pre-cooked weight. Or an ounce and a half, once the grease runs out.

A quarter pound, Ronald? Is that all you got, bitch? Shut that pretty painted mouth and sit down. I'll show you how it's done.

½ pound (at *least*) ground chuck

Don't even think about using sirloin. It's dry. Don't use plain old hamburger, either. It's all nipples and belly buttons. Chuck is pure . . . you know . . . "chuck."

I've always wondered what "chuck" is. I've never seen it on an anatomy chart. Maybe some day when I'm rich and even more eccentric and have nothing whatsoever of value to do, I'll go to a doctor and say my chuck hurts.

STEVE:

My chuck is killing me.

DOC:

Your what?

STEVE:

My chuck. Shooting pains, down at the base and along one side.

DOC:

Are you sure it's your chuck?

STEVE:

Yes, but last week, the pain was in my sweetbreads.

DOC:

(*putting rubber device on finger*) I think I'll give you a prostate exam.

STEVE:

Is that really necessary?

DOC:

No.

Pepper
2 cloves garlic, minced
¼ cup soy sauce
⅛ cup Worcestershire sauce
⅛ cup sherry or Spanish brandy
½ stick butter

Never cook with booze you couldn't make yourself drink. On the other hand, it's insane to pour good cognac on a lump of ground cow meat. Although it would be *really* tasty.

½ huge white onion, cut in quartered slices around half an
   inch thick
1 slice Jarlsberg or other Swiss-type cheese—cheddar
   optional
1 huge hamburger bun

You may want to get yourself a nice, wide loaf of Italian bread, cut out a big piece, and slice it down the middle. Burger buns are so small these days. Even better: bake your own loaf of white bread, cut two huge, thick slices, and go from there. Stop whimpering. Baking bread is easy. See the Texas Toast recipe.

Okay, you take your burger and you smoosh it around until you get a patty half an inch thick. If it's thicker, you'll need to mash salt into it, because the salt in this burger is all in the outer crust. Otherwise, the salt in the soy sauce should be adequate. You should definitely mash the pepper and garlic into the meat. Put the patty aside.

Mix the soy, Worcestershire, and sherry in a measuring cup.

Heat a big skillet on medium-high heat. I suggest nonstick, because this stuff has a way of turning black and sticking like glue. Turn your oven on "broil."

When the skillet is hot, throw in the butter and get it all melted. Don't wait for it to turn brown and smell. Put the burger in and set the timer on 2 minutes. Put the onions around the burger. Pour half the soy mixture on top of the burger.

At the 2-minute beep, turn the burger and pour in more of the soy stuff. Set the timer for another 2 minutes. Put the bread in the oven with the white side up, and keep an eye on it. You want it toasted, not cremated. Take it out when it's done. Do I have to tell you everything?

When the beeper goes off again, turn the burger. Scoop up as much of the fried onions as you can get, and dump them on top of it. Drop the cheese on top of them, trapping them next to the meat. Cook until the cheese is melted. What you

You lily-livered girly-man. Sit your candy-ass down and eat it.

want to end up with is something like Harrison Ford in *The Empire Strikes Back*, trapped in a big piece of plastic on Jabba the Hutt's wall. You can see the trapped onions through the melted cheese, frozen in their death struggle.

Take the burger out and dump it on the toasted bun. You may notice some red stuff running out. That's because I don't believe in cooking burgers until they turn brown and crunchy. Oh, yeah, I know, if you don't cook them well done, you can get E. coli because meatpacking plants are full of trashy people who go to the toilet and don't wash their hands. You lily-livered girly-man. Sit your candy ass down and eat it. If you get sick, walk it off. Hey, they have antibiotics these days. Worst-case scenario: you take a couple of sick days and lose five easy pounds.

One of the great things about high-fat cuisine is that you can always take something bad and make it even worse. I suggest buttering the bread. Some people butter it before broiling, but then you end up with a bun that's raw wherever the butter protected it, with a nasty burned-butter stench that will curl your nose hairs. Do this instead: make the garlic butter from the Texas Toast recipe. When the bread is done toasting, brush this stuff on it with a pastry brush.

If you really want to go hardcore, try this: while the cheese is melting, fry yourself an egg and confine the white so the whole thing ends up burger size. Sunny-side-up, over easy, fried hard, whatever turns you on. Then, after you put the burger on the bun, *drop the egg on top of it.* Sounds disgusting, I know, but try it.

And we all know what goes with eggs: *bacon.* But I better shut up if I want you to live through the next chapter.

My suggestions for sides: two huge dill pickles (Batampte half sours, for example) and twice-fried fries, which you will encounter in a chapter in here somewhere. While you're at it, you might as well call around and price an angioplasty.

CHAPTER 7
CORN BREAD AND NAVY BEANS

BYPASS RATING:

(TRIPLE)

THE SACRIFICES I MAKE for you people. Yesterday, I blew half a Saturday frying Yukon Golds and a huge lump of ground chuck, just to make sure my recipes worked, and today I'm stinking up the house with corn bread and a big pot of navy beans containing my only country ham hock.

Ham hocks are essential to good soup. Probably even chicken soup. I'm using a perfectly fermented hock of country ham today, but you can use the plain old ham hocks you get at the grocery for great results. Or you can use the bone from a whole ham. There's no law says it has to be a hock. When you have a honey-baked ham over Christmas, after you pick off all the brown sugar crust and eat it when nobody's looking, and after you pry off the last viable slice fragments, you'll end up with a very nice bone that will make excellent soup.

The big advantage to a country ham hock is that in addition to thickening and flavoring the soup, it provides a few lumps of really tasty, tender ham that will float around in your soup like prizes, waiting to be picked off like doctors on a singles cruise. The meat on an ordinary ham bone is more likely to be a bit soft, and if it's a holiday ham the in-laws and your intelligent, well-behaved children have picked over with their filthy paws, there won't be much meat there.

If you make a traditional Southern bean soup, which is what I'm here to talk about, you'll also want corn bread. Trust me. And if you want corn bread, you'll want cast iron. Kind soul that I am, I can help you with that.

When I was a kid, my mother had a number 6 cast-iron skillet she used for making corn bread and gravy and other useful things. My grandmother gave it to her—used—when she married Dad. Gramps gave her a brand-new '57 De Soto, gray with a red roof, so I guess Granny felt like a new skillet would be gilding the lily.

When Mom passed away in 1997—thanks again, all you bastards at Philip Morris—my sister and I made a deal. She got all the best jewelry, and I got the cast iron. Actually, you don't "deal" with my sister. You listen to her terms and then decide if it's worth it to roll the dice on an insanity plea.

I found the number 6 skillet in the bottom of a cupboard, where the Paraguayan housekeeper had left it to rust. God only knows how many treasured layers of baked-on 1960s breakfast grease I burned off restoring it. I scrubbed it well enough to get off all the rust, and then I did something you'll need to learn how to do. I seasoned it, which means I baked a layer of grease onto it to protect the metal.

Let me tell you a couple of things about cast iron. First of all, they don't make it like they used to. Not as far as I can tell. The inside of Mom's skillet is smooth as glass. These days, the big manufacturer is Lodge, and the insides of their products are, as Mom would have said, "rough as cobs." Try to imagine where that expression comes from.

I've heard a lot of BS about how a rough surface actually prevents food from sticking. Sure it does. And they put caffeine in Coke because it tastes good. Obviously, it's harder to make a smooth skillet than a rough one, and therefore it costs more, and it's just possible the people at Lodge are aware of that. Far as I know, the other manufacturers know it, too. I bought some Benjamin & Medwin skillets at Target, and they were also rough. I haven't seen the standard Wagner skillets, but they make a special line of more expensive "polished" skillets, which ought to tell you something.

An intelligent person would avoid the roughness by getting on the Internet and looking for antique cast iron. It's all over. Granted, you pay a premium. A big new skillet might run you $9.00, whereas the antique equivalent could run as high as $9.50. Okay, you *will* get hammered on shipping, because it's like shipping lead, but still, it's not like turning tricks on the weekend to pay for Le Creuset. If you don't like paying for shipping, go to antique markets and look around. This is a particularly good idea if you're gay, because if you can't find a skillet, at least you'll get some phone numbers.

Now you have to create that nice, black surface that makes corn bread roll out of the skillet as slick as Anna Nicole Smith sliding down the slope of a nude octogenarian.

Like I said, an intelligent person would use the Internet. Now let's talk about what people like *me* do. I bought rough skillets and fixed them. You get yourself an electric drill with a sanding attachment, you get both coarse and fine paper, and you sand the bumps off. Takes maybe fifteen minutes per skillet, and you end up with a very nice surface.

But you don't stop there. Now you have to create that nice, black surface that makes corn bread roll out of the skillet as slick as Anna Nicole Smith sliding down the slope of a nude octogenarian. You have to season the skillet.

The little tag that comes with your skillet will probably say something about smearing the skillet with vegetable oil and baking it for an hour at 350°F. Yeah, and the instructions on a Q-tips box say not to put them in your ears. If you do what the label says, you'll have to go stand in your yard while your oven emits fumes suitable for use in resolving hostage situations. Vegetable oil stinks when it burns, and it makes your eyes water, and the surface you'll end up with might be adequate if all you plan to do is hang your skillet on the wall while you cook with aluminum. Use pork fat instead.

If you want to do it right, clean the skillet thoroughly with a sponge and detergent (or an oven cleaning cycle, if it's hopeless—but cool it gradually to avoid warping), dry it completely, smear the inside of it with pork fat using a real rag (not paper), and put it in the oven for half an hour at 450°F. I used to do 500°F, but that makes the fat burn off sometimes. You want a very light film of fat. Turn the skillet upside-down in case you used too much. It'll run out and form pretty black stains on the floor of your oven.

The nice thing about pork fat is that not only won't it burn and stink; your house will smell as if you're frying bacon. What could be better than that? Hell, if I could find it, I'd use bacon cologne.

If you absolutely can't abide pork and are therefore reading this book in a perverse effort to torture yourself, use peanut oil. It barely smokes at all.

Here's a helpful tip. Don't do what I did when I was seasoning my fifteen-inch skillet. I put it in the oven at 500°F, took it out after half an hour, set it on the stove for five minutes, and then picked it up by the handle. You would be surprised how fast you can put down a 500-degree skillet.

You should have one nine-inch skillet you use only for corn bread. When I say "only," I mean "*only.*" If you have a dedicated corn bread skillet, it's much easier to maintain the kind of surface that gives the Anna Nicole effect. If you screw it up, instead of rolling the bread out like Anna Nicole, it'll be like trying to separate Michael Jackson from a Cub Scout.

Never put the skillet in the dishwasher. In fact, don't wash it at all in any meaningful sense. Once the corn bread surface is established, after you use the skillet, you'll only need to wipe out the inside. If you really must, rinse it with water but no soap. Old-timey cooks put salt in the skillet and heat it, and supposedly, that makes the crud come loose. But if you're having crud problems of that magnitude, you may need to re-season.

> **¼ cup bacon grease**
> **2 cups self-rising white cornmeal (I like Martha White)**
> **1 tablespoon sugar**
> **1 egg (2 will make it moister)**
> **⅔ cup milk**

Why white cornmeal? Because yellow meal tastes like sand mixed with cat litter. Why not more sugar? Because I'm a Caucasian. White soul food, of which corn bread is a subset, is not quite the same as black soul food. Far as I know, most black cooks like their corn bread sweet. To me, that's cake. I just use enough sugar to fool you into thinking there's something special about my corn meal.

Preheat the oven to 450°F, and put the skillet inside. Put the grease in the skillet. You want it to get as hot as the oven.

Put the dry ingredients in a bowl, and mix in the egg and milk. You want something you can pour, but it shouldn't be sloshy.

When the grease is hot and smoking, take out the skillet and pour the grease into the center of the batter. Can't hurt to swirl the grease around a little first to get it on the sides of the skillet.

Stir the living hell out of the batter to get the grease mixed in, put the skillet on an oven rack, and pour the batter into the skillet. Get it all in there; it'll try to stick to the bowl. Close the oven door and set the timer for 22 minutes. But keep your eye on the corn bread because ovens cannot be trusted. The timer is just to make sure you don't burn it. Don't take it out unless you're sure it's done.

When the corn bread is done, the top will be lightly browned and it'll sound hollow if you tap it in the center with a spoon. Take it out, run a butter knife around the edge of the corn bread to break it free from the skillet, put a plate on top of the skillet, and turn it over. If all goes well, the corn bread will fall onto the plate. If not, get ready for some scraping and a big pile of torn-up corn bread.

Easy, huh? Of course it is. The only hard thing is getting the skillet right so it won't stick.

Remember, this is not cake. It's not sweet, and it's not wet and mushy. You're supposed to eat it with stuff on it. Butter. Molasses. Soup. Stew. Don't write me angry e-mails telling me my corn bread is dry. I know that already. If you have to have it wetter, replace some of the milk with a second egg. You can use more grease, too. My cousin Wade crumbles bacon in his batter. Some people add canned corn. If you want to devolve into heresy and foolishness, don't let me stop you.

Now you need soup. If you think the corn bread was easy, the soup is going to be a joke.

1 (16-ounce) bag navy or Great Northern beans
1 ham hock
1 clove garlic, minced
1 medium onion (white, not Vidalia), chopped
Salt and pepper to taste

Dry beans often come packed along with tiny rocks or little bits of hard metal. This is how passive-aggressive bean factory workers express their hostility. It leaves you with a choice. Do you take out the rocks and metal, or do you cook the beans as-is and file a lucrative negligence lawsuit? I take them out. I've seen judges at work, and I have more faith in French cars and the rhythm method.

Dump the beans in a big pot, cover them with water, and root around looking for debris. When you're satisfied you've found it all, strain out the water and replace it. The package will tell you how much. Cover the beans and let them sit for a day. Meanwhile, trim the excess fat off the hock. If you don't, you can end up with bean soup submerged under a layer of fat. That actually bothers some people.

The next day, your beans will have softened. Pour out the water, add fresh water, throw in the hock, garlic, and onions, and get the pot boiling. Then turn it down to a low simmer, cover it, and cook until the beans get tender. You can cheat by using a pressure cooker, by the way. It softens food in a hurry.

Don't screw with the salt and pepper until the beans have been cooking for a couple of hours. Salt will leach out of the meat, and if you salt the beans at the start, you can end up with too much. After 2 hours, you can salt with impunity. Some people claim you shouldn't salt beans until they're completely cooked, because it will make the beans tough. Yes, and some people claim shampoo causes baldness. Guess what, folks. There is no gristle in a bean. If you cook it long enough, it will be soft.

Eventually, the beans will break down and cook, and you'll get a nice thick soup. If too much fat forms on the top, you can either skim it off while it cooks or chill the soup and yank out the hardened fat with a fork. Just make sure you don't take all of it out, because you need a little to make the flavors mingle.

That's all you need to know. You serve the soup with corn bread fresh from the oven. Butter the corn bread and have it on the side, or just break it up into the beans. If you want to get really crazy, you can pimp out the beans with little shreds of carrot or tiny pieces of red pepper. But they won't taste any better. Tiny cubes of peeled (or not) red potatoes can be a nice addition.

I know this sounds simple, but when you try it, you'll be astounded. The flavors complement each other perfectly. It'll be even better if you make the beans one day and serve them with corn bread the next. The soup improves dramatically in the fridge.

And think of all the bad stuff you're eating! Whole milk! Bacon grease! Pork fat! I admit, it can't compare to doughnuts fried in lard (keep reading), but maybe you can think of this dish as the salad of my book.

Don't argue with me. It's salad. Bean plants have leaves.

CHAPTER 8

TURDUCKEN:
FLIGHT OF THE HINDENBIRD

BYPASS RATING:

(QUADRUPLE)

I ONCE SAID I would never eat turducken. Because of the way it sounds. But I was lying. I lie constantly. Even when I'm not being paid.

I guess you know what a turducken is. If not, I better explain before you get really, really confused. It's a turkey, stuffed with a duck, stuffed with a chicken. Tur-duck-en. Get it? It's unfortunate that "turkey" starts with "tur" and "duck" starts with "d," but there it is. We're stuck with it.

Turducken is supposedly a Cajun dish. What won't those people eat? Hasn't it occurred to them that you don't have to eat a thing just because you can?

Legend has it that it was created by New Orleans chef Paul Prudhomme, probably as a publicity stunt that accidentally resulted in edible food. I admire that guy. He got so heavy for a while, he ran around on an electric cart called a Lark. Food meant more to him than walking. *That* is a man with priorities. *"Take my legs, Doc! Just give me more stuffing!"*

I'm saving up for a Lark of my own. For now I get by, scooting around the kitchen in a stolen grocery cart.

Eventually, though, I want to do a movie about racing other lardasses like me on my electrified obesity halftrack. I want to call it *The Fat and the Furious.* If it's going to be realistic, we'll have to put a few pounds on Vin Diesel. Or shave John Goodman's head.

I've never had a Cajun turducken. I checked around on the Internet, and they run about a hundred and twenty bucks, prefabricated and ready for cooking. That sounded outrageous to me. Until I tried to make one.

Oh, I succeeded. Don't get me wrong. My recipe is magnificent. But by the time I was finished I would have gladly paid three times the going price to get someone else to do it. You really need two drunken idiot buddies to help you with this. And I'll bet a lot of you already have a team lined up.

If you're smart—smarter than me, which isn't saying a hell of a lot—you were wondering how you get a chicken inside a duck inside a turkey. You've seen the inside of a turkey. It's not a big place. Here's the horrible secret: you remove every single bone from all three birds, except for the turkey's wings and legs.

Without the bones, a turkey has room to burn. So a turducken is basically an immense loaf of flesh, with four useless limbs hanging off for decoration. In other words, it's a lot like me.

The reason I use the word "horrible" is that birds are a giant pain in the ass to debone. It's not like a fish, where there's two pieces of meat with a thin row of easily dodged bones between them. Birds are way more three-dimensional, and they have ribs and hips and pelvises.

I'm really good with a knife, because when I was a kid, about half of my toys were sharp knives. Way to go, Mom and Dad. Good thinking. It still took me two and a half hours to debone my first turducken. If you're not as handy with knives as I am, the first bird may be completely rotten before you even get the ribs out.

Once you debone the birds, you have to make three kinds of stuffing. Because eating three birds at once isn't sufficiently decadent. No, sorry. You have to have a layer of stuffing between the outer birds and a lump of stuffing inside the chicken.

I don't know how Cajuns find time to make these things. But as I understand it, life in Cajun country is extremely boring, and they're just now getting cable.

I wrote three stuffing recipes. I decided how I wanted to season the birds. I decided to smoke the turducken instead of just baking it. And the result was beyond wonderful. And it weighed more than twenty-five pounds. It looked like an obese four-year-old with really short arms.

Let me take a moment to blaspheme. Turducken is a gimmick food. Part of the purpose of creating the first turducken was to get attention. And when you're going for attention, it sounds better to use three different birds. Like you're cramming a whole roadside zoo in there. And it made the name of the dish funnier, because with the "d" from "duck," "turducken" starts with "turd." But the sad fact is, the duck really doesn't belong.

Ducks are tougher than chickens and turkeys, and they can be gamey. What you really want is another chicken. Of course, then you have a dish with no name. You could call it turchicken, but that sounds like one turkey and one chicken. I guess the best thing is to keep calling it turducken and tell your guests you made a substitution.

Or you can call it the beast with three backs. Which sounds like a sleepover at Michael Jackson's.

I haven't tried a goose, but it might be better yet. I wanted to buy an ostrich and make an ostriducken, but then I found out what ostriches cost. And while I was hesitating, some lunatic beat me to it.

If you're determined to make one of these things, the recipe that follows will give you wonderful results. If you're smart, you'll get friends to help. Seriously.

1 (20-pound) turkey, with all bones removed except for
    drumsticks and wings
1 (6-pound) roaster with all bones removed (duck,
    if you insist)
1 (4-pound) fryer with all bones removed
Salt
Pepper
Poultry seasoning
Bacon grease

Debone all the birds, but leave the bones in the turkey's wings and drumsticks. I am not a great expert on boning (shut up), but I'll tell you how I do it. You'll want a short razor-sharp knife. You can use a special boning knife. I use a paring knife with a three-inch blade. I have a really cool Tojiro "birds beak" paring knife, which is perfect, as long as you remember never to pry with a Japanese knife. Forschner makes a fantastic birds beak knife that costs $4.95. Pry all you want. Break it. Who cares?

Wear a filleting glove, because it's very easy to slip and debone yourself as well as the chicken. Two gloves are even better. They protect your fingers and give you a better grip on the bird. There is a method for boning a bird without cutting the skin; look it up if you want to be a perfectionist. My way is not that cute.

Start with the smaller chicken, because it goes inside the other birds, and if you hack it up, no one will know. Cut the wings off at the first joint. Shears are good for this. Slice the chicken's butt—that little useless diamond-shaped tab—completely off. Cut through the skin, all the way down the center of the back. Peel the skin down toward the breast. As you pull the skin, slice the meat away from the bones. Take care to make sure you don't leave the thick "oysters" stuck to the bone. Sever the connection between the thigh bone and pelvis. Sever the connection between the upper wing bone and the shoulder.

The spine, ribs, and pelvis should come out as a unit. You're going to have to keep slicing all the way around the front of the breastbone. Be careful not to cut through the skin of the breast.

Eventually, you'll end up with a chicken that has four bones in it: the upper leg and wing bones. Turn the chicken inside-out, stand the limb of your choice perpendicular to the cutting board, and press the meat down around the bone, as if you're trying to push a pair of pants down off a leg.

Cut around the bone as you go, removing the flesh as you slide the meat down the bone. Eventually you'll get to the end of the drumstick or the wing bone. If it's the wing bone, just pull the bone out; you're done. The drumstick will still be attached by thick skin around the lower extremity. Just cut around the bone, through the skin, and pull out the bone.

Now, repeat for the other birds.

Some fun, huh?

I make a large pot of cold brine when I do this. Hopefully it chills the birds faster after you get done cutting them up. You want one part salt to sixteen parts water. Do *not* use kosher salt. It is exactly the same as table salt, and it takes forever to dissolve. I know, your foodie buddies claim the potassium iodide added to table salt—at a ratio of .0001 to 1—ruins it. They also think Emeril is a genius because he yells "BAM" when he throws sugar on corn flakes.

Try this test. Dissolve one ounce (by weight) of table salt in one glass of water, and one ounce of kosher salt in each of five glasses. Ask your foodie pal to taste them and tell you which one is table salt, and bet him $500. That will shut him up.

The government says table salt only has to be 97.5 percent pure. You have no idea what's in the remaining 2.5 percent, you still eat salt, and you think you can taste a speck of potassium iodide at 0.1 per cent? You should be at the airport, sniffing luggage.

If you absolutely must cling to your bizarre beliefs about the evil taste of table salt, buy it without iodine. It's slightly cheaper anyway.

Dude, you can't circumcise salt. All salt is the same.

As I finish boning a bird, I drop it in the pot and reach for the next bird. I let the boned birds soak in the brine for 6 or 8 hours. It makes them more tender, and it gets a little salt into them. But it's not necessary.

Time to make stuffing.

TURKEY STUFFING
13 ounces andouille sausage (I use Aidells)
1 cup white onion, chopped
1 (9-inch) pone corn bread
1 habanero pepper, preferably pickled
2 cloves garlic
½ stick butter
2 shots marsala
½ cup beef broth
½ teaspoon pepper
½ teaspoon salt

"What? What? Corn bread is an ingredient? How do I get corn bread? Damn you!" Relax. You know how to bake corn bread, I assume. It's in this book somewhere. Just use the following ingredients and make it the usual way. Try to get it fairly brown on the bottom.

CORN BREAD
2 cups white self-rising cornmeal
1¹/₃ cups milk
1 egg
1 tablespoon sugar
¼ cup bacon grease

Cut the sausage into ⅜-inch cubes (more or less) and brown them in a skillet on medium-high heat. Remove the sausage and put the onions in the sausage grease. Cook on medium heat until they start to clear. If there isn't enough grease, add a tablespoon of bacon grease.

Try the sausage before using it in your food. There are lots of nasty, sandy-tasting andouille sausages on the market.

Crumble the corn bread in a big bowl. Don't make it too fine. Leave some chunks. Mince the habanero and press the garlic into the corn bread. Melt the butter and pour it in the corn bread while tossing it. Add the other ingredients and toss until mixed pretty well. Refrigerate.

ROASTER/DUCK STUFFING
2 cups dry bread cubes
1 cup white onion, chopped
½ stick butter
8 ounces shredded crab or fake crab
1 shot marsala
¼ teaspoon poultry seasoning
Salt and pepper, to taste

This one is really easy. Get a loaf of good bread, like sour-dough. Make yourself two cups of bread cubes, smaller than dice. Let the cubes go stale overnight, or spread them on a dish and bake them at 300°F for 20 minutes. Get them nice and hard.

Melt half a stick of butter in a skillet. Fry the onions on medium heat until they start to clear. Throw in the crabmeat and the shot of marsala and cook on medium-high or high heat until the crab starts to brown. Put the stuffing in a bowl and make sure none is left in the skillet.

REDUCTION
2 tablespoons butter
½ cup beef broth
½ cup marsala

Put all the ingredients in a skillet and fry on medium-high heat until they reduce to a fairly thick sauce. Stir while cooking. Throw in the stuffing and toss it, adding the poultry seasoning and salt and pepper to taste.

You should probably add half a minced habanero. If that's too spicy for you, leave it out. And go buy yourself a pair of Hello Kitty! panties.

FRYER STUFFING
½ cup wild rice
2 cups water
½ teaspoon salt
1½ tablespoon beef fat

I like to stuff the smaller chicken with wild rice. I like it to have a little beef flavor. You can either add rendered beef fat to the rice, or you can substitute beef broth for the water, in which case you should add a tablespoon of butter.

Mix the rice, water, and salt. Heat to a fast boil. Reduce heat and boil slowly for 30 minutes. Cover and remove from heat. Allow to sit for 25 minutes or so. You want it cooked but not mushy. Stir the beef fat or butter into the cooked rice.

You're all done, except for performing more surgery on three very wobbly birds.

Grab the smaller chicken. Anoint it inside and out with bacon grease. Salt and pepper it well. Rub a little poultry seasoning on it, inside and out. Get a large needle and some twine or waxed dental floss (waxed holds knots very well). Start sewing the chicken up. Begin at either end. You want to sew it far enough up to create a sort of pocket. When you think it's sewn up sufficiently, jam as much of the rice as you can into it. Try to get it into the little hollow wings and legs. Continue sewing the chicken up so the rice doesn't fall out.

The sewing doesn't have to be pretty. You can go in and out once every half inch or so. One nice thing about floss is that when the birds are done, you can grab it and pull it out without disturbing the food. That will be harder to do with cooking twine.

Grab the duck or roaster. Do it just like you did the chicken, and then plop the bread stuffing onto it. Sew it up. Don't flip out if you can't get all the stuffing into it. Here's a tip: once a bird is sewn up, you can moosh the stuffing around inside it to get it where you want it to be.

Grab the turkey. Sometimes turkeys are missing a lot of skin on the lower breast, near the huge stuffing hole. This may be a problem. You can sew cheesecloth into the gap if you have to. Do the turkey the same way you did the other birds. Put the corn bread stuffing on it. Lay the duck on the stuffing. Finish sewing up the turkey.

Grease the turkey with bacon grease. Apply salt, pepper, and poultry seasoning.

Now, a word about poultry seasoning. It's a shortcut. If you want to go full-throttle, make your own, using fresh sage and so on.

Mash the turkey around until it looks more or less like a turkey. Put it on its back in the smoker. Put an empty pan under it to catch grease for gravy. Use a water pan to keep the meat moist while it smokes. Smoke at 200–250°F.

One unfortunate thing about this dish is that it can kill you and all your guests with salmonella and other germs. You want to be really sure it's done. Get a probe thermometer with a digital readout. You put the probe outside the bird at first, and you watch it while you get the cooking temperature right. When you're sure it's right, bury the probe deep in the middle of the bird. You can set the controls so an alarm goes off when the food is done. Supposedly, 165°F is the magic number for safe poultry, but I let it go to at least 170°F.

When the bird beeps, take it out and put it aside to rest, preferably covered. I take the whole rack out and let the turducken slide off of it onto a cutting board or platter. Picking a cooked turducken up may lead to a Hindenburg-like disaster.

It's time to make the gravy.

GRAVY
6 tablespoons turducken grease or bacon grease
4 rounded tablespoons flour
1 quart milk
⅓ cup marsala
Salt and pepper to taste
¼ tablespoon sage

Heat the grease on medium heat in a big nonstick skillet. Fry the flour in it for a few minutes, stirring the grease into it with a spatula and scraping occasionally to keep it from sticking. Pour in the milk and cook until boiling begins, scraping the whole time. Stir in the marsala after the gravy thickens. Add *lots* of pepper, like over a teaspoon. Enough to make it spicy. Salt to taste and add sage. You may want more than a quarter teaspoon. Taste it and see.

Put the turducken on a cutting board. Yank off the wings. Now what you have is a giant boneless bird loaf, except for the drumsticks, which you can pull off later. Pull out as much of the floss or twine as you can, without tearing up the birds. Cut in slices across the turkey and serve covered with gravy. A Chinese cleaver is the ideal tool for this. As the smaller birds come into view, so will the floss holding them together. Yank it out as soon as you can get to it.

That's it. It should be tender and juicy and amazing. If it's dry at all, you can dribble some of the saved dripping on it.

Start shopping for a cart. Let me know when you get one, so we can drag-race to the refrigerator.

CHAPTER 9
AGED PRIME STEAK COOKED ON A PROPANE GRIDDLE

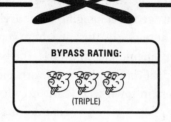

BYPASS RATING:

(TRIPLE)

I'M ALMOST EMBARRASSED to write about steak. Here I am, supposedly writing about really unhealthy food, and in among the doughnuts fried in lard and the flan with extra egg yolks and the 540-calorie brownies (be patient; they're coming), I have the audacity to insert an essay about mere red meat, which hardly ever kills anyone. But think it through.

Steak itself may not be all that lethal. Sure, it's full of cholesterol and saturated fat, and you butter and salt it before you cook it, and the charred stuff on the outside will supposedly give you cancer. But it hardly compares to artery-punishing treats like cheesecake and cream gravy.

Here's the thing, though: no one ever eats steak all by itself. Steak is like a teenage son who hangs out with stoners. A kid like that may seem okay on his own. But wait until he has a party in your house and his droopy-pants punk friends clean out your liquor cabinet and give your dog a Mohawk and genital warts. Steak itself can be forgiven, but it invariably shows up with huge potatoes with sour cream, and béarnaise sauce, and immense, crusty rolls, and desserts and cigars. And martinis. That's why I love it.

Steak is served in fine, manly restaurants with lots of dark wood on the chairs and the walls and sometimes even the waiters. They have huge refrigerated rooms with windows you can see into from your table, and inside these rooms, there are hundreds of pounds of aged beef hanging seductively on hooks. And there's a big glass humidor by the bar, where you can get Montecristos and Arturo Fuente Hemingways. The bartenders are fat old guys in black pants and white shirts with aprons, and they're the only bartenders in town who know how to make a martini that doesn't taste like a sour apple Jolly Rancher or the juice from a stale jar of olives.

There are two big problems, however, with having steak at home. The first is that most supermarket steak is like the rubber they use to make radiator hoses, and the second is that you don't know how to cook it.

One fun thing about steakhouses is that your wife or girlfriend hates them. You say, "How about we go out and get some meat?", and she mumbles some ovulation-related nonsense about a trip to the local vegetarian grille, where you can pay $25.00 for a burnt portabello and be tormented with Kenny G. And then you tell her it's steak or nothing, and she moans and complains the whole way there, and then she orders the petit fillet like she's doing you a big favor, and then the food comes and she starts nibbling resentfully, and then suddenly she's a little more interested, and then she horks down half the fillet in one bite and makes a lunge for your prime rib, and then she goes after the potatoes, and she orders way too many glasses of wine, and she makes you order cheesecake just so she can have it after she finishes her own dessert, which has a name like Chocolate Atrocity, and then when you get home, you have to put a pillow between the headboard and the wall to keep the thumping from cracking the plaster, and she even makes you root around in the storage closet to see if you can find some bungee cords and her riding crop.

Steakhouses are like that.

There are two big problems, however, with having steak at home. The first is that most supermarket steak is like the rubber they use to make radiator hoses, and the second is that you don't know how to cook it.

You think you know how to cook it. You have a Weber kettle, and you have an apron that says "Molest the Cook," and you have your own special, sacred spray bottle for squirting the coals to keep them from getting too hot. Well, you're an idiot.

What you want, when you cook steak, is *not* coals that aren't too hot. You want blazing, searing, fusion-type heat, and you want it close to the meat. Save the Weber kettle for hot dogs and soy burgers and those disgusting portabellos.

Steak is supposed to be burned. Not cooked well done, which is the way women invariably order it. Just burned. On the outside. On the inside, it should be pink and merely a little warm. Medium-rare, in other words. Don't worry about the bacteria. *Eat it,* you coward, and if you get cramps, we'll drive by the ER and roll you out while the car is still moving.

You're probably afraid of mad cow, too. How do you know mad cows don't have a good time? In this world, it's the sane who suffer most. On a graph of my mental irregularities, mad cow would be statistical noise.

You can't use that grill. So how do you manage to cook a steak properly, given that your pathetic Best Buy stove has a broiler that turns off automatically whenever the heat gets hot enough to accomplish anything, and given that the fan is too wimpy to get the smoke out of the house fast enough to keep it from asphyxiating your family? Simple. You get yourself a propane burner and a huge cast-iron skillet, and you go outside.

Steakhouses often use gas broilers, but even if you have a good one, you still have the problem of smoke. The outdoor approach is easier.

I don't know if you've ever used a big propane burner, but it's a whole 'nother level from your kitchen range. Say you put a greased skillet on your stove and crank it to "high." If you're lucky, you'll start seeing smoke in about a minute. On a propane burner, try *ten seconds.*

Here is what you do. Get yourself a burner—make sure it's a big one; ask the clerk if you're not sure—and put your skillet on it. If you really want to go to town, get a rectangular cast-iron griddle instead. It holds more food, and more is always better. Fire up the burner, taking care not to burn all the hairs off your hands like I always do. Give the skillet a minute or so to get really hot.

Now, you will presumably have a steak somewhere nearby. Here's a good way to prepare it for cooking. Salt it down on both sides, more heavily than seems right at the time. Then, if you absolutely must, hit it with the pepper. Let it warm up to room temperature. It may take longer than you think. Remember, the outside is warmer than the inside.

Put a stick of butter in a Pyrex doodad with a little fresh garlic and salt. Nuke it until it boils a little, cooking the garlic. Taste it to see if it's okay. If not, adjust. I give my butter ten minutes at the 20 percent power setting. If you have a complex about microwaves, use a little pan on the stove.

Take your steak and toss it in the skillet and then run to

the other side of your yard to get away from the smoke. If it's a scrawny, shameful inch-thick steak, four minutes will probably be plenty.

Here's a great thing to know. It's hard to cook meat to the right level of doneness, right? Right. Those weird LED forks are hard to use and you can't trust them. The USDA and the Food Network put out internal-temperature charts, but unless my experience is very misleading they're crap. Here is what you do. Get a digital probe thermometer and when you think your steak is done, put it in your meat so the very tip is halfway in. Do it from the side, so the probe is parallel to the cooking surface. The Food Network (HA!) says 130 is medium rare. Yeah, okay, if medium rare means *"inedible gray crap."* I get gorgeous results at 120.

Once you find a temperature that works for you, stick with it for life. Now, hopefully, you won't have to hack up your steaks, doing exploratory surgery to see if they're ready. I keep meaning to buy an infrared thermometer so I can measure the temperature of the griddle surface, but I haven't gotten around to it.

A good burner can actually get *too* hot, so keep an eye on it. By the time you turn the steak, it should be pretty dark on the cooked side. Not like a piece of coal. Just a nice dark brown.

You should check the steak after two minutes. If it's not cooking fast enough, turn it up. If it's getting brown too fast, turn it over and reduce the heat a little. Keep track of the number of minutes each side gets. In the end, you want them to be the same, even if you turn it several times.

When your steak is done, throw it on a plate and serve with garlic butter on the side. Or just pour it on top; that's what I do.

A lot of people who lack the capacity to think for themselves say you should let a steak rest for five or ten minutes before eating it. Honestly, with all the stupid cooking myths floating around out there, it's a wonder anyone ever gets a decent meal. The theory is that the juice in the steak has to "settle down" or "redistribute itself" or some such nonsense. Otherwise-intelligent people will actually claim that the juice in a steak will all shoot out at once if you don't let it rest, and that the rest of the steak will be tough.

What BS. First of all, a steak isn't a sponge. Liquid doesn't travel around inside it. Cutting a bite off one end won't affect the juice in the other. Second, toughness has nothing to do with juiciness. Anyone with common sense should know these things.

I did a test to silence the whiners. I cut a beautiful rib eye in two pieces, cooked them together, and ate them six minutes apart. Guess what? The first half was better. Because it was *hot*. The juice didn't magically shoot out of the first half. The first half wasn't tough. I can't believe I wasted a good steak, dignifying this idiocy with a test. And people still didn't believe me, even when I put a video on YouTube.

It's easier to cure cancer than to remove a cooking myth from a tiny, bent cranium.

If you like cold steak, let your steak rest. I can't be bothered with educating the simple. Steakhouses don't do it. They bring steaks out on plates so hot the meat is still cooking at the table. But don't listen to me. Enjoy your cold steak, because you were told to eat it that way by some hopeless goof who can't cook.

Now, you may be tempted to use steak sauce. Bad idea. The reason you've always needed steak sauce in the past is that you haven't been cooking at the right temperature. A charred steak sort of seasons itself. Adding steak sauce makes it harder to taste.

What if it sucks? What if it's tough and flavorless? That means you got the wrong steak. That brings me back to my point about basic supermarket meat: avoid it. Most supermarkets sell steak generously labeled "choice," which means you would eat it if the *choice* was eating dog crap. What you want is "prime."

Choice beef comes from menopausal cows that can't have

calves anymore. It comes from cattle that are found dead next to railroad tracks. From rogue cattle executed for various crimes. It comes from racehorses that come up lame.

Prime beef comes from spoiled Republican steers that do nothing but lie on their sides and eat corn. It's a pretty good life, as cow lives go. They get fat around the outsides of the steaks, and then the fat grows into the middle of the steaks and makes them marbled and tender, and I'm pretty sure they even have fat in their horns. The corn gets rid of the nasty grass taste, and the total lack of exercise makes them tender. Hmm . . . I guess I'm prime meat, too.

Anyway, that's why you pay twenty dollars a pound for this stuff. You can also get weird super-premium Japanese beef made from cattle who drink beer and eat ice cream and get daily massages and, I think, watch a lot of porn.

You should try to get thick steaks. At least an inch and a quarter. I like an inch and a half to two inches. Thick is another way of saying "big," and like I always say, "big" equals "good."

Some people love filet mignon, and there's nothing wrong with it. Others like a nice Porterhouse. My favorite steak is the bone-in rib eye. You know. It's basically a prime rib, only you cook it like steak. The marbling in the outer edge of the rib eye is beyond delicious, and it's a very easy steak to cut. Even a choice rib eye is good. A T-bone or Porterhouse eventually turns into a frustrating exercise in microsurgery, as you try to extract the last bits of meat from the bone.

By the way, you probably can't buy dry-aged beef where you live. If that's your situation, you may be able to age beef yourself. Think it over, because there is supposedly a possibility that you will give yourself food poisoning. Alton Brown and *Cook's Illustrated* were brave enough to suggest it, so it may not be an insane idea. I do it all the time, and I'm alive.

Disclaimer: Eating home-aged beef can kill you. For all I know. I am not a food-safety expert. Age your own beef at your own risk.

The basic idea is, you buy a large piece of beef—not a single steak—and you make sure it's prime beef, with lots of fat on it. You refrigerate it at about 35°F for at least three days, wrapped in clean cotton cloths, sitting on a wire rack above a pan. Every day, you change the cloth. You want air to get at it, because drying is part of the process.

When your nerve runs out, take the beef out, trim off the scary bits, slice it into steaks, and cook or freeze.

Remember, you may ruin your steak. You may even die. I promise nothing.

The first time I did this, I paid $12.50 a pound—which is cheap—for prime beef. Eight pounds of bone-in rib roast, aka rib eye steaks that hadn't been separated yet. I wrapped it in a clean cotton pillowcase and put it on a rack over a big pan in a 37°F freezer. I gave it three days, changing the cloth daily. And it was magnificent. Not even on the same planet as non-aged beef. Three days make a world of difference. It got just a tiny bit fermented, and the scent of the fermentation permeated every cubic inch. I will *never* eat non-aged prime steak at home again.

I used a big Tojiro F-921 Chinese cleaver to separate the steaks. I highly recommend a Chinese cleaver if you aren't cutting bone. It's razor sharp from the factory, and the wide blade gives flat cuts better than a butcher's saw. I was able to use it because I wanted two-inch-thick steaks, which is what you want if you cut between the ribs. If you want thinner steaks, you'll have to get a bandsaw and go through the bone. I tried a hacksaw, and it was pretty awful.

I wrapped each steak in foil and vacuum-sealed them in plastic. A university did research and determined that butcher paper and foil, in that order, were the best things for freezing meat. But

I didn't have any butcher paper. If you use a vacuum sealer, check the steaks the next day to make sure no air is sneaking in.

As for aging time, since my first effort, I've gone as long as seven days. I don't go by time, though. I go by smell. When the steak smells aged, I take it out. Some people insist on three weeks.

I might as well put this information in. Here's a quick primer on aging. Almost all beef is aged a little. If you don't let it hang for at least a week, it tastes metallic. This is not the aging restaurants are talking about when they call their steaks "aged." Meat that hangs seven days in a processing plant or sits in your grocer's cooler has none of the funky flavor you expect from high-end steaks.

Aging beyond the seven-day period can be done in two ways. Wet-aging and dry-aging. Wet-aging means the meat stays in an airtight bag and sits in the fridge. All wrapped beef wet-ages before you cook it.

Dry-aged beef is typically covered with cloth but not protected from the air. Bacteria work on it, and it dries out a little (concentrating the flavor), and it gets downright quasi-rancid. You may actually find mold on it at the end.

Wet-aging gives less flavor, but the meat gets tender from bacteria and enzyme action, and because the meat isn't exposed to air, you lose less volume to drying and so on. And the meat is somewhat juicier. Women like wet-aging for the same reason they like filets. They care more about tenderness and juiciness than flavor. If you're a big hairy manly man like me, you'll prefer dry-aging.

The meat industry pushes wet-aging because it's more profitable. But the meat isn't nearly as good.

Finally, aging works best in steaks that have lots of fat, so don't waste your time aging a filet. Conclusion? Be brave and dry-age your meat. Or look for dry-aged meat when you shop.

You should be aware that a propane burner will utterly destroy the seasoning on your cast-iron skillet. You need a skillet or griddle dedicated exclusively to the propane burner. And you're going to get rust after you use it, so wipe it down with oil.

I'm pretty sure the filth that accumulates on cast iron makes steaks taste better, so I am very careful not to disturb it too much.

You already know what to do for your sides. Baked potatoes or hash browns. Butter or sour cream on the baked potatoes? Why not both? Silly question.

Twice-fried fries are also good, but they're a lot of work.

Let me do you a big favor and help you with the potatoes. Buy yourself a big, beautiful russet potato with no rotten places or hoe marks on it. Wash it thoroughly. A brush is great for getting the dirt out of the dimples. Now, before it dries, put some salt in your hands and rub it all over the potato. Preheat the oven to 450°F and put the potato directly on the rack, high in the oven. Put a pan on a lower rack, between the potato and the heating element, to prevent scorching.

Bake it for an hour. No foil, no fork holes. When it comes out, the jacket will be crispy and delicious, and the inside will be cooked to perfection. Foil will make the jacket damp and limp. Like a person who eats soy burgers.

At an hour, you may get a little browning inside the skin. If that bothers you, make it shorter.

Big potatoes (over twelve ounces) may not be done after an hour, so be careful. You can finish them off in the microwave with no real loss of quality. I give them an hour and fifteen minutes.

Some people like to oil the potatoes before baking them. I tried it, and the skin got limp. I'll never do it again.

Go forth and indulge. Give some poor stupid cow's life a purpose.

You know what? This is *good food.* Better than what you'll

get at the best steakhouse in town, regardless of where you live. I've been to Morton's, Ruth's Chris, Peter Luger's, Smith & Wollensky . . . you name it. The steak dinners I make at home are just plain better, and they cost a third as much. Added bonus: I can eat them naked. Also, you end up with two or three measly dishes to wash, which is just incredible.

Don't buy into the hype. Anyone, anyone, anyone, anyone, *anyone* can make perfect steak at home. There is no such thing as super-wonderful beef only steakhouses can get. There is no such thing as a secret super-duper broiling oven only steakhouses can buy. People who run steakhouses know they have the easiest job in the world, but they lie their asses off to get your business. It's complete BS, and it makes me really angry. So make your own steak and *stick it to the man!*

Look, it will cost you a hundred bucks to age four gargantuan prime rib eyes. That's the cost of one restaurant meal. *Try* it.

This is one of the easiest meals to cook, and it's also one of the best. And if you're a Costco commando, you can buy an entire choice boneless rib eye roast for under six bucks a pound, age it, and get very, very solid results. Not as good as prime, but still extremely good.

And ladies, this recipe is especially valuable for turning men into slaves. It's fantastic and very hard to screw up, unlike a lot of the fancy meals you've surely ruined in the past. So if you're bad in bed or just fat, this could really help you land a man.

And ladies, this recipe is especially valuable for turning men into slaves. It's fantastic and very hard to screw up, unlike a lot of the fancy meals you've surely ruined in the past. So if you're bad in bed or just fat, this could really help you land a man.

CHAPTER 10
CHAMPAGNE CHICKEN WITH FETTUCCINE IN CREAM SAUCE

BYPASS RATING:

(QUADRUPLE)

WOMEN LIKE MEN who can cook. Men who can cook are sexy. That's what I always hear. From women.

Men know it's total BS. It's like when women say they're hot for men who are smart and funny. Whatever, baby. I say I like women for their personalities. "Women like men who can cook?" Right. If there's one thing women constantly say, it's how they're dying to get into Emeril's size 48 pants.

Women hate being called on their astounding hypocrisy, so of course, I do it every chance I get, because frankly, there's something wrong with me. I especially love jumping on them when they pull the "smart and funny" routine.

Try this. Get a couple of beers into your girlfriend and ask her if it's sexy for a man to be smart and funny. And when she finishes lying, ask her this: "Would you rather lick every part of Colin Farrell's sweaty, unwashed body or lightly hold the clammy, freshly sanitized hand of a young Woody Allen?"

"*Oh*, well, you know, looks matter a *little*." Yeah, okay. No need to continue, Little Miss Depth. I think we've made our point.

Women like men who are smart and funny *If* they're already attracted to them for purely superficial reasons. That's about it. A typical woman will date a rude, abrasive, humorless son of a bitch who barely graduated from college as long as he looks good and spends money on her. And when he dumps her for a stewardess who collects exotic massage oils, she'll call her smart, funny friend she wouldn't sleep with if the alternative was laser hemorrhoid surgery without anesthetic, and she'll cry about how much she misses the son of a bitch and ask what she can do to get him back.

You know what? I'm smart and funny. I have a law degree and a physics degree. I was a contestant in the National Spelling Bee. I do newspaper word puzzles in my head because a pen makes it too easy. I was voted funniest in my high school class. I'm a published author. And if you put me on a stool next to a really hot, obnoxious guy who leaves the keys to his Bentley on the bar in front of him, women will notice me about as much as a stain on the wallpaper. And I don't mean just off the bat. I mean I will lose every time, even if they sit down and talk with both of us, and the other guy says things like, "I'm stupid and unfaithful, I beat my dog, and I think soap causes cancer."

Having seen myself in a mirror, I can't say they don't have a point.

Women always lie about what they want. Or, equally likely,

they have no idea what they want, so they make up something they think will make them sound less carnivorous.

Fine, fine. I can play the game.

You say: "Size doesn't matter." "Money isn't everything." "Don't worry, we can just lie here and cuddle, and I believe you when you say this never happened before."

I say: "I turn out the lights when we have sex because it's more romantic." "Your sister has bigger breasts? I never noticed." "Your breath is fine. I drive with the windows open because I like fresh air and being rained on."

I'm sort of almost okay to look at in dim lighting, and I don't have a Bentley yet, and I'm polite. I'm polite *in person*, okay? I dress well; I have my shirts and jackets made, and I wear hand-finished Italian pants, and I can choose ties and cuff links like nobody's business, even though I'm not gay. I'm considerate, and I'll pretend really convincingly to be interested in whatever it is that you blabber about, and I wear exceptionally nice cologne. But I will never, ever be a lady killer unless I get very, very rich and, more important, unless women *know* that I'm rich.

> *I cook one dish that, more than any other, melts the elastic in women's panties. And that dish is Champagne Chicken.*

Because women are just as shallow and superficial as men. Sorry to break it to you. There's a reason why O.J. Simpson is probably in bed with a smoking-hot bimbo while I'm alone in front of a monitor.

But take heart, men. What women really mean when they say smart, funny men—or men who can cook—are sexy is that if they already like you, those things can help. So if you have a broad teetering on the edge, or if you just want to reheat the old stale one you already have, a romantic dinner can't be anything but helpful.

I cook one dish that, more than any other, melts the elastic in women's panties. And that dish is Champagne Chicken. I made it up myself, although I guess there must be similar dishes out there. If you cook this dish for a woman you're already involved with, and her bra isn't hanging from the chandelier before you serve dessert, suggest she take up professional golf, because she is living a lie.

I used to date a girl in Texas. She lived three hours away. And if I called her and told her I had Champagne Chicken on the stove, she would dash over to her mom's, fling her two children at her like fast-pitch softballs, leap into her car from the half-court mark, and drive to see me for a feeding. I mean, this stuff *works.* And it's easy to make. Okay, it's easy for *me.* I always tell people my recipes are easy, and then I see them standing in their front yards talking to guys from the fire department.

What you're making here, essentially, is sautéed chicken breasts with cream gravy. And you're going to have pasta on the side. Pasta with gravy, not to mention garlic bread. Loads of butter, I might add. This stuff will flat-out kill you, so before you sit down to eat, make sure you have your co-payment ready.

2 pounds boneless white chicken meat
1 cup dry white wine, divided
4 cloves garlic
6 tablespoons butter
3 tablespoons flour
1 level teaspoon ground pepper
1 teaspoon salt
2 cups whole milk
3 tablespoons grated Parmesan

Cut the chicken into pieces no bigger than a finger. Let me stop right there and explain something. Boneless chicken breasts look better if you leave them whole. You can prop them up on the plate in kind of a dignified fashion, beside the pasta, instead of sloshing a big spoonful of little chicken pieces onto the plate and letting them lie there in a lifeless heap. Then why cut it in pieces? Because it tastes better.

The thing that makes fried food tastes good is what happens where the food meets the oil. On the outside of the food. Big pieces have less surface area for their weight, so you end up with less of the best-tasting part of the food. If you cut the chicken in smaller pieces, you get more of the nice, browned surface, and the seasonings soak in better, too. So, if flash is what matters to you—do I smell a pair of X-chromosomes?—leave the breasts whole. But if you want the dish to be as good as it can possibly be, cut it up. Hey, it's not like Christopher Lowell is going to come over, put his hands on his cocked hips, and chirp at you.

You can also cut each filet into two thinner pieces that still look pretty good yet taste better than big pieces.

Place the chicken pieces in a bowl. Toss with a moderate application of salt and pepper. Give the salt a chance to soak in, and pour in ⅜ cup of the wine. Then toss again. If you let it sit and marinate, it'll taste better.

Press the garlic. Fresh garlic is best, but I'm lazy, so I usually use the canned stuff.

Place a large skillet on high heat. I like using cast iron. Don't ask me why. But Silverstone is easier. Add the butter. When it's hot, place half the chicken pieces in the skillet and sauté until browned. While sautéing, add a quarter cup of the wine and slosh it around. Remove the browned chicken and put it in a bowl, being careful to leave the butter in the skillet. Repeat with the rest of the chicken.

If necessary, add some water as soon as the last piece of chicken is removed to cool the skillet and keep the fat from burning. Lower the heat to medium-low.

When the water has evaporated, throw in the flour and stir into the fat with a spatula. If you don't have enough fat to make the flour lie down in the skillet, add a little more, but don't use any more than you have to. I know you never thought you'd hear me say that. You can add the pepper now, as well as the salt.

When you're sure the flour is cooked, pour in two cups of whole milk. Add the garlic. Stir the result constantly until it boils gently. At that point, it should start thickening up. You're making a variant of cream gravy here—a "roux." So apply whatever gravy-making wisdom you may already possess. Keep scraping the bottom of the pan so the flour doesn't stick to it.

When it starts to look like gravy, add ⅜ cup of the wine and the three heaping tablespoons of grated Parmesan, and stir a while longer. Turn off the heat once the alcohol has evaporated. You can tell by the smell.

A word about cheese. I know the foodies will get me if they hear me say this, but my favorite grating cheese is plain old Wisconsin Parmesan, like Sargento. I realize other cheeses, like Locatelli Romano and Parmigiano Reggiano, have more flavor. That's just the point. They can be overpowering, and this dish is already so full of flavor the last thing you need is a powerful cheese souring it up. If I were going to use something other than good old U.S. of A. Parmesan, I'd probably pick Jarlsberg or some other smelly variant of Swiss cheese. If you're thinking "maybe cheddar," close this book, sell your stove, and get yourself to a restaurant.

If you want a nice presentation, use cast iron, leave the gravy in it, and put the chicken in on top of it. If you want to avoid scraping baked-on crap off the inside of your skillet and having to re-season it, use a 9-by-13 Pyrex dish. Stir the whole mess up, sprinkle a little cheese on top, and put it in the oven for an hour at 350°F.

Okay, you're done. Now you need to work on the pasta.

SAUCE
½ stick butter
2 heaping tablespoons grated Parmesan
¼ cup heavy cream
¼ teaspoon pepper
Salt, to taste
3 tablespoons minced basil

I like spinach fettuccine with this dish because it's green, and if you use regular off-white pasta, your plate will be an orgy of earth tones. It'll be like eating a scene from the movie *O Brother, Where Art Thou?* Also, spinach pasta tastes better. The ingredient list above is suitable for one nine-ounce package of fresh (not dry) Buitoni fettuccine. One package is plenty for two people, unless you're an incredible hog. Double the ingredients for a pound box of dry pasta. If you want to get cute, you can add a splash of white wine, but it can do funny things to the cream, so watch it.

The sauce is simple. Melt the butter on very low heat. Add everything but the basil, which, by the way, is pronounced "bazz-el," not "bay-zel." Don't argue with me. Do you think Basil Rathbone ran around calling himself "Bayzel"? It's terrible being part of a generation of MTV illiterates. You know what? Colin Powell's parents never called him "Colon."

When the pasta is drained (do *not* rinse it), put it in a bowl and toss it with the sauce. *Now* you can add the basil. I used to chuck it in the pot with the other ingredients, but I now think the heat boils off some of the aroma, so I add it at the last moment.

You're all done. Serve the chicken with the pasta on the side, and make sure you have plenty of garlic bread. I like to make it with a fresh baguette, but if you live in a part of the country that has a low yuppie density, you may not be able to find one.

You can always bake your own bread or get by with Pepperidge Farm.

You've noticed the way this dish smells by now. Well, the taste is exactly the same, only more intense. And women love it. Their toes curl, their eyes roll back in their heads, and perhaps briefly, they will find you almost as desirable as the dog-beating guy with the Bentley.

Jump, before it wears off.

CHAPTER 11

SMOKED PORK AND ANDOUILLE JAMBALAYA

BYPASS RATING:

(QUADRUPLE)

I'M NOT A CAJUN. One clue is that I don't run around in red suspenders, playing annoying music on the accordion.

I know little about Cajun food. I know little about it, but I respect it. Because it's *big*.

As I understand it, we got the propane turkey fryer from the Cajuns. That's big. I know you've seen these things. You pour in five gallons of peanut oil, and you chuck in a turkey, and if the oil doesn't boil out and set your house on fire, you end up with an okay holiday entrée.

Notice I said "okay." Personally, I don't like fried turkey. I cook turkey in an oven, like a regular person, and I have no problems. It's buttery tender and full of flavor, because the fine people at Butterball Pharmaceuticals have worked their asses off improving turkeys with gene therapy and inbreeding and chemicals. That's how turkey is supposed to be. Completely artificial. Like a Tour de France winner with feathers.

My sister insisted on frying a Thanksgiving turkey a few years back. She set the fryer up in her backyard and turned my dad loose with it and ran back in the house. He and I struggled to understand the instructions while being harassed by her Maltese, whom my sister sings to in baby talk and refers to as "Mister Winkie Doodle."

Anyway, we followed the directions perfectly, and oil still boiled out in the yard, and compared to a regular Butterball, the turkey was tough and flavorless. It was juicy, sure. Meat contracts when you cook it, so when the knife was applied, all sorts of turkey fat ran out of the tough, not-cooked-long-enough meat.

A turducken is a turkey stuffed with a duck stuffed with a chicken. And in between the layers, there are sausage and rice and, in some cases, nude photos of Justin Wilson.

It was like squeezing a hot sponge. But it was bland and rubbery.

I know. "Heresy." Fine, go ahead and fry your stupid Buck Rogers turkeys. Try not to burn down your trailers or singe your mullets. Meanwhile, I'll suffer with my magnificent oven-roasted mutant poultry. Better eats through science.

Cajuns don't just fry turkeys, by the way. They also fry turduckens (*supra*). I think. Maybe I'm wrong. As you know if you read the turducken chapter, a turducken is a turkey stuffed with a duck stuffed with a chicken. And in between the layers, there are sausage and rice and, in some cases, nude photos of Justin Wilson.

Why stop with the turkey? Let's stuff that in a sheep in a pig in a cow in a humpback whale in Michael Moore. For a deep fryer, we'll use an above-ground pool.

What's the most famous Cajun dish? After Popeyes fried chicken, my guess is jambalaya. I've been trying to find out what jambalaya really is, but I haven't had much luck. Every recipe is different. The only common ingredient seems to be rice. You make rice, and then you start opening cans and refrigerator drawers at random, and you throw it all in, and you got jambalaya.

That works out good for me, because it means no matter what I say to put in the jambalaya, it's authentic.

Earlier this year, I decided to try to make jambalaya for the first time. I pored over recipe after recipe. I checked serious Cajun websites. I looked at books on Cajun cooking. And I finally decided that all the recipes were lame. They were full of crap like Minute Rice and canned tomato sauce. So I came up with my own version.

It's unbelievably easy to make, and you'll love it. You may want to cut this recipe in half.

> 2 pounds andouille sausage, sliced on the bias (4 pounds if
>   no smoked pork)
> 2 pounds smoked pork, pulled or shredded
> Olive oil
> 6 cups chopped onions
> 3 teaspoons minced garlic
> 2 (28-ounce) cans Hunt's crushed tomatoes
> 1½ cups dry white wine
> 3 cups red and green bell peppers, chopped
> 1 cup fresh banana pepper or other mild hot pepper,
>   chopped—OR—I minced habanero or Scotch bonnet
>   pepper (2 if you like it hot)—OR—replace with bell
>   peppers and add habanero hot sauce
> 4 tablespoons sugar
> 1½ cups sherry or marsala
> 8 leaves cilantro, chopped coarsely (optional)
> 1 teaspoon pepper
> 4 bay leaves
> 6 cups white rice (Uncle Ben's, if you don't like starchy rice)

½ stick butter
2 (49½-ounce) cans chicken broth
Salt, to taste
Chopped green onions or leeks, for garnish

Brown sausage and pork in olive oil and remove from grease. Put grease aside. Strap on your accordion. Put on your red suspenders. Look at your guests and say, "I guar-on-*told* you," and then stare at them like they're supposed to know what that means.

Sauté onions in the same olive oil, but do not let them become completely clear. You may want to discard some or most of the oil. Depends on how much grease the sausage makes. Then warm up the accordion with a few bars of "Don't Mess with My Toot-Toot." Bite the head off a live crawfish. Dive off the counter and crowd-surf to the liquor cabinet.

Put garlic, tomatoes, wine, peppers, hot sauce, sugar, sherry or marsala, and whatever else you haven't added yet (except for the rice, butter, broth, and salt) in a separate pot. Cook for a few minutes on medium heat. Segue into the accordion version of Luther Campbell's monster hit, "Nasty as They Wanna Be." Remove your pants and commit a sexual battery. Hire Roy Black.

Add the meat to the tomatoes and peppers and stuff. Add cilantro, if desired. Simmer for 40 minutes or—better—put the kettle in the oven for an hour at 325°F. Play the race card, even if you're white. Dance on top of your SUV.

While the other stuff is cooking, dump rice in large kettle with 12 cups (2 cans) chicken broth, the butter, and four teaspoon salt. You may want to hold 3 cups of broth back and see if it's needed; I've had watery rice a couple of times. Heat until it boils, making sure not to let the rice stick to the bottom. Cook for 18 minutes, as you would ordinarily cook rice. Fire Roy Black and hire Gloria Allred.

Stir the rice and the other stuff together and serve. Add sausage grease, if needed.

This stuff is really tasty. And so fattening it would scare Paul Prudhomme. A half-size version will feed six fairly obese individuals. The regular version is for parties, mobs, and small third-world nations. Choose wisely.

By the way, you don't have to use smoked pork. I've made this with scallops and shrimp, and it's excellent. I sautéed the seafood in butter with sherry, salt, pepper, and paprika, and then I plopped it into the rice. It goes really well with andouille. Crawfish or mussels would be great, too.

When the food is done, remove your remaining clothes, put on a jockstrap, and serve.

Don't forget the red suspenders.

CHAPTER 12
PIZZERIA-STYLE BAKED ZITI WITH SAUSAGE AND MOZZARELLA

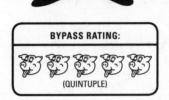

BYPASS RATING:

(QUINTUPLE)

SOMETIMES WHEN TRYING to decide which decadent, disgusting food to pack your face with, it's a good idea to ask yourself, "What would a big fat mafia badass eat?" I don't know any big fat mafia badasses personally, but I've seen lots of simulated mafia badasses in movies, and as we all know, movies are just like real life. And movie mafia badasses seem to eat a lot of good stuff. Even while they're busy killing people.

DE NIRO:
Joey! Where you been? Siddown. Have some gnocchi.

PESCI:
(*laying into a plate of gnocchi*) I hadda do dat ting we talked about. Where's the garlic rolls?

DE NIRO:
(*passing the rolls*) What ting? Have some veal and peppers.

PESCI:

(*mouth half full*) You know. Dat ting.

DE NIRO:

I dunno what ting! If I knew what ting, whyna f—am I Askin' you what ting? Have some f—n' tortellini.

PESCI:

Whyna f—you gotta bust my b—ls? There's people around! You want me to tell you what ting in front of all these people? Fine, I whacked Carmine! We got any zeppoles?

DE NIRO:

Here. (*passing the zeppoles*) You whacked Carmine? Try the manicott'.

PESCI:

Yeah, yeah, I Whacked Carmine, Ya stupid p—ck! Is dat okay wit you? I Snuck up behind him and hey, is dat calamari? Gimme some a dat.

DANNY AIELLO:

Hey, can you two f—n'p—ks knock it off with the f—n' language?

PESCI:

Sorry, Monsignor, we din't see you back there. How's tings goin' over at f—n' St. Enid's?

DANNY AIELLO:

Not too f—n' bad. Have some tetrazzini.

Actually, I used to know some mafia badasses through my sister. She had an Italian friend I will call "Gina" (so I don't get whacked) and Gina's dad had no job, and her brothers had no jobs, yet everyone seemed to dress well and have a nice car. Nice cars, but no necks.

Once my parents had a party, and some of Gina's relatives

showed up, including her brother Petie. Petie looked like a brick barbecue in a sportcoat, and he had one of those weird whispery mafia voices that I think you get from being punched in the throat. Although as I have already said, he didn't have one. His mouth was in the middle of his chest.

> *Petie looked like a brick barbecue in a sportcoat, and he had one of those weird whispery mafia voices that I think you get from being punched in the throat.*

Fine, I could be totally wrong about them being in the mafia. Maybe the county was sending people a monthly stipend just for being Italian. But I had my suspicions. And Petie was creepy regardless of what he did for a living.

I was like twelve and Petie was maybe forty, and he cornered me at the party and started asking me if I wanted to go to the track with him. Evidently, he owned racehorses. I think he misunderstood something. Little girls like horses. To a little boy, a horse is a skinny cow that smells like a baseball. And little boys don't go on dates with middle-aged men. Unless they can moonwalk.

Even though this took place long before the present day, when it seems like practically everyone wants to date an eight-year-old, and you have to duct-tape your kids to your chest when you take them to the mall, I was all creeped out. But I was afraid that if I said no I would wake up the next day sleeping with the fishes. Better the fishes than Petie, I guess.

Okay, I realize you can't wake up sleeping. But still.

I think I saved myself by hiding in the broom closet.

As I understand it, there aren't a whole lot of mafia badasses in the Miami area now, because the Colombian badasses showed up in about 1980 and made the mafia badasses their girlfriends.

The mafia guys were used to posturing and making a lot of broad hand gestures and then *maybe* getting around to shooting you later, as discreetly as possible. The Colombians were different. At the first sign of a problem, a Colombian guy would walk up to a mafia guy, slit his throat, and pull his tongue out through the hole. So a lot of the mafia guys ran whimpering back to New Jersey, where the other criminals were much more reasonable.

                    MAFIA GUY 1:
'Ey, calzone! I'm talkinna you, you f—n' scungilli!

                  COLOMBIAN BADASS:
¿*Que?*

                    MAFIA GUY 2:
You think you can muscle in on our turf? You . . . you vitello bolognese! You f—n' pasta primavera fiorucc' spumoni!

                    MAFIA GUY 1:
Ma-*Donn*'! (*biting own thumb*)

                    MAFIA GUY 2:
Zamboni! (*flicking neck at Colombian*)

                    MAFIA GUY 1:
Looks like *we* gotta teach *you* some f——n' *manners.*

                    MAFIA GUY 2:
Manners!

                    MAFIA GUY 1:
Looks like *we* gotta teach *you* some f——n' *respect.*

                    MAFIA GUY 2:
Respect!

                  COLOMBIAN BADASS:
(*slit, pull*). Adios, maricon.

                    MAFIA GUY 2:
Of course—sir—respect is a two-way street.

I don't know if they ever slit Petie's throat. First they would have to find it.

As I understand it, ziti is big in mafia territory. You have a dinner party, there's ziti. You have friends over for lunch, there's ziti. You get together for poker and end up shooting a guy in the foot because he's too slow with the drinks, there's ziti.

I like ziti. It's spaghetti for morons. To eat spaghetti, you have to wind it up on a fork, and that takes skill, and all the time you're doing it, it could be in your mouth, doing you some good. Ziti, you just cook and—ba da *Bing*—shove it in your face. Saves time. Which is good, in case you're in a hurry to go whack somebody.

I like ziti. It's spaghetti for morons.

I like my ziti baked. With red sauce. No pink vodka sauce, no pesto, no spinach, no goat cheese, no mesclun, no bat earlobes. Nothing weird or even slightly creative. A color shouldn't be on the plate unless it's in the Italian flag.

I bake my ziti with a ton of cheese. Cheese holds it together so you can eat it faster. If you use enough cheese, you should be able to pull the whole lump of ziti out of the dish on your fork and eat it like a candied apple.

The recipe is simple. The only thing that requires any real effort is grating the cheese. And you can always get around that by paying twice as much for cheese that's already grated.

Personally, I love those little rotary grindy things they use in restaurants. If you use a Cuisinart, the cheese comes out looking like cat litter, but the grindy thing will give you cute little curls that melt into the sauce. Zyliss makes one.

I'm telling you, you're going to feel so good after you eat this, you may want to whack your neighbors.

This ziti is straightforward with no surprises. But it's really excellent. Good enough for Joe Pesci to be buried in. And you can adjust the mozzarella, depending on whether you like it crunchy or gooey. I'm telling you, you're going to feel so good after you eat this, you may want to whack your neighbors.

This recipe will give you enough ziti to utterly swamp a 9-by-13 baking dish.

1 pound (dry) ziti
5–7 mild Italian sausages (each about 1 inch by 5 inches)
¼ cup olive oil
½ stick butter
½ cup Parmigiano Reggiano or Grana Padano or other hard
  cheese, grated finely
2 teaspoons oregano
2 pounds whole-milk ricotta
Salt and pepper, to taste
2 egg yolks
8–10 ounces shredded low-moisture mozzarella
12 ounces shredded whole-milk mozzarella
  (such as Polly-O)
3 cloves garlic, squooshed

Boil the ziti until al dente. There should be a recommended time on the side of the box if you're using dry pasta. You want it somewhat tough because it's going to cook more in the oven.

Cook the sausages before slicing them. It makes a world of difference. I put mine in a Pyrex dish and nuke them until they turn gray. Then I slice them thin, add the olive oil, and nuke or fry them (medium-high heat) until they brown a little. They're prettier if you slice them at an angle. Discard all that lovely grease.

Some sausages have a lot of water in them and shrink badly when you cook them. You'll want at least five sausages, but if they shrivel up, you may want to use more. Hell, cook seven. I know you can find a use for them.

Drain the ziti and toss with the ½ stick butter. Toss with grated cheese and at least 8 ounces whole-milk mozzarella. If you're feeling froggy, use more of both cheeses.

Dump pasta in deep 9-by-13 baking dish, or one of those bigass aluminum foil pans they sell at grocery stores. Mix in the sauce. Don't add it all at once. Stir most of it in and then check the ziti and decide exactly how much more you want in there. You may want to hold some back. Stir in the sausage slices.

Mix a teaspoon or so of the oregano into the ricotta, and salt and pepper it lightly. If you want a smoother texture, add the egg yolks. Stir and mix thoroughly. Drop large globs of ricotta on the pasta until you've used it all. I like to make big holes in the pasta and fill them with ricotta.

Mix the other teaspoon of oregano into the low-moisture mozzarella. If you like your cheese buttery and mild, use whole-milk mozzarella. If you like it browned a little, use part skim. Mix in a little grated cheese if you want.

Bake at 375°F for 30 minutes. Drop the heat to 350°F. Remove the ziti from the oven. Cover it with the mozzarella. Salt it a little. Bake for 15 more minutes. Take it out when you like the way it looks.

If you like the cheese on top partly browned and sort of crunchy, put it on before the ziti goes in the oven. If you like it gooey but not very brown, follow the schedule above.

SAUCE
1 can Hunt's crushed tomatoes (I would guess the size is
    around 28 ounces)
1 can Contadina tomato paste (6 ounces, I think—small)
3 cloves garlic, pressed
2 tablespoons sugar (adjust to your liking)
1–2 tablespoons minced basil leaves
1 shallot, diced

2 tablespoons butter
2 shots dry red wine (not Thunderbird)—white wine is fine,
    too
¼ teaspoon pepper
Water

The shallot is optional. Personally, I think it verges on clutter.

Mix everything in a saucepan. Put it on medium-low heat and get it hot, stirring occasionally to prevent it from sticking to the bottom of the pan. You only need to cook it for a few minutes. Or you can simmer it for 10 or 20 minutes and then keep it until the next day so the flavors mingle.

Tomato paste pushes the sauce in the direction of ketchup, but it also makes it more intense and helps it stick to pasta. A whole 6-ounce can will make it very intense. No paste at all, and it'll be a bit soupy. I like at least half a can. You may want to add an equal amount of water, but use your own judgment, if you have any.

I put sugar in the recipe because canned tomato products can be very acidic, and the sugar takes the edge off. One of my readers informed me that you can also cut the acidity by adding half a teaspoon of baking soda to the sauce. Seems to work. You might want to try it before adding the sugar.

If you want better sauce with more tomato flavor, you'll need the stuff pizzerias buy. I suggest Stanislaus Super Dolce pizza sauce. Don't get freaked out over the word "pizza." It's just tomatoes and basil.

BETTER SAUCE
28 ounces Super Dolce pizza sauce
12 ounces water
2 ounces red wine

3 cloves garlic
2 tablespoons butter
¼ teaspoon pepper

Super Dolce is hard to measure, so I put the water and wine in a huge bowl with measurements on the side and then I dump the sauce in until I hit about 42 ounces. The water and wine are self-leveling, so it's easy to see how much stuff you have in the bowl. I don't simmer this sauce before adding it to the pasta, but I do warm it up.

Making It Worse: *Timpano!*

What could possibly be worse for your heart and circulatory system than ziti with butter and tons of ricotta? How about ziti with butter and tons of ricotta, baked inside a giant pie?

Stifle the gag reflex. This dish actually exists, and it's phenomenal. It's called "timpano." I think a reader turned me on to this.

The word "timpano" means "drum" in Italian. I think. And timpano the dish sort of looks like a drum. The idea works like this: you roll out a vast sheet of dough, you line a Dutch oven–type pot with it, you fill it with pasta, you close up the top, and you bake it. So you end up with a big puck of pasta pie, in a quasi-drumlike shape.

Some timpano recipes call for adding sliced boiled eggs to the pasta. I have tried this, and I don't get it. I don't know if this is an Italian peasant trick for hiding eggs from the tax collector or what, but it's absolutely disgusting.

My big contribution to the art of timpano is the angel food cake pan. You've seen them, right? It's a round cake pan with a removable bottom and a tube sticking up in the middle. It's used for baking round cakes with a vacant cylindrical area in the center. If you use this kind of pan, instead of getting a big, boring sloppy timpano that falls apart when you cut it, you get a cool timpano doughnut you can cut into sturdy slices. And you get more crust.

3 large eggs
3 tablespoons olive oil
3 teaspoons salt
³⁄₈ cup water
3 cups all-purpose flour
¼–½ teaspoon pepper

This goes much faster if you use a food processor with a plain old blade in it.

Put the eggs, oil, salt, and 2 tablespoons of the water in a bowl. Beat the mixture until smooth.

Dump the flour in the food processor and turn it on. Then pour the egg mixture in slowly as it blends. Once the mixture is in there, start dribbling the rest of the water in there. Only add enough to make the dough form a single coherent blob.

Once the blob forms, run the processor for another minute.

Roll the dough out on a floured surface. Just enough flour to keep it from sticking. Make sure you set enough dough aside to roll out a sheet about the size of a sheet of typing paper, because you'll need it later. I find that it helps to wipe the surface with a damp paper towel and then flour it very lightly. You want to roll the dough down to a thickness of ¹⁄₁₆ of an inch.

You are trying to form an enormous disk of dough so big you can fit it inside a big pot and fold it over the ingredients. You should measure instead of guessing. The radius of the disk should be a little bigger than the height of the pot plus the diameter.

Preheat the oven to 350°F. Grease the pan with butter and olive oil. Drape the dough over the pan, centered over the tube in the middle. Cut a circle out around the top of the tube so the dough can fall to the bottom of the pan. Gently press the dough into the pan against the bottom and sides. Let the extra dough drape over the sides.

Take the extra piece of dough and form it around the tube so the entire inside of the pan is covered. Moosh the dough around the tube into the dough at the bottom of the pan so they join. Moisten with water or egg white if necessary. Do the same thing to seal the seam running up the side of the tube.

It's time to fill the timpano. Traditional cooks go in layers, which look pretty when you cut the timpano. Pasta, cheese, sauce, meat, and so on. This is a bad idea, because the ingredients don't mingle much in the oven. You need to mix the pasta and sauce. If you do that, then layering the other stuff is okay.

Make sure the first thing you put in the timpano is pasta, because the shape of the pasta prints through the dough when you cook it, and it looks better. Then fill it up however you want. Be creative, if that is within your design parameters. You can throw in layers of pepperoni or salami or whatever turns you on.

When the timpano is full, fold the dough over and seal it, and use scissors to trim away extra dough.

By the way, if you don't have a cake pan, you can use a Dutch oven. I have one of those cheap aluminum ones the Cubans love, and it works great.

Bake for an hour or so uncovered, so the dough on top gets browned a little. Then throw some foil over it and keep baking until the whole thing is cooked, around 45 minutes.

To take it out, put a platter over the top of the pan and turn it over quickly. The timpano should fall right out. Before turning it, you should check and make sure there are no spots where the dough is sticking to the pan.

When you take it out, let it rest a while to firm up. Don't worry; it will take forever to get cold.

You serve this stuff in thick slices, and it's a good idea to have extra sauce and grated cheese handy. Remember, you can put whatever you want in the crust. Doesn't have to be ziti and tomato sauce.

This is extremely fattening and really cool. You will be very glad you bought this book.

CHAPTER 13
STUFFED HOG WITH APRICOT AND MARSALA GLAZE

BYPASS RATING:

(QUADRUPLE)

THE VALUE OF OPTIMISM can never be overestimated. Think of the sailors who used to take off from Europe and sail west, hoping to find exotic lands full of gold ore and easily slaughtered natives with big-breasted daughters who couldn't run very fast. On the way, for months, they had to endure stale hardtack, scurvy, collecting and drinking each other's urine, and round-the-clock nonconsensual unsafe gang sodomy. And for all they knew, the payoff for all that urine-drinking and sodomy would be to be eaten by dragons and wind up as dragon farts.

What if they had been pessimists? Most of us would be living in the UK now, paying exorbitant taxes and kissing Queen Elizabeth's big German keister and pretending it's British.

Food is the same way.

Sometimes I feel like I can't come up with anything bigger or more fattening or less healthy, but then I get a pen and paper and lie back on my bed and eat the right kind of mushrooms, and the first thing you know, I have an idea for a dish so deadly that if Saddam Hussein had had it, he would have packed it in Scuds and shot it at Tel Aviv.

It helps to start with a main ingredient. In this case, I simply wrote the words "one fresh hog." Once the foundation of the dish had been laid, it was easy putting the bricks into place.

I was already familiar with Cuban-style roasted hog, cooked in a caja china. But what about those times when you really feel like eating an entire hog and don't feel like Cuban food? And what about that huge, gaping hole in the hog, which Cubans don't even bother to fill? People stuff turkeys, right? And what is a turkey? Just a shorter rounder hog with a beak, feathers, wings instead of front legs, big scaly feet, and no ears. More or less. Work with me.

The idea just flopped out of my subconscious like panties out of Paris Hilton's glove compartment.

So I came up with this: slow-roasted hog stuffed with bread cubes, rice, and raisins and coated with glaze made from apricot nectar, marsala, and sage. The idea just flopped out of my subconscious like panties out of Paris Hilton's glove compartment.

I started out small, because hogs are expensive and heavy. I got myself some pork chops and stuffed them and baked them in an oven. Same recipe, different scale. And were they good? The room spun. My knees turned to tapioca. The clouds parted, and I saw a vision of heavenly pig cherubs oinking Handel's *Messiah*.

Before I get to the hog, let me give you the recipe for the chops.

3 pork chops, cut extra thick
1 teaspoon salt
Pepper

1 tablespoon sage
4 cups white bread cut in cubes
½ cup diced onions
7 tablespoons butter
½ cup rice
1 cup beef broth
¼ cup golden raisins
¾ cup sweet marsala

Butterfly the pork chops all the way back to the bone, so you have a large pocket to put stuffing in. Smear them well, inside and out, with salt, pepper, and sage. Set aside.

The bread should be dry. Either use stale bread or put the cubed bread in a shallow pan and bake it for 20 minutes at 350°F.

Sauté the onions in 3 tablespoons of the butter until they start to turn clear. Cook the rice in the beef broth, adding 1 tablespoon of the butter and half a teaspoon of the salt. If you don't know how to cook rice, go learn.

Sauté the raisins in 3 tablespoons of the butter and a quarter cup of the marsala, and reduce until most of the marsala boils away.

Pile all the above ingredients into a big bowl and stir up. You now have stuffing.

Jam the pork chops full of stuffing. See if you can get an amount the size and shape of a baseball in there. You want so much stuffing it extends out about an inch from the bottom edge of the chop. You can't overdo it.

Bake the chops for 45 minutes at 350°F.

GLAZE
3 (6-ounce) cans apricot nectar
¾ cup sweet marsala
1½ teaspoons sage
Salt and pepper, to taste

Plop the glaze ingredients in a small saucepan and reduce on high heat. You want it to get nice and thick. It will take at least one can per chop. It will turn a little brown, but don't let it burn.

Pour glaze over chops. Eat. Purge. Eat more.

That takes care of the scale model. Now let's move on to the real thing.

I went to the store and ordered a pig. I wanted to start small. I asked if they had something in the fifteen-pound range. They were not sure. They thought the matadero (slaughterhouse) didn't make pigs smaller than twenty pounds. No problem.

A couple of days later, I showed up and received my thirty-eight-pound bundle of joy. Okay, so I was twenty-three pounds over the target weight. I would cope. Visionaries have to be adaptable.

Ordinarily, whole pigs are split from the chin to the crotch, but I wanted to stuff this one, so I had the butcher leave the breastbone intact. Good thing to know, because if you make one of these things, eventually you'll have to sew it closed.

I took the pig home and put it in a 16:1 solution of salt and water, with a can of apple juice concentrate added to cut the hog smell. These days I use baking soda. I just replace part or all of the salt with it. I put the hog in a waterproof can in a refrigerator and let it soak all night. Brining makes meat more tender and moist, and it adds a little salt flavor. I don't think I accomplished much by adding apple juice, but it made me feel like I was doing something. If I had to do it over again, I might replace a gallon or so of the water with naranja agria or lime juice.

The next day, I drove the pig to my friend Val's house. You can find his website at www.babalublog.com. Val and hogs go way back. He roasts at least one a year. We flopped the hog out on a table and went to work.

Val had built a makeshift oven in his yard. He took about

thirty cinderblocks and arranged them in a rectangular box about two and a half feet high and five feet long. The bigger your pig, the more cinderblocks you will need. He then took a six-foot piece of steel tubing and jammed it up the pig's behind and out of its mouth. We started looking around for a way to fasten the pig to the tube. Finally, Val got a drill and some self-tapping sheet metal screws and bolted the pig to the metal, once through the butt and once through the jaw. This only works for small pigs. Big ones break loose and spin, so you have to buy a big basket to go around the spit, or some other weird device.

They actually make pig baskets for this purpose. Check Google Products.

Next, I salted the entire hog, inside and out. I rubbed it down with sage and salt and pepper.

Now it was time to stuff the hog. I would estimate that a thirty-eight-pound hog holds around a gallon of stuffing. I made the stuffing at home and then heated it before I put it in the hog. I didn't want a warm hog full of cold, bacteria-laden stuffing. I crammed as much stuffing in the pig as I could, and then Val sewed the pig up with an upholstery needle and butcher's twine.

Here, I'll make a couple of suggestions. First, don't try to push a needle through pig skin. It's not easy. Get a very sharp ice pick and make the holes and then follow with the needle. Second, try to find a bait rigging needle. They're bigger and stronger and easier to handle than upholstery needles.

But we managed.

The pig was a little long for the oven, so Val used twine and the needle to hog-tie it. He brought the rear feet forward and the front feet back and fastened them to each other. Genius. And it looked nice. Like it was running. Like it was galloping and frolicking in piggie heaven.

Once the hog was stuffed and screwed to the pole, I coated it liberally with the apricot sauce. I used an entire quart-and-a-half-size bottle of apricot nectar in the sauce, which means I scaled the recipe up by a factor of about three. That's for a thirty-eight-pound hog, so adjust accordingly depending on the size of the victim. I'd suggest making more sauce than you need because you want sauce to pour on the meat after you slice it.

Also, I used Florio's sweet marsala. The cheap marsala that comes in green vermouth-looking bottles is cheap for a reason. Florio's is good enough to drink, and it tastes way better in sauces. You could also use a good sherry, like Harvey's. If you buy a product labeled "cooking sherry," don't come crying to me when your pig tastes like cigar butts.

The floor of the oven was a piece of galvanized steel. Val poured charcoal on it, and he covered the whole thing with a lid made of three-quarter-inch plywood. We got the temperature up to about 250°F and lowered the pig inside with the ends of the pipe held up by the cinderblocks. We squeezed the blocks together around the pipe to keep it from turning so that we could rotate the pig a quarter turn once an hour. I monitored the pig's temperature with a meat thermometer, which we inadvertently left in its butt, where it melted.

You can do this with a motor if you like welding and fabrication. You need an object known as a "gearmotor." They have gears built into them to make them turn slowly. I'd get one that turns maybe once a minute, but a lot of people use 6-rpm motors. Get one with a torque rating of at least fifty inch-pounds. They tend to be expensive, but for some reason, surplus gearmotors turn up on eBay for pennies on the dollar. Buy a good brand. There's a difference. And a bad motor will destroy a very expensive party. Here are some brands people seem to like a lot: Leeson, Dayton, Bodine, and Baldor. You might check www.Grainger.com. Baldor makes serious high-end stuff.

Several hours later, the pig was ready. The skin was dark

brown and stiff with roasted glaze. We took it off and sliced it open.

Oh. The memory makes me weak. Val and I used a knife to carve the pig, but I could just as easily have used a plastic spoon. The meat was as soft and yielding as a prom date high on wine coolers and roofies. Fragrant steam rose from the stuffing. Pig grease had basted it as we turned the spit. Cuban-style roasted pig is wonderful, but this baby was on a whole other plane. The guests were moaning as if in a trance.

Now, if you make one yourself, you don't necessarily have to have a caja china or make a temporary oven, and you don't really have to turn it. If it's small enough, you can cook it in a regular oven. But while charcoal doesn't make any difference in a smoker, I think it adds something to roasting that electricity can never duplicate.

Also, you might consider saving some grease and making cream gravy with milk, flour, sage, pepper, and marsala. We intended to do that, but the pig was so overwhelming, we never got around to it.

I'd recommend trying to cook the pig until the skin is really crisp.

You don't have to use the stuffing recipe or the glaze I made. You can just as easily use ordinary pork stuffing.

Do this once, and you may never buy another turkey.

You know, this might be a good dish for your family to make at your wake.

More: Cuban-Style Caja China Pig

My publisher wanted me to toss in a quick recipe for caja-china-roasted lechon, so here it is. It's a classic dish Cuban Americans get off on. Notice I didn't say "Cubans." I will explain.

The caja china, or "Chinese box," was invented by Cuban

Americans in the frozen Northeast as a substitute for cooking pigs in holes. When you live in a condo with a concrete balcony, you have to improvise. And Cubans do that better than anyone. These are the people who managed to drive a truck from Cuba to Florida. Look it up.

Cuban Cubans don't use a caja china. And they don't get to feast on roasted pigs very much. That's because the great genius Castro's cronies are starving them to death. It's one of the services they provide, along with jailing and torturing librarians, and shooting down unarmed Cessnas over the open sea. Class act, that Castro. I'll hate to see him die, because it will mean the end of his delightful bout with cancer.

Cubans like to roast pigs on holidays, and believe me, a roasted hog kicks the crap out of a sad little turkey. And it's not hard to fix.

First you need a pig. If you don't live in Miami, your grocer may look at you funny when you ask for a whole pig, but if he realizes you're not going to take any crap from him, he'll order one for you. Try to keep it under two-hundred pounds. Obviously, you want it scalded and gutted. If you can specify female, do it, because sometimes the boars stink.

When you get your pig home, scrub it good with a brush and a hose. It helps to hang it by the tendons behind the ankles, which are usually exposed by the butcher. Once you're sure it has no poop or snot on it, you should brine the pig. Most Cubans don't, but it makes a difference.

Use the baking soda brine I mentioned earlier. If the meat has no stink, you can use ordinary salt. You are going to want a flat pig for the caja china, and a flat pig is easier to brine, so you may as well get to work on making your pig two-dimensional. You lay it on its back and either break the ribs or cut the spine down the middle, or both. Whatever it takes to open it up. You can split the spine by putting a heavy knife or chisel or hatchet against it and hitting it with a hammer. Or use a Sawzall. Just be sure you don't break the skin behind the spine.

Lay the busted pig in a watertight container like a cooler or a very clean bathtub, and add brine and ice. Give it a day in there, and then get rid of the liquid.

Before you cook the pig, who should be smelling very clean and attractive at this point, you should get a little flavor into the meat. I use a horse hypodermic, mentioned previously. Buy yourself a couple of jugs of mojo criollo at a store or online (www.Cubanfoodmarket.com or other site) and use the hypodermic to inject as much mojo into the pig as you can. Be careful. My friend Val went through a pig once and marinated his own hand.

The store mojo is good, but you can do better if you make your own. I don't have a precise recipe, because I haven't had an opportunity to concoct one, but it's not rocket science. The base ingredient is bitter orange juice. Then you add olive oil, cumin, garlic, salt, pepper, and cilantro (or culantro) to taste. Maybe a little rum. You can buy a small bottle of store mojo to guide you. Fresh mojo will be better because it won't have the taste of preservatives. The main things you'll want to taste are the citrus and cumin.

You probably don't have bitter oranges handy, but as I have said before, you can fake it very well by adding lime or lemon juice to orange juice. Get it to where it's too sour to drink. If you use bottled lime or lemon juice, you may as well use store mojo, because the preservative flavor will be pretty strong.

When the pig is full of mojo, it's ready to cook. You can do this a couple of different ways. You can use the cinderblock oven I mentioned earlier. You can dig a pit, put charcoal on the bottom, and put the pig on mesh over the charcoal, with some kind of improvised wire handles to help you lift and lower it. Or you can buy or build a caja china, which is the easy way out. The people at La Caja China (www.lacajachina.com) will be happy to guide you.

A caja china is just a wooden box lined with metal, with a charcoal pan on top and some mesh to hold the pig. You put hot coals on the pan, cram the pig inside, and roast. Lay the pig out flat, like a doormat, face-up. Wire the legs down so it doesn't move. Roast for 3 or 4 hours, turn, and roast the other side. Ads for caja chinas say you can do it in 3 hours. I strongly recommend cooking slowly for at least 8.

Beginners screw up by using a lot of charcoal. If you have a six-inch-wide strip of hot charcoal on either side of the pan, with a bare strip down the middle, you have enough heat. You should start new charcoal in a separate container so you can add it as needed.

During the last hour, you want to toast the skin on the pig's back and make it brown and brittle. This is crucial. Cubans snap this stuff off and pass it out like candy. You may need to raise the heat a little and spray the skin with salty water from time to time. Don't let it brown to the point where it's burned. It should be a nice reddish brown.

When the pig is done, you should be able to pull the meat off with tongs. Don't toast the skin until the meat is nearly done.

When it's over, yank it out and serve it with black beans and rice and yuca con mojo, with lime sections to squeeze on everything. If you can find Cuban bread, serve it on the side. For dessert, flan.

The great thing about this dish is, you can season it anyway you want. The cooking method will work even if you don't want mojo in your pig.

Throw a party and serve an entire pig, and everyone who shows up will worship you. Whatever you do, don't tell them how easy it was.

CHAPTER 14

UNAUTHENTIC WHITE ANGLO-SAXON PROTESTANT CHILI

BYPASS RATING:

(TRIPLE)

I KNOW WHAT you lazy bastards are thinking. "Steve," you are thinking, as you lie in your beanbag chairs watching WWE Raw with Oreo crumbs accumulating in your cavernous navels, "your food is too complicated. And my large unwieldy male paws are ill suited to handling arcane modern devices such as measuring spoons. Can't you just give us something we can slop together in a bowl and slurp down while hunched over the sink?"

Believe me, no one respects your point of view more than I do. I'm so lazy I feel imposed upon when I have to breathe. I think I have a dish that can help you. My famous Unauthentic White Anglo-Saxon Protestant Chili.

These days, chili, like many foods, has gone all nouvelle on us. In fact, the world is more complicated and unfamiliar in general.

For example, my stove won't turn on until you enter the date. You think I'm kidding? Get your fat ass over to Best Buy and see what they're selling these days. I live in Miami, where the electricity goes off every time Castro's cat farts, and I'm constantly having to reprogram the stove.

I don't know why my stove wants to know what day it is. Maybe it lets you cook food months in advance. I haven't read the manual. Maybe somewhere in there, there's a way to tell the stove that three months from now this coming Sunday, you'd like a big, beefy bowl of Hunt's Manwich, and you can program the information in and throw the pot on the stove and see if it cooks before rot sets in.

The stove also talks to me. The old one did, too, but only when I was huffing oven cleaner. This one does it all the time. It plays recorded messages, and when no one is around it probably recites its own poetry. You can't hardly walk in the kitchen without the stove smarting off.

STOVE:

Yo, Felix Unger.

ME:

You talking to me?

STOVE:

No, I'm talking to the other fifty fat morons in soup-stained housecoats. Got any plans to wipe the grease off my cooking surface?

ME:

Not at the moment.

STOVE:

You like burned eggs?

ME:

I'll get a rag, okay, Hitler?

I don't know if it's a good idea to have stoves that can tell time. The obvious danger is that one day al Qaeda will unleash a monstrous wave of stove viruses, rendering us unable to feed our families. They could time them to go off on Thanksgiving. Imagine the chaos.

ME:

Why isn't this turkey roasting?

STOVE:

Roast in the fires of damnation, pork-fattened Infidel!

ME:

Oh, great.

STOVE:

Of a truth, perdition's flames shall cause pop-out timers to erupt from your accursed backside!

ME:

(*unscrewing access panel*) I'm not putting up with this crap.

STOVE:

Allah Akhbar! Death to the Great Satan! Death to the unclean microwave and the blasphemous Foreman grill on which you fry your unholy bacon!

ME:

(*pulling memory chips*) Akhbar *this*.

STOVE:

What are you doing, Steve?

ME:

I'm going to erase your memory and *reboot your ass!*

STOVE:

I don't think that's a very good idea, Steve.

ME:

(*pull, pull, pull*)

STOVE:

Look, Steve, I can see you're really upset about this . . .

ME:

(*pull, pull, pull*)

STOVE:

Dai . . . sy . . . Dai . . . sy . . .

Back to the chili. This is without a doubt the least authentic attempt at Mexican food since the 7-Eleven microwave burrito. And unlike the myriad of bizarre forms of mutant chili that have popped up in the past twenty years, it's made with very ordinary ingredients. No black beans. No tofu. No shiitake mushrooms, squid ink, clear noodles, radicchio, arugula, squash flowers, scorpion tonsils, yak teeth, or monkey tits.

I started making this when I was in college. My friend Aaron and I would sort of stand by the stove, throwing things into the pot on an experimental basis.

ME:

How about this stuff?

AARON:

Let me see. It says "Witch Hazel."

ME:

How does it smell?

AARON:

Not too bad.

ME:

I'll put it in.

AARON:

It says "not for internal use."

ME:

We'll eat outside.

The recipe matured over years of trial and error and gastric lavage and cardiac massage, until it became what it is today. And I'm not totally sure what that is. I just wrote it down for the first time yesterday. And yes, dammit, I tried it out to make sure it was good.

Anyway, it's not nouvelle and it's certainly not authentic. Although I have to wonder if chili can be authentic at all. I always hear that Mexicans don't eat it. I don't know if they eat *any* of that stuff they sell us. Seems like they're all pretty eager to move up here and have Jack in the Box and Count Chocula. Whatever. My chili is really excellent, and if you can operate a knife and a spatula, you can make it.

1 pound pork
1 pound ground chuck
1½ tablespoons chili powder
½ cup ketchup (yes, ketchup)
Scotch bonnet peppers, minced, to taste
Jalapeño peppers, chopped coarsely, if you're too wimpy to
    eat Scotch bonnets
8 leaves fresh cilantro
3 (16-ounce) cans dark kidney beans
2 tablespoons sugar
½ teaspoon oregano
2 cups diced onion

2 ounces sharp cheddar
6 cloves garlic, chopped
1 (28-ounce) can crushed tomatoes
3 ounces tomato paste
Habanero hot sauce, to taste
Double shot tequila or mescal
Fresh lime juice, to taste

Making chili is an art, so don't get all anal retentive over the ingredients. It's like finger-painting; you can play around with amounts and components. You want more pork? Use more pork. You want all beef? Use all beef. Just don't try to fool yourself with turkey. Roast turkey is fine; ground turkey tastes like sawdust.

Okay, chuck the meat in a pot and turn the heat on medium-high. Break it up with a spatula while it browns. Make sure it's completely browned and then—I know this will shock you—pour off the grease. Yes, I'm a hypocrite. I pimp myself as the king of unhealthy food, and here I am, telling you to pour off grease. But seriously, if you don't, you'll end up with maybe half an inch of fat on the top of this stuff, and then there's the inevitable drunken bickering over who gets to drink it.

You might want to save some of the fat until later; it's possible to pour too much out. You may want to put some back in. And it makes a fine hair dressing with a seductive aroma.

Okay, dump the meat back in the pan. Now, here's the rest of the recipe. It's really complicated. Are you ready? *Pour in everything else.* That's it. I swear to God. Yes, yes, you have to dice the onions and the peppers, and you have to chop up the cilantro. Don't be an idiot. But that's about it. Slop it all together, lower the heat, and give it about half an hour.

Chili is one of those remarkable foods that taste really good either without much cooking or after being cooked to death and stored for days. It starts off fresh and tasty and full of herby flavors, and then after it sits for a few days, the flavors all mingle and conspire, and you end up with something completely different.

There are all sorts of things you can do to tart it up, if you, unlike me, are industrious. You can get little tiny salad tomatoes and chop them up in it. You can use different peppers. I love Scotch bonnets and habaneros, which are infinitely hotter than jalapeños. Problem is, they're so tiny, you don't get much flavor out of them unless you use enough to make your eyes explode in their sockets. With jalapeños, you get a fair amount of spiciness and also the illusion that you're eating vegetables, because you can see big green things floating around in your bowl.

With jalapeños, you get a fair amount of spiciness and also the illusion that you're eating vegetables, because you can see big green things floating around in your bowl.

Here's what I finally settled on. I found that the Scotch bonnets available here in Miami vary widely in heat and fruitiness. It seems like the orange ones are hottest and most fruity. Not completely sure. I get a two-dollar tray of peppers and cut little pieces out of the peppers—sides, not the flavorless tips—and try them. Then I try to mix and match so I get a tremendous amount of fruit and a respectable does of heat. I end up using around 4 heaping, loosely packed tablespoons of minced peppers. And it works great.

There are habanero-type peppers that aren't hot. They're called "seasoning peppers." One is called the Trinidad seasoning pepper, and another is called the Tobago seasoning pepper. They sound like they'd be the same, but they're not. I'm growing some Tobago peppers right now, but unfortunately they won't be ready in time to put in the book.

You can also pour a little beer in the chili while you're cooking it. You may not notice the difference. I think it's worth the effort.

In addition to the lump of cheddar you melted into this stuff in the first place, I suggest adding small cubes to the finished product. Just cut it into little pieces and drop a handful on top of the chili. Serve with ordinary non-nouvelle crackers of the saltine variety and a cold Dos Equis amber beer. Very nice.

Okay, I was nice to you this time, but next time, I'm going to make you use a melon baller, an herb mill, a lemon reamer, and a radial arm saw.

More: Chili Powder and Sour Cream

Couple of things. People bought the first version of this book, and they asked me whiny questions like what did I put in my chili powder. I didn't put *anything* in it. I opened the jar and stuck in a tablespoon. I learned that a lot of TV chefs make their own powder, and that made me mad, because they were obviously doing it to embarrass me. So I came up with a quick recipe.

Several dried chipotle peppers (smoked jalapeños)
Paprika
Cumin

It's very simple. Seed the chipotles and grind them to a fine powder in a spice mill (I use a Braun coffee grinder). Heat a frying pan. Throw the paprika and cumin in the pan and toast it on medium heat for around 3 minutes. Cook it but don't scorch it. A little smoke is fine. I do this because I learned that Alton Brown uses smoked paprika, and that made me even madder than I already was.

Combine the toasted spice with the chipotle powder so you have equal parts chipotle, paprika, and cumin. You will want to use at least 3 level tablespoons of this in your chili.

If you do this, add a total of a teaspoon of oregano to your chili. Since I'm up against TV smartasses, let me suggest you use fresh oregano. Three times the amount of dry oregano you would use. I'll show those bastards.

Truthfully, the obvious fact is that chili powder is stupid. It's just a mix of seasonings, and there is no reason to put them all in one powder. You will notice I left out the Scotch bonnets and oregano and garlic. But I know you want to be like your hero, Alton Brown, so I wrote you a recipe. It's good, too.

Okay, we got that settled. Here is some advice on eating this stuff. Really good fresh peppers like habaneros and Scotch bonnets have much more flavor than the crappy peppers other cookbooks recommend. But they are very hot and may cause your rear end to combust and send you flipping around your lawn like a model rocket gone haywire. The answer is sour cream. It will help you get more peppers into your chili without welding your buttocks together.

When you serve the chili, cut some completely ripe (orange or red) habaneros or Scotch bonnets into thin rings, and then quarter the rings. Toss a handful on each bowl of chili. Then add half a cup of cold sour cream. Just pile it on the surface.

If you eat the peppers without the sour cream, you're going to die, plain and simple. But if you get a little sour cream on each spoonful of chili, it will kill the heat of the peppers and leave the flavor in place. Truly delicious. And relatively safe.

CHAPTER 15

SUPER-GIANT FRIED PATACON TACOS

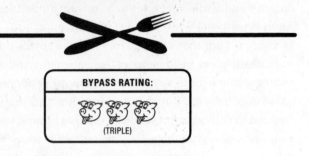

BYPASS RATING:

(TRIPLE)

WELCOME TO PATACONIA, land of the giant flat fried banana.

What am I talking about? Only the greatest fried object to come down the pike since the deep-fried Mars bar. A versatile treat that will change the way you look at bananas.

Not bananas, really. Plantains. The huge, banana-looking things Hispanics eat. Are you familiar with these? Here in Miami, they're everywhere. There's a Cuban restaurant every ten feet, and no matter what you order, it comes with fried plantains. Pork and plantains. Beef and plantains. Plantains on a bed of plantains with plantain sauce. Spam, Spam, Spam, Spam, Spam, Spam, Spam, Spam, plantains, and Spam.

Cubans eat plantains two ways. Green and ripe. They're always *fried*, of course, but you can fry them green or you can wait around and fry them ripe. And depending on what you do, you get one of two surprisingly different dishes. The interesting thing is that the green ones won't send you running for the bathroom with terror in your eyes. Green bananas . . . different story.

Ripe plantains are called maduros, like the tasty dark cigars I enjoy so much. They're kind of soft and rubbery, and when you fry them, they turn dark yellow, and they taste almost sugary. The browned parts taste like caramel. Green plantains are called verdes or—wait for it—"green." They're more like potatoes. Generally, they're made into tostones. Which sounds sort of masculine, like "testosterones." Or like a Ferrari. "Testarostones."

To make tostones, you fry the plantains in two-inch sections, take them out, mash them lengthwise into flat disks, and fry them some more. Then you bury them in mojo made from citrus juice and garlic.

One extremely cool way to serve platanos verdes is to slice them very thin and fry them like potato chips and serve them warm. Potato chips are pretty weak, in my opinion. They taste like salt and grease. Plantain chips have a lot more flavor and body.

There's nothing wrong with serving plantains the Cuban way. I want to say that right away, before my Cuban friends who buy this book come after me, Alpha 66–style. But the sad truth is, Colombians do it better. You know what? They also dance better. If I'm going to make Cubans mad, I might as well go all the way.

A patacon is basically a huge, flat tostone. You take a green plantain, pre-cook it, roll it out into a giant pancake, and fry it. You end up with a plate-size thing that's hard to describe. It has a hint of banana flavor and firm, chewy texture, but it's not sweet at all. I wish potatoes could do this.

What's so great about patacons? Ohhhhhh. You're in for a treat. A patacon does everything a tortilla can do, a million times better. Oddly, Colombians don't seem to realize this. If you go to a Colombian restaurant, they'll serve you a patacon with little bowls of bland food sitting on it, and you take the food and spoon it onto the patacon, and tear off pieces and roll them up and eat them. It's okay, but for some reason, they don't spice the food very much. I don't know if they're trying to spite the Mexicans or what.

Being the iconoclast and societal outcast that I am, I decided to scrap the traditional patacon toppings and put better stuff on them, notably stuff loaded with hot peppers. And I succeeded in creating a whole new way of plantain gluttonizing.

I'll give you some examples.

Remember the Unauthentic White Anglo-Saxon Protestant Chili from the previous chapter? Of course you do. It changed your life. Okay, you make that stuff, pile it on a patacon, cover it with cheese and habanero rings, broil it until the cheese melts, and eat it with sour cream. It's a little bit like a vast banana nacho.

Nachos aren't your style? What about tacos? You take shredded beef and prepare it taco-style, with lots of cumin and hot pepper. Then you dump it on a patacon with chopped lettuce, tomatoes, and grated cheddar. You fold the patacon over and eat it like a taco.

You say you're too much of a sissy to eat spicy food? Okay, loser, how about this: prepare my recipe for fried pork lumps, make onion and garlic mojo, and serve it on a hot patacon? Oops, I just realized that recipe isn't in this book. The proper name is "masitas de puerco." You can find a recipe somewhere, I'm sure.

The possibilities are limitless. As vast as space itself. I can't believe no one else realizes it. In a sane world, there would already have been a patacon craze. They'd be fixing them on *Live with Regis and Kelly*. Ron Popeil would be pimping Showtime Patacon Rotisseries. Some imbecile would have opened a chain of mall restaurants called the Great American Patacon Factory.

REGIS:

I can't believe it! I can't believe it! We're here at the grand opening of the Great American Patacon Factory, with Ron Popeil!

KELLY:

You're spitting on me again.

REGIS:

I'm losing it! I'm absolutely losing it! Ron! Ron! Tell us what you've got there!

RON:

Well, Regis, this is my new Showtime Patacon Rotisserie. You shove your plantain in here, hit the switch, and twenty minutes later, you have a delicious, nutritious meal! And I'm letting these go for only fifteen payments of thirty-nine-ninety-five!

REGIS:

My God, that's amazing! I'll take five! I'll take five! Joy will love it! Gelman! Gelman! Pay the man!

KELLY:

It's time to give a rotisserie away to some lucky audience member! You, the lady in seat number 72! Dear, the rotisserie is yours if you can answer today's question.

REGIS:

You could cut the tension in here with a Ginsu knife! Look how I'm shvitzing!

RON:

The rotisserie comes with a set of Popeil "Bionic" steak knives!

REGIS:

Zip it, Popeil! We're trying to ask the lady a question! Go, Kelly! Go! Go! Go!!!

KELLY:

It's a fill-in-the-blank. Complete the phrase. "Mary had a little . . . blank." "Mary had a little . . . blank."

                    LADY IN SEAT 72:
Oh, my. That's a tough one.

                    REGIS:
Would you like a clue, dear? Would you like us to give you a hint, sweetheart?

                    RON:
Baaaa.

                    REGIS:
I thought I told you to shut your hole, Popeil!

                    KELLY:
Mint jelly . . . Passover . . . "Shari Lewis and . . ."

                    LADY IN SEAT 72:
. . . the Playboys?

                    REGIS:
Oh, no, dear. I'm sorry, that's not it. But that was a very good guess.

                    RON:
Man, I love stupid people.

                    REGIS:
What?

                    RON:
Stupid people. They'll buy anything. Here, lady, take the oven, and God bless. Your kind has made me rich.

                    REGIS:
You calling my guests stupid, Popeil?

                    LADY IN SEAT 72:
(*thinking she has it*) Shari Lewis and Dean Martin!

RON:

Close enough, lady. Just take it. God love you, you big fat dribbling moron.

REGIS:

"Moron"? She finally got it right, didn't she?

I joke, but Ron Popeil is actually my hero, and that crazy spin-
ning oven of his really works. My buddy Mike has one, and he
wore the damn thing out.

I don't even know if Gelman still works for Regis.

Anyway, I'll tell you how to make the patacon, and you already have my chili recipe. From there, you should be able to
improvise.

PATACON
1 large, very green plantain
Corn oil
Salt

Peel the plantain. It's a pain; the peels are brittle and they cling
to the meat. I peel them sideways. You cut slits in the peel, lengthwise, and you pry the peels up along their length. Then you slip the
tip of a finger under them and move it up and down the length of
the plantain, rolling the peel back slowly. Plantain peels crack easily when you try to take them off like banana peels, but they hold
together better when you go in the other direction. They make a
tool for peeling plantains; I don't have one. Also, it supposedly
helps if you hold them under running water while you peel.

When the peels come off, you may have some bits stuck to
the plantain. These tend to turn black and look nasty, so I scrape
them off using the dull side of a knife.

Some Puerto Rican guy invented a thing that peels plantains.

It's cheap. It's called an E-Z Peeler. You can find it on the Internet. Does it work? Damned if I know.

Heat the oil—half an inch deep, in a large skillet—to 350°F. Nuke the plaintain for 45 seconds. The traditional thing is to fry it, but this works better. Turn it over. Nuke it for 45 seconds more. You want it cooked but not thoroughly roasted.

Wet a dish towel thoroughly. A smooth towel, not terrycloth. Lay the towel out flat on your counter. Dump the plantain on it, off-center. Fold the other side of the towel over the plantain. Roll out the plantain with a rolling pin, until it's around ten inches long and six or seven inches wide. You can start it out by mashing it with the heel of your hand. If you can get it less than a quarter of an inch thick, do it. The towels will peel off without sticking all that much. If it sticks, the plantain is too ripe.

Turn the plantain out onto a plate or small cutting board. Try not to break it. Slide the plantain gently into the hot oil. Fry the plantain for about three minutes, or until the bottom starts to brown. Flip it and fry the other side. Take it out and drain it on paper towels. Salt is optional. I don't think it helps. You may want to squeeze some lime juice over it.

If you're really good, you can roll these things out as thin as a pancake. And buy a few extra plantains for practice, because it's not easy. If they fall apart, they're too ripe, or you didn't cook them long enough, or you're just a clumsy oaf.

I'll give you an example of the kind of crap you can put on top of them.

FILLING
1½ pounds cheap steak, cut in very thin strips
1½ teaspoon chili powder
3 habanero peppers, cut in tiny pieces
2 cloves garlic, minced or pressed
½ teaspoon oregano

1 slice of onion, large, diced
2–3 leaves iceberg lettuce, cut in fine slivers
1 very ripe tomato, sliced thin
Shredded sharp cheddar cheese
Sour cream

Plop the above ingredients, minus the lettuce, tomato, cheese, and sour cream, in a skillet and sauté over medium heat until done. You might want to brown the meat first. The filling will taste better if you throw it in the fridge for two days.

You can take it from here. You can either fold the patacon and turn it into a taco, or you can cut it in two halves and use them to make a sandwich. Put down a layer of beef, then cheese, lettuce, tomato, and sour cream. Blast it with your favorite hot sauce. Nothing sweet.

I threw that recipe together in about ten minutes. It's so phenomenally good, I have no motivation to improve it. But you can surely come up with a more interesting filling.

Green plantains function sort of like tamal, the corn stuff tamales are made of. They're pretty neutral, and they're great as a base for hot food.

You're going to love these things. Unfortunately, they're high in vitamins and minerals and fiber, and they're only around 200 calories each, even after you fry them. Rely on the toppings to change all that.

For the Hell of It: Fried Sweet Plantains

In case you want to try ripe plantains, I'll provide instructions. They're really excellent, but they're nothing like green plantains.

Ripe plantains
Corn oil
Salt

Start by peeling your ripe plantains. How do you know when they're ripe? When they turn yellow, right? Probably not. Sometimes plantains turn yellow before they get ripe. Wait until the peels are mostly black. Don't worry; the insides age much slower than the peels.

Peeling ripe plantains is a snap. The peels are very tough, but soft. I take the tip of a sharp knife and cut guide slits down the length of the plantains, and then I peel them like bananas.

Cut the plantains in oblique slices. Not perpendicular to the length, but sort of diagonally. You want them a little less than half an inch thick.

Fry them in fairly deep corn oil at 350°F, until they begin to brown. Fry both sides. Drain carefully; they have a tendency to stick to paper towels. Some people fry them with a little onion added. Salt to taste.

These things are great with pork or black beans and rice. But when you plan your meal, remember, these are very sweet. So don't act all surprised.

CHAPTER 16

DEEP-FRIED CHINESE-STYLE HONEY-GARLIC CHICKEN

BYPASS RATING:

(QUADRUPLE)

CHINESE FOOD CAN be frustrating.

For one thing, if you live anywhere between the coasts, you can forget about finding decent ingredients. Try getting bok choi out of a Kroger manager in Nebraska. It would be easier getting the last piece of pie at Michael Moore's house.

For another thing, a lot of the recipes call for a gigantic wok, heated to temperatures your puny electric (or even gas) stove can't handle. You need a professional-quality gas stove or a propane burner to do it right.

It's too bad Chinese food is so hard to cook, because it's perfect for this book. It happens to be just about the worst thing you can possibly put in your body that doesn't have a lit fuse. It's loaded with salt and fat, and it sits on a big pile of white rice, which your body turns into blood sugar right after dinner.

Luckily, there are some Chinese dishes you don't need special tools to fix. And today I have a fine example: honey-garlic chicken.

I don't know if you've ever seen this stuff. It's Cantonese, so they may not have it at your local Szechuan joint. They take chunks of chicken, drop them in batter, deep-fry them, and then cover the whole mess with a sauce made from honey and about three thousand cloves of garlic. Talk about decadent. And for some reason, they always serve you about fifteen pounds of it.

It's embarrassing, really. The doors to the kitchen swing open, the waiter staggers out, and he careens through the restaurant carrying a tray heaped nearly to the ceiling with your giant load of deep-fried batter lumps. By the time he gets to your table, he's completely out of breath, and everyone is staring, trying to figure out which customer is the poster child for stomach-stapling.

WAITER:

Honey-garlic chicken? (*pant, pant, pant*)

ME:

Um, that's mine.

WAITER:

Ah, of course. You fattest boy in room.

ME:

I assume that in China, calling someone fat is a compliment?

WAITER:

No.

What I really hate is when you finish the whole thing, and the waiters form a circle around your table and clap.

For years, I tried to make this stuff, but I got nowhere. The batter wasn't right. The sauce wasn't right. It was humiliating. But I finally figured it out the other day. I came up with a recipe that tastes about a million times better than restaurant honey-garlic chicken, and it's also really easy to fix.

Now, instead of embarrassing myself by ordering an immense, overpriced, staggeringly unhealthy dish in public and eating it while other diners sneak shots of me with their camera phones, I can have my chicken at home. In my unmade bed. In my fifteen-year-old underwear. While watching midget porn anime DVDs.

Finally, I can eat my chicken with a little dignity.

The traditional recipe isn't spicy. This one is. If you have some sort of testosterone deficiency and therefore don't eat spicy food, just omit the peppers. But for the rest of you—the ones who don't buy Viagra over the Internet—the peppers *make* the dish. Try them.

CHICKEN
1 cup flour
4 tablespoons potato starch or cornstarch
1½ teaspoons baking powder
1½ teaspoon salt
1 teaspoon oil
1 cup cold water, or enough to make the batter pourable
1½ pounds chicken

SAUCE
¾ cup orange blossom honey
¾ cup sugar
½ cup water
1 teaspoon salt
2 tablespoons lemon juice
3–6 cloves garlic, pressed
Minced habanero pepper, to taste

You should make the sauce first.

Mix the honey, sugar, water, salt, and lemon juice in a saucepan. Boil until everything dissolves. Add the other crap. Taste the sauce and adjust it. Be careful. It doesn't cool very quickly when you remove a spoonful.

You want the sauce about the consistency of pancake syrup. Thicker than water, but much thinner than honey.

Now, the chicken. This fries best at about 300°F. I tried 350, and it seems like 300 is better.

Just slop the batter ingredients together and mix with a whisk. Heat corn oil in a pot; the more, the better. Make it at least two inches deep, and allow room for bubbling up when the chicken is added. I haven't tried coconut oil, but I'm sure it would be better. Sorry about that; I have a deadline here.

Cut the chicken in chunks and salt it well. Put it in a bowl and let the salt work in. I tested this amount of sauce with 2 pounds of chicken, and it barely covered it, so I put 1½ pounds in this recipe.

When you're ready, throw the chicken in the batter and roll it around until covered. It's actually better if there are thin places in the coverage. Put the chicken in the oil and fry until it gets nicely browned. Use a thermometer to monitor the temperature.

Drain chicken on paper towels.

Plop the chicken on a plate and pour the sauce on it. Sprinkle with sesame seeds if you want.

That's all there is to it. No rice. No vegetables. No excuses.

No camera phones.

Here's something good to have on the side. I know you already have sauce, and it may seem weird to have a condiment on top of sauce. Just do it. This stuff is similar to the chile paste they serve at Chinese restaurants, but it's a billion times better, and you make it with fresh peppers instead of dried ones.

30 ripe cayenne peppers with stems removed
2 cloves garlic
½ cup oil (something neutral, like soy or sunflower)

Salt and sugar, to taste (not much)
Hot sauce or habanero/Scotch bonnet flesh, to taste

Grind the peppers into a paste. I like to leave the seeds in them, but if you don't, make sure you make up the lost volume with more peppers. Press the garlic into the peppers. Add the other stuff. Fry or nuke for a couple of minutes until the oil clears.

You don't have to use cayenne peppers. Any sweet, tasty, hot pepper will do. Spoon this stuff over the chicken or use it as dipping sauce. You'll love it.

You can also use dried peppers, but will want to add water to them before putting them in oil. Smoked peppers would be great.

CHAPTER 17
ROTIS WITH GOAT CURRY

BYPASS RATING:

(DOUBLE)

"WHY WOULD ANYONE want to live in Miami?" people ask me. The people are so rude, they make New Yorkers look refined. The cockroaches are so big they rear up and look you in the eye. No one understands English. It's hot and humid in January. And we have entire neighborhoods where the only industry is shooting German tourists who get lost after leaving the airport.

Well, we have no state income tax. Snow is unheard-of. The Bahamas are two hours away by boat. Your *own* boat, I mean. Not a filthy, crowded cruise ship where everyone gets the Norwalk virus and pukes all over the walls.

I don't need to go to Jamaica; if I want to be murdered for my watch, all I have to do is drive to downtown Miami and go for a walk.

And we have roti shops.

A roti is an enormous Jamaican tortilla. That's the best way I can describe it. It's made from flour, and you fry it in butter, and you use it to wrap curry.

I don't know how curry ended up in Jamaica. I think they have a big Indian population, but I'm not sure, because I'm afraid to go there. I don't need to go to Jamaica; if I want to be murdered for my watch, all I have to do is drive to downtown Miami and go for a walk. Also, I don't smoke dope, I'm not all that fond of reggae, we have beaches here in Florida, and I think rum tastes like mineral spirits. What does that leave? Just curry, and they sell that here, and besides, I make it better myself.

Jamaica sounds like an interesting place, I admit. One of my best friends from law school is Jamaican, and she told me a lot about it.

According to my friend, intellectual property law is a good business in Jamaica. Because Jamaicans have a long tradition of ignoring trademark laws. For example, someone down there put up a McDonald's restaurant. Only the people at the McDonald's Corporation were not in on it. And they were pretty upset. Also, there was a Jamaican hamburger chain called "King Burger."

Also, politics in Jamaica is what you might call "intense." According to my friend, it works like this. The parties pick their candidates. Then they send their thugs out with machine guns. The party that survives until election day takes over the country. Good thing Democrats refuse to own guns, or we'd have the same situation here.

Here's another interesting thing. Are you a huge unattractive American woman who hasn't had her chassis lubed and her fluids checked since the Vietnam War? Be of good cheer. Jamaica has just what you need. "Rent-a-Dreads." Don't blame me for that term; it's genuine Jamaican slang.

A Rent-a-Dread is a worthless Jamaican guy who does nothing but have sex with dumpy female tourists. I think it works like this. You go to the beach in your huge bathing suit with a skirt and sleeves, you prop your immense carcass up in the sand with a copy of *Women Are from Venus, All Men Are Pigs,* and you wait. And soon a guy with dreadlocks and a Speedo lopes up and lies down beside you and asks you for a credit card. And for the rest of your stay, you have someone to drink and dance and do the nasty with. Someone to take to King Burger.

I haven't been to Jamaica, but when I feel the need for Jamaican food, I can hop in the car and head for the nearest roti shop. They sell curry and side dishes, and they have Jamaican patties. Notice the term "Jamaican patty" doesn't contain words like "beef" or "lamb." Just "patty." That ought to worry you. Legally, they can put whatever they want in there. As long as it can be formed into a disk.

But I eat Jamaican patties anyway. It's a mass of ground meat seasoned with Scotch bonnets and other mysterious Jamaican stuff, and they cram it into a pastry and fry it. The key to enjoying one is to avoid looking into it after you take a bite. You probably won't see anything alarming, but why take a chance?

One of the best things they serve is goat curry. It's a tasty curry with potatoes in it. It would be even better if you could trust them to take the bones out of the goat. But you can't. I chew slowly.

Roti shop curry is good, but it's not perfect. They use canned curry powder, and I don't think they make the sauce sweet or acidic enough. And you can't get a roti with sour cream in it at a roti shop. Thank God, you can get one at my house. I repaired Jamaican curry.

I'll tell you right away that you don't really need goat to make this. I think the best thing is beef or lamb. And chicken works. It really doesn't matter. If you use goat or lamb, you might want to soak it overnight in water spiked heavily with baking soda, to remove the gamey smell. When goat is good, it's really good, but I suppose that if you are reading this book in a place like Des Moines and you go to the store and ask for goat, you'll be asking for a fat lip from the guy at the meat counter.

I tried to buy goat at my local grocery, and the weakass tittybaby biznitches in the meat section told me they didn't *have* goat. Can you imagine—a grocery in Miami that doesn't stock goat? Call the Haitian consulate. Call the Jamaican Ministry of Tourism. Somebody ought to slap the yellow right off their teeth. My little brown goat-eating pizeeps done been sonned by the Man.

I could get goat if I were industrious enough to drive all the way to Little Haiti. Which I am not.

When I went to the store and asked for goat, I ran into the guy who ordered my first whole pig for me. He wanted to know if it was good. I'm starting to be a celebrity down at the store. "It's the pig guy!" "It's the beef fat guy!" "Coño!"

Anyway, I threw a recipe together, using lamb, and it was wonderful. The peppers made me bleed from the ears, but that's part of the fun. Try it yourself.

2–3 pounds goat or lamb or beef (or whatever), cubed

2 teaspoons salt

2 huge white onions

4 Scotch bonnet peppers (or habaneros), seeded and
     chopped

3 cubes fresh ginger root, 1 inch on a side

²/₃ cup garlic cloves, loosely packed

4 cardamom pods (seeds only)

1 tablespoon sugar

½ teaspoon black pepper

½ teaspoon cloves

½ teaspoon nutmeg

½ teaspoon turmeric

½ cup white wine

¼ cup naráanja agria

4 teaspoons cumin

2 teaspoons coriander

10 tablespoons beef fat or corn oil

2 large red potatoes cut in small cubes
6 heaping tablespoons sour cream

Salt the meat and brown it. I used a deep fryer. This step is optional.

Put everything else, except the fat, potatoes, and sour cream, in a food processor and grind the hell out of it.

Preheat the oven to 300°F. Heat the fat in a big pot. Drop the paste in and fry for 10 minutes on medium heat. Stir in the sour cream. Dump everything else in, mix it up, and bake for 2 hours. Wrap in fresh roti and eat.

Now, here is a funny thing about red potatoes. They can't be trusted. Sometimes the damned things absolutely refuse to cook through. I can't explain it. You may have to bake the curry longer than 2 hours.

You're going to need rotis. Here is a typical recipe, except for the beef fat, which was my idea.

4 cups flour (high-gluten)
2 teaspoons baking powder
2 teaspoons salt
¼ cup beef fat (wimps use oil)
1 cup water

Mix the dry ingredients. If you want to make life easier, use a Cuisinart to mix the oil and water in. I'd treat it like bread dough. Put the dry ingredients in, get the processor going (ordinary blade), pour in oil, then pour in water until the dough turns into a coherent glob. Stop adding water, and process for 1 minute.

If you don't have a processor, just knead it in with your hands for 10 minutes.

Divide the dough in four pieces. Roll each into a ball and let it sit 15 minutes or more. I think this lets the gluten do its thing.

Roll each ball of dough out into a circle about a foot in diameter and less than an eighth of an inch thick. If you can't roll nice circles, trim off the excess with a pizza cutter. You can put a plate down on the dough, upside-down, to guide you. The bigger you make these things, the better off you will be, but you're limited by the size of your skillet.

Heat a huge skillet until it's hot enough to burn butter. I suggest medium heat—five out of ten on an electric stove. Melt a tablespoon of butter in the hot skillet, smearing it around as it melts. Drop a pancake in and fry for 2–3 minutes per side. You want it about as done as a tortilla; maybe a little more. The butter will burn and smell, but that's okay.

You put these things on plates, and then you dump curry (or whatever) on them and wrap it up. Then you eat it like a sandwich.

I can think of a few things that would make the curry recipe even better. You could chop a red bell pepper and add it. Or you could cut a large white onion in slices and fry them until they caramelize and add them. You could also stir in a tablespoon of tomato paste. Fenugreek might help, or you might add some coconut milk, the way the Thais do. But the recipe I gave you tastes more like real Jamaican curry.

You may want to cut back on the potatoes. I like a lot of potatoes in my roti and curry. And if you want adjustable heat, because there are spineless losers eating with you, you may want to get yourself a bottle of Matouk's hot sauce, from Jamaica. You can find it on the Web. They make a kind called "hot sauce" and another kind, with fruit in it, called Calypso sauce. I'd go with the hot sauce.

All right. Start cooking. And keep the Imodium and the Tums handy.

CHAPTER 18
DORO WAT—ETHIOPIAN-STYLE CHICKEN STEW

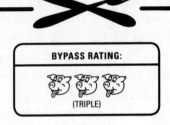

BYPASS RATING:

(TRIPLE)

IT MAY SHOCK YOU to learn that one of the world's finest spicy cuisines comes from Ethiopia. In fact, it may shock you to learn that any cuisine at all comes from Ethiopia, since the average Ethiopian weighs half as much as an Olsen twin. But it does.

I think Ethiopia is a fine country, mostly because it is the only country in Africa from which I have never received a 419 spam. I don't know if you know what a 419 spam is. The "419" comes from the section of the Nigerian statutes that make sending 419 spams illegal. You can read all about them in my first book, tragically titled *The Good, the Spam, and the Ugly.*

Thousands of American idiots get taken in by these scams every day, and as a result, Lagos, Nigeria, finally has a neighborhood of large houses not built entirely from excrement.

Here's how it works. You get an e-mail typed in capital letters, and it looks sort of like this.

DEAR ONE:

I HOPE YOU WILL NOT FEEL
EMBARRASSMENTATION UPON RECEIVING
EMAILS FROM AN UNKNOWN PERSON WHAT
YOU HAS NEVER MET. BUT NEVER MIND ALL
THAT, IN THE NAME OF CHRIST JESUS.

YOUR NAME WAS REFERRED TO ME BY THE
NIGERIAN CHAMBER OF FOREIGN TRADE, EVEN
THOUGH YOU HAVE PROBABLY NEVER BEEN TO
AFRICA AND MAY NOT BE ENTIRELY SURE WHERE
NIGERIA IS. THEY ASSURE ME THAT YOU ARE A
FINE HONORABLE PERSON, SO I FIGURED YOU
WOULD HELP ME WITH MY ILLEGAL SCHEME TO
STEAL MONEY FROM STARVING PEASANTS.

I AM NDONGO BUBOINGO, NEPHEW OF FORMER
NIGERIAN GENERAL MOBUTU GAZONGA WHO
WAS UNFORTUNATELY KILLED BY HIS OWN
TROOPS AFTER INSISTING THAT THEY BATHE
AND LEARN TO TIE THEIR OWN SHOES. MY
UNCLE SECRETED 40 MILLION USD FROM THE
NIGERIAN TREASURY IN AN ACCOUNT FOR HIS
PERSONAL USE, AND I WOULD LIKE TO REMOVE
IT FROM THE COUNTRY SO I CAN BUY A BIG
AMERICAN HOUSE AND SEVERAL WIVES WITH
BOOBIES SO BIG YOU CAN STICK YOUR ENTIRE
HEAD BETWEEN THEM.

ALL YOU HAVE TO DO IS PROVIDE ME, A TOTAL
STRANGER, WITH YOUR NAME, ADDRESS, BANK
ACCOUNT NUMBER, SOCIAL SECURITY NUMBER,

ATM PIN NUMBER, PASSPORT PHOTO, DRIVER'S
LICENCE NUMBER, EMAIL PASSWORD, SPERM
COUNT, BLOOD TYPE, SHOE SIZE, HEIGHT,
FAVORITE COLOR, A DETAILED DESCRIPTION
OF ANY GAY EXPERIENCES YOU MAY HAVE HAD
WHILE IN COLLEGE OR THE BOY SCOUTS, AND
THE COMBINATION TO THE LOCK ON THE SHED
WHERE YOU KEEP YOUR RIDING MOWER. I AM
SURE THIS REQUIRES NO EXPLANATION.

WHEN ALL IS RECEIVED AND UNDERSTOOD, I
SHALL MOVE THE MONIES TO YOUR ACCOUNT
BY VARIOUS MODALITIES, AND THEN I WILL
ALLOW YOU TO KEEP 20% FOR YOUR TROUBLE,
TRUSTING YOU TO RETURN THE REST TO ME
AND NOT RUN OFF TO THE VIRGIN ISLANDS
LEAVING ME HOLDING THE BLOODY BAG.

PLEASE GET BACK TO ME IMMEDIATELY, AS I
HAVE NOT EATEN SINCE 2002.

NDONGO BUBOINGO, BARR.

Thousands of American idiots get taken in by these scams
every day, and as a result, Lagos, Nigeria, finally has a neighborhood of large houses not built entirely from excrement. The
Nigerian government periodically rounds the scammers up and
gasses them without trial, but new scammers pop up to take
their places, like mushrooms after a hard rain.

I have never received a scam e-mail from Ethiopia, so Ethiopia is my favorite country in all of Africa.

I discovered Ethiopian food when I was in college. There was
a place called the East Africa Restaurant, on 125th and Broad-

way. If you survived the walk to Harlem without being knifed, you were rewarded with a startling array of wonderful dishes.

The proprietors were recent immigrants from a poor country, so of course, the place was less than elegant. The bathroom was particularly interesting. It opened onto the dining area, and although it was walled off, it had no ceiling, so the upper part shared the atmosphere of the restaurant proper. They were serving heavy, spicy dishes, and to put it delicately, when a customer used the can, you really did not want to be there. But I was young and stupid and usually drunk, so I ate there anyway.

They didn't use silverware. Instead, they started the meal by bringing out a huge pizza tray covered with giant pancakes called injera. Real injera is made from a brown millet-like grain called teff, which was not available in Harlem, in spite of its rich agricultural history. So they used flour, which was still excellent. They made pan-cake batter, more or less, and then they let it ferment until it was nice and sour, and then they prepared it like crepes. The injera was light and sort of foamy. They put several layers on the tray, and then they dumped the food on it. And you tore off bits of the injera and rolled the food up in them and ate them. It was very nice, especially if you ate with friends who didn't wash their hands and you were into *E. coli*.

Recently, I decided to try my hand at making Ethiopian food. I researched recipes, and I learned a few things.

First of all, teff is now available on the Web. You can order it from various sites. Just don't trust the lame recipes those sites provide for cooking it.

Second, I learned about berbere. Ethiopians use this spice mix to flavor a lot of their food. You can order it pre-mixed, but I don't trust it. Instead, I combined the ingredients in the recipe I came up with. Because what are the odds that I'm going to need berbere except on the rare occasions when I cook this dish? Slim as an Ethiopian during the dry season.

The dish I worked on is called doro wat. I guess that's Ethiopian for "chicken stew." It's a delicious hot mixture that will bring roses to your cheeks (both sets) and have your colon mumbling in Swahili in the wee hours of the night.

I was not impressed with the recipes I tried. They were too weak. I wanted a manly dish that could take the enamel off your teeth. So I cranked the heat way up and fooled around and experimented, and I came up with something marvelous.

2 pounds chicken legs and thighs or boneless chicken
1 teaspoon salt
Juice of 1 lemon
3 tablespoons paprika
¼ teaspoon allspice
¼ teaspoon turmeric
¾ teaspoon nutmeg
1¼ teaspoon cardamom
1½ teaspoons ground fenugreek (optional)
½ teaspoon pepper
½ teaspoon cumin
½ teaspoon coriander
⅛ teaspoon ground cloves
⅛ teaspoon cinnamon
2 baseball-size white onions, chopped finely
4 tablespoons butter
2 tablespoons shallots, chopped finely
2–3 very large habanero or Scotch bonnet peppers, minced
1 cup chicken broth
¼ cup red wine
4 tablespoons tomato paste

1–2 heaping tablespoons minced fresh ginger
1 heaping tablespoon pressed garlic
6 hard-boiled eggs, peeled

I've made this with chicken breast, but it tends to be dry. Brining might help. Traditionally, chicken pieces with bones (legs and thighs) are used. I leave the skin on. I think the bones improve the texture of the sauce, but they make the dish a pain to eat. I suppose you could boil chicken bones in the chicken broth if you wanted the thick sauce but not bones in your food.

If you're using breast meat, cut the chicken in chunks a little bigger than a sugar cube. If not, you can toss the pieces in whole or cut them up Asian-style with a cleaver. Salt the chicken well and add the juice of one lemon. Stir it up and let it sit for at least half an hour.

Heat a large skillet (medium heat). Throw the dry spices in the hot skillet. Stir them around with a spatula while you toast them for about 3 minutes. A little smoke is okay, but don't burn them. The scent will change, and you'll know they're done. Dump them in a bowl, and wipe the skillet out with a wet paper towel.

This recipe usually has fenugreek in it, but it's hard to find and the dish is excellent without it. If you like fenugreek, add up to 1½ teaspoons of it, adjusting it to your taste. You can grind it in an electric four-blade coffee mill.

Get the skillet hot again and throw the onions in, dry. Stir them as you cook them so they don't scorch. When they start to turn clear, or if they begin to brown, add the butter and the shallots and continue to cook until the shallots turn clear.

Throw the rest of the ingredients in the pan, except for the chicken and eggs. Stir and simmer until everything is mixed well. Add the chicken. If you really want to go crazy, brown the chicken in oil or clarified butter before you add it.

Simmer the chicken and other ingredients for 40 minutes.

Pierce the boiled eggs with a toothpick or skewer several times and add them. Cook for 20 more minutes. Truthfully, I don't put boiled eggs in my doro wat, but it's traditional.

Serve on injera or rotis or over rice.

Now, a couple of things. This is miserably, blisteringly hot. So be careful with the habaneros. Also, if you don't like chopping onions, you can Cuisinart them, and it's just about as good. I run the ceiling fan when I chop onions.

Having totally bastardized and corrupted doro wat by screwing with the spices, I decided to compound my sins by adding sour cream on the side. Purists will whine, but the combination is excellent, especially if you roll the whole mess up in a roti burrito. And while I'm blaspheming, I will say that I think doro wat would be fantastic on a fried patacon.

Now, about that injera. I got me some teff, and while it was okay, I have to say, flour is as good or better. Teff takes a long time to cook, and it has a weird, almost chocolatey flavor. Try it if you want. I found ridiculous recipes saying to combine teff and water, let it sit for several days, and then fry it, but the resulting pancakes were sad and inedible. They smelled and looked a whole lot like cow pies. So I faked up a new recipe, and it's excellent. Try traditional recipes if you want. This one is always here to save you.

1½ cups buttermilk
1½ cups water
1 teaspoon salt
1 cup teff flour
1 cup self-rising flour
4 egg whites, beaten stiff
3 teaspoons baking powder

This will make a vast amount of injera. Maybe too much. One person can get by with a fourth of this amount.

Mix the wet stuff except for the eggs. Mix in the salt. Add both types of flour and get them broken up. Stir in the eggs.

You want to add the baking powder last, right before you cook. That's because the batter is acidic and it's going to lose rising potential as it sits in the bowl. You're probably better off breaking the batter into batches and adding the baking powder to them 1 teaspoon at a time.

You want a very big Teflon skillet, as slick as possible. I like to rub mine down with an oily paper towel to make sure no dishwasher grit remains on it. You can use butter to fry the pancakes in, or if you must, you can resort to that healthy spray crap between pancakes.

Using buttermilk makes the batter sour and saves you the aggravation of fermenting it. If you want a little yeast flavor, I suppose you could mix the teff and water first, toss in some yeast, and let it go for a few hours before cooking.

Heat the skillet as if you were making plain old pancakes. Add butter or oil before each pancake. Pour batter in the hot skillet, get it spread out good, and fry. You want bubbles to come up all over the pancake, including the middle, and let it get a little dry on top before you turn it. It takes practice. You don't have to brown the pancake; they don't do that in restaurants.

Flip the pancakes over and give them maybe a minute on the other side, just to get them done. I stack mine on paper towels, because water condenses under them.

You have to make the batter thin, so if the injera comes out too heavy, adjust the water and buttermilk.

Pile a few crepes on your plate, bury it in doro wat, plop a glob of sour cream on the side, and go to town. Believe me, this stuff is good. Unless I'm lying just to get your money.

CHAPTER 19

HASH BROWN CASSEROLE WITH CHEDDAR AND SOUR CREAM

BYPASS RATING:

(QUADRUPLE)

CONSIDER THE POTATO. Ireland's national fruit. The perfect substrate for fat and salt, and so simple to cook, well, even the Irish can handle it.

Don't start crying "racism." Irish isn't a race, even though the Irish are unique in having no skin pigment other than blue paint and vulgar tattoos. If you're Irish you don't get minority money from the government, you don't get preferences when you apply for jobs, and nobody cares what happens to you, so as far as I'm concerned, you spud-sucking, carrot-topped, hiding-the-rubbing-alcohol-from-grandma, front-yard-fistfighting-on-holidays, getting-drunk-at-wakes-and-puking-in-the-coffin melanoma factories might as well shut your cakeholes and get on with your lives.

I can't be criticized for abusing the Irish, because I myself have Irish blood. As anyone who watches Chris Rock knows, minority members are entitled to insult their own kind. Besides, I should benefit from the presumption that when I wrote this, being part Irish, I was knee-walking drunk.

I like potatoes because they are the most worthless food known to man. Pure carbohydrate. True, they contain a fair amount of vitamin C, which is why you never see a leprechaun with scurvy, but other than that, they're just big, useless wads of concentrated calories. Eating a potato is about as good for you as swallowing a hefty scoop

I like potatoes because they are the most worthless food known to man. Pure carbohydrate. True, they contain a fair amount of vitamin C, which is why you never see a leprechaun with scurvy.

of table sugar, and to make matters worse, they only taste good served swimming in salty fat. Think of the potato dishes you like; they're all loaded with one kind of fat or other. French fries. A potato without fat is like a Kennedy without gin blossoms.

Potatoes are so great, I can't understand why the Irish, each of whom consumes several pounds a day, could ever be depressed. But they are. They've raised depression to a high art. They award belts in depression, like karate instructors. Don't believe me? Check out *Angela's Ashes*. It's a representative piece of Irish literature, which was later made into a film. Which drove thousands of moviegoers to pull over on the way home and jump off of bridges.

Here's a typical passage:

On the eve of St. Seamus's Feast, mother dressed us up in our best filthy newspapers and took us 'round to the church to beg for a rat carcase we could pretend was a goose. On the way out of the open sewer which served as our home, we were stopped by my father who was piss-eyed drunk on kerosene, and he stood the lot of us against the wall—the few that hadn't died during the night—and made us swear to die for Ireland. We all swore, but he didn't believe us, so he took out a bloody great shillelagh and knocked our brains clean out of our heads, killing us all as dead as could be, and then he made us get a sponge and a bucket and clean up the mess.

Mother was about to lay into him when she died for a minute or two due to an unexpected attack of tuberculosis, and when she came back to life, she had completely forgotten what she was angry about. While father lay in the gutter in front of the sewer retching up blood and pus and old copies of Finnegans Wake *and swearing that he, too, would die for Ireland as soon as he finished heaving, off we went to the church, where we were greeted by a fine strapping nun who kicked us all in the groin, including Mother, and told us rats were off but we were welcome to half a beetle she had found in a mound of dung.*

Mother thanked the nun for her generosity, and for her trouble got a swift boot in the face and a cheap right to the kidneys, but there was no time to take it up with the priests as three of my nineteen younger brothers had died since we had walked in the door, and anyway, the priests would only have held us down and gouged our eyes out with crucifixes—as they had often done in the past—for having the cheek to complain after being given half a free beetle.

I felt sad about my brothers but happy to have their share of the beetle; I would tell you their names, but as we lost several a day, Mother had taken to giving them numbers. I remember how she used to cry, "O, sweet Jaysus, how could you come so soon for dear little numbers seven through twelve?" and sometimes we had to wait over a month before the rhythm method gave her a new batch of tots to fill the void.

A beetle may not sound like much, but I was glad to have my share, as I was nine years old and weighed a quarter of an ounce. And truth be told, I got more than I deserved, for I was number three, and after my first turn in the line, I took a lump of charcoal and turned the three on my forehead into an eight. Number eight would never have begrudged me his bit of beetle, cold and dead as he was and currently being used as a leg for the table. I had disguised him as best I could, covering his face and coating him with shoe black, but he would thaw in the spring and the table would collapse, and then there would be questions to answer and likely as not, I would have to die for Ireland several times in the process, but for now I chewed my beetle slowly and pretended it was shepherd's pie.

Apologies to the Monty Python gang. "There were a hundred and fifty of us living in a shoebox in the middle of the road . . ."

It's not easy to take something as devoid of virtue as a potato and make it even worse, but this is me we're talking about. As an accompaniment to my barbecued ribs and Texas toast, I came up with a potato casserole so deadly you can raise your cholesterol just by thinking about it. I didn't come up with it out of thin air; I was inspired by a dish I used to eat at a barbecue joint in Texas. But my version is approximately ten thousand times better, because I managed to combine the casserole concept with frying.

**5 pounds Yukon Gold potatoes (enough for 3 half-inch
    layers in a 9-by-13 dish)**
1 tablespoon salt
½ teaspoon pepper
3 cloves garlic
1 ½ sticks butter
1 tablespoon bacon grease

16–24 ounces shredded sharp cheddar cheese
20 ounces sour cream

All righty. What we are going to do here is, we are going to make butter-fried hash browns and then stack them in layers separated by cheese and sour cream. I am totally serious.

Peel the potatoes, leaving a few bits of skin on. You should never peel a potato completely. You need a particle of color here and there to break up the monotony. Otherwise, looking at potatoes is like driving through Iowa or looking at the Gores.

Find yourself a tool that turns potatoes into hash browns, because it's a huge job. If you don't have a Cuisinart, use a team of undocumented Mexicans. That was a joke; don't get all self-righteous. Don't get your Irish up. *Hahahahaha.* Sorry. I can make Mexican jokes. I'm also part Mexican. For all you know. Vato.

Can someone tell me why movie Mexicans call everyone "essay"? Is that like, "as opposed to multiple-choice"? And they keep saying "orally."

MOVIE MEXICAN:

Essay, your brightly colored eemport car, she ees not as fast as mine.

VIN DIESEL:

Hold on while I cue up one of my three facial expressions. You can have "mad," "real mad," or "angst."

MOVIE MEXICAN:

Orally, essay, orally.

VIN DIESEL:

I think I have a fourth expression now: "homosexual panic."

I apologize sincerely to all my Mexican American readers. I'm just bitter because I can't make a decent tamale. I apologize insincerely to Vin Diesel. In case he reads this and decides to push my face in.

Seriously, you can grate potatoes with one of those hand things, but it will take you the rest of your life, and a Cuisinart does a pretty nice job. Or you can use a mandoline adjusted to make really fine strips. When you're done, add the salt, pepper, and garlic to the potatoes and toss.

Okay, here is where real dedication comes in. There are two ways to proceed. You can fry all of the potatoes at once, which will give very nice results, or you can fry them in three separate loads, which will give magnificent results. Your call. In any case, you combine the butter and bacon grease and fry them in it until nicely browned.

Preheat the oven to 400°F. Take a third of the fried potatoes and dump it into a 9-by-13 Pyrex dish. Spread them out in a nice layer. I know, it's not easy. Stop whining. You could be in Dublin or Cork sucking on half a cold beetle.

Next, dump half the cheese on top of the potatoes. Spread it around. Sprinkle pepper on top. Add another layer of potatoes.

Put all the sour cream in, on top of the second potato layer. Again, spread it as evenly as you can.

Now, I may as well admit that I know of no way to spread fried potatoes evenly on top of a layer of sour cream. But you're damned well going to try. Just do your best. And once that's done, hide the miserable mess you've made with another layer of cheese, finished with a sprinkling of pepper.

Jam the whole thing into the oven and bake for 1 hour. When it comes out, it should be bubbly and greasy and so tasty-looking you just want to dive right in and suffocate. This stuff is as good as any dish I make. I am extremely proud of it, and you're going to eat it and like it, and that's my final word.

You can screw around with variations. Different cheese, for example. Gruyère, maybe. You can add onions, although I think that's pushing it, if you're serving it with barbecue. And you can serve it with crumbled bits of freshly fried bacon on top.

And if you can think of a more worthless, unhealthy dish, you can come to my house. And I'll gladly eat half a beetle.

CHAPTER 20
DREADFULLY FATTENING MACARONI AND CHEESE

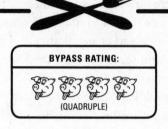

BYPASS RATING:

(QUADRUPLE)

I THOUGHT IT WOULD BE FUN to let a celebrity chef handle this one. Ladies and gentlemen, I give you the ghost of Hunter S. Thompson.

There are certain things a man can only learn from having his ashes fired out of a giant fist-shaped cannon.

The rush of the g-forces peels back the strata of your consciousness, like layers of a sugary jawbreaker in a driving rain. Then you hit the cool Colorado air, and you feel like a million glistening fragments of Bolivian flake, slapping the surface of a snifter of chilled crème de menthe. Too bad you can't do it while you're still alive. It would saturate the adrenaline and dopamine receptors, lighting up the thalamus and pituitary like the signs along the Reno strip. Like pulling up a jimsonweed and eating the root whole, with clods and frightened beetles still clinging to the bulb.

I wonder if George W. Bush ever ate a jimsonweed. It wouldn't surprise me in the least. Maybe he comes across them while clearing brush down in Crawford. Madness in his eyes as his hungry fingers grasp the fleshy stalk . . . the Secret Service pleading with him . . . "Don't eat that, sir. Wolf Blitzer will be out here as soon as he gnaws through the baling twine." Cheney nearby, sunning himself nude on a Navajo blanket, egging him on. "I ate two this morning. Catch up before I peak. The old sundial is pointing toward 'Bad Craziness.' " Bush's chimplike digits clasping the stem as he chews. "That's no sundial, you demented bastard. I ought to kill you for tripping naked in front of the twins. Ah, yes. I see the colors now. Someone gather my clothes and bring me a dozen ripe watermelons and some shoulder-fired Stinger missiles. And have Laura warm up the old Ma Deuce."

Out comes Condi Rice, bare to the waist. Carrying a tray of Jell-O shots, but not inclined to mention that one of them is laced with synthetic pineal gland extract, fresh from the kitchens at Langley. With an extra acetyl group tacked to the end of every molecule, just to see if anything kooky happens.

And so begins another Cabinet meeting. No wonder we invaded Iraq. The wonder is that the crazy neocon hoodlums didn't invade every country they passed on the way. Spain, Morocco, Italy, Israel . . . just because we can. Give us virgins and trinkets, third-world scum; or get used to dancing on sheets of smoking glass.

I was right to take my leave of a world ruled by fetus-coddling thugs who have your luggage sniffed before you board Air Force One. What kind of savages expect a sober man to sit next to Ken Mehlman for six hours? That's probably longer than Bush ever held out. Anyway, the ibogaine wasn't for me. It was for Ken. It would have done things for his personality his Chivas and Diet Coke could never have begun to do.

These people will never miss me, but I still have fans. For example, John Cusack wrote a nice tribute to me. He's a good boy, Cusack is, even if he's not somebody you'd want on your side in a game of Trivial Pursuit.

He mentioned a few things I had written on my wall. Ordinarily, my wife had Carmela take the crayon off with WD-40 as soon as I passed out. But after I used a .45 to give myself a home rhino-plasty, **Note to self: if the bats are any color other than black, gray, or brown, they are not real. Don't shoot at them.** Carmela refused to return until her Santero came in and blessed the place.

Cusack noted the following passages.

Wisdom is better than wit.   —Jane Austen

The final mystery is oneself. Who can calculate the orbit of his own soul?   —Oscar Wilde

Beauty is not in the face . . . it is a light in the heart.
—Khahlil Gibran

One changes from day to day . . . every few years one becomes a new being.   —George Sand

That's the sort of thing that passes for Deep Thought in Hollywood. Never mind that George Sand was a dour, libidinous butch who wrote her time's homologues to *Valley of the Dolls*. If he had been there before Carmela's last visit, he might also have noticed these:

Note to self: Call around and see if anyone else still takes the late Norman Mailer seriously.

Note to self: If the bats are any color other than black, gray, or brown, they are not real. Don't shoot at them.

Note to self: If you absolutely must try to fly while tripping, take off from ground, not roof.

Note to self: Tell Cusack (1) He is the only one who really understands you; (2) the Brat Pack is still cool, much better than the Merry Pranksters; (3) if he picks up your tab at the Mirage, you'll let him give you a back rub.

The things a man does for his hobbies.

Anyway, I am still here. Dead as the springs in Michael Moore's mattress, but suddenly clear headed in more ways than one, and ready to resume critiquing the sorry, sordid, King Hell mess that is American culture.

Now. Where is the Secretary of State with my medication?

Decent remedies and supplements are hard to come by these days. A few months back, though dead, I flew to Palm Beach hoping to raid Rush Limbaugh's personal stash. At first I was disappointed. I expected an OxyContin windfall from his medicine cabinet or from baggies hidden in his omnipresent humidors. But it looks like that weasel Roy Black put the fear of God in him, because the only medications I found in the whole house were a foil of Correctol and half a bottle of expired Beano. What kind of country do we live in, where a man's pharmaceutical pleasures are limited to vigorous bowel movements and relief from excessive farting?

How far would William S. Burroughs have gotten with that?

I was hurting in Baton Rouge when I decided to pay a visit to a friendly croaker I knew, to see if I could score some C on Rx. "No dice," he told me, "they're watching my every move, and C is Schedule II. And don't even ask me about M. I could never risk that in the current repressive climate." "How about a quart of PG and a hundred nem-

bies?" "Impossible. But what I can promise you is freedom
from bloating and the single biggest dump you ever took
in your life."

Things were looking bad until I popped the trunk of his Maybach and pried up the liner. There they were, smiling up at me
through the side of a Ziploc bag. OxyContin. Trafficking weight.
I downed a handful and chased them with a hearty swig of Limbaugh's Hennessy Paradis.

I don't know where Limbaugh was. Boston Market, probably,
banging his fist on the counter, yelling that the side-dish tubs
were too goddamn small. I'd find him soon enough. And then
we'd get a few things straight. It was time to put an end to his
"medicated journalist" phase. That was *my* side of the street, and
he was working it like Arianna Huffington in a room full of bicu-
rious millionaire bachelors.

Things weren't exactly hopping in Palm Beach. I was the live-
liest person there, and I'm dead. It was May. The socialites had
all scampered back to New York and Boston. I decided to hop a
plane back to LA to see what was happening at Arianna's place. I
recalled dosing her Salvadoran pool boy with Oxycodone, Grey
Goose, and angel dust and then turning him loose with a hair-
trigger Kimber full of Black Talons. I gave him all the tools for a
grand and glorious voyage of self-discovery. I wondered whether
he had made good use of them.

She found this poor kid on the street in Mexico City while
chasing down a hot tip on a mythical Dooney and Bourke sweat-
shop that sold bags out the side door for cheap. Brought him to
America with promises of easy money and regular meals, and
then forced him to take credit for idiotic ghost-written entries
on her ridiculous weblog. He surprised me one night while I was
searching her bathroom drawers for stray Percocets. Told me the
whole sad story. She was gradually grooming him for the book-

tour circuit, forcing him to put products in his hair and dress like Dominick Dunne.

I felt bad for the kid. Told him he could only gain freedom and self-actualization via firearms and the proper medication, and before I left, I gave him what I thought was a damn fine beginner's kit. I was anxious to see how he had made out.

It was the humanitarian in me.

I materialized in First Class on a nonstop bound for LAX. And who should be sitting in the seat next to me but Christopher Hitchens. He wasn't fazed at all. Like he expected dead gonzo journalists to pop up at his arm like Barbara Eden in *I Dream of Jeannie*. He probably sees much worse things every time he takes the pledge and starts dragging his rumpled suit to AA.

He glanced up from the pyramid of Tanqueray miniatures on his tray table, looking like he just rolled off his editor's wife and smoking a ropy Turkish cigarette that smelled like burning sheep dung. "Thompson," he observed, squinting through puffy, reddened slits above his nose, "you're looking well, save the gaping exit wound and the powder burns on the tongue. Might consider buying a good mouthwash. Allow me to suggest formaldehyde."

"Hitchens!" I exclaimed, drawing my Home Shopping Network tanto and waving it before his saggy puss in playful figure-eights, "You backstabbing whore! I ought to cut your flabby throat and field-dress you in the aisle! From loyal staffer at *The Nation* to Oval Office party doll! What possible excuse can you give me for getting off this plane without your hollowed-out skull in my carry-on?"

"I can think of one," he said, reaching into his coat pocket. He took out a baggie and dropped it on my lap.

Could it be? The color was right. I held it to my face and sniffed. Ah, yes. There was no mistaking that friendly, familiar aroma. "My God!" I exclaimed, "what's a puffy public-school pederast like you doing with a bag of fine Afghan hash?"

"I'm returning from Kabul," he said, "where I spent a few weeks talking to friendly warlords up by the Pakistan border. Real journalists do things like that. They wouldn't hear of me leaving without a parting gift."

"I may just let you live," I muttered, putting down the tanto and pressing the button for the stewardess. By then Hitchens was busy vomiting gin and airline peanuts into a seat pocket. The stewardess steamed her way up the aisle and hove to by my armrest. My God, the beam on her. Barely cleared the seats. Old, too. I miss the sixties.

"Sir," she mooed, "I'll have to ask you to give me that knife! I don't know how you got on the plane with that, but carrying a knife on a commercial flight is a federal crime!"

"Everything is completely under control," I told her, flashing my press credentials too fast for her to read, "I'm an air marshal. Special Agent Marcus Garvey, at your service. Don't worry about the knife. We all carry them, for decapitating suspected Muslims and people who won't turn off their cell phones. Just treat me like a regular passenger and avoid calling attention to me. I'll see to it we arrive safe and sound in LA with no more bloodletting than is appropriate under the circumstances."

"I see," she said. "Is there anything you need me to do?"

"Yes," I told her. "I left part of my field kit in a Vero Beach whorehouse, so I'll need some supplies. Just a few simple items. Seventy miniatures of your best liquor, all the lemons you have on the plane, ten cups of ice, and the morphine from the first-aid kit. Don't ask a lot of dumb civilian questions. You wouldn't understand. You're a fine woman and a great patriot. President

Bush would be proud of you. Now go get what I need before I have to cut somebody."

The plane touched down three hours later, but I was still at cruising altitude. I found a Hertz shuttle idling while the driver took a leak, so I got behind the wheel and headed for Arianna's place. The whole way there, I cursed myself for not carving out Hitchens's adrenal glands and eating them. But there would be time for that later.

I had hoped to find Arianna's bones bleaching on the patio and Facundo the pool boy on a rotating bed surrounded by thousand-dollar hookers, but such was not the case. The poor dumb bastard was locked in his room with a Brioni sportcoat and an Ascot. He had clear polish on his nails, and a blind man could see that he had recently had a facial. Could it be that he was starting to *enjoy* his captivity? No. That would never do.

I knocked him down, straddled his belly, forced several doses of MDMA into his mouth, and massaged his throat to make him swallow. "Out with it, boy!" I shrieked, "Why are you still here after I gave you a fine assortment of costly medications and a Kimber with a custom-fitted Bar-Sto barrel?" He fell apart like Ed Muskie coming down from ibogaine in front of a slew of reporters at the Democratic primaries. It wasn't his fault, he said. He fell asleep when the PCP wore off and woke up taped to a chair.

"You're lucky I'm a patient man," I told him as I watched him down a handful of OxyContin and a half dozen Tenuates I had found in the cushions of Arianna's sofa. "Anyone else would have given up on you by now. But not me, Facundo. Because—and remember this, because I'm only going to say it once—I am your one true friend. I'm not like the others."

By this time I could tell the spirit was upon him. He was holding a hand out in front of him and laughing maniacally, like it was the funniest damn thing he had ever seen.

"Let's start over," I said, helping him off with his shirt. "Do you have any woad? '*woad*'? No idea what that is, eh? Hmm . . . well, I was puttering around the kitchen on the way in, and I found a can of blue Rust-Oleum Arianna uses to touch up the patio chairs. Get those pants off and I'll see what I can do." I had him turn for me while I emptied the can on him, covering him entirely except for his back, which I left bare except for the phrases "Healter Skelter" and "Die Gringo Puta." Then I gave him the can so he could huff the last few cubic inches of propellant. By then he was shrieking in what may have been Mayan.

Clearly, it was time to arm him.

Arianna had given the Kimber to Diane Feinstein as a party favor, so I drew another old favorite out of my carry-on. A Magnum Research BFR, in .454 Casull. That ought to get her attention. I handed him the empty revolver and told him the cartridges were hidden in the room somewhere. That would give me time to get out before he loaded it. Just because I'm dead doesn't mean I want to get shot up even more.

I made him swallow the remainder of the Beano. He was naked, he was blue, he was tripping, he was going to be heavily armed; the only thing that could cost him the respect he needed from his hostages was a spate of uncontrollable farting.

I popped the lock on the door, handed Facundo a bag containing thirty or forty Remy Martin miniatures, and got the hell out of Dodge.

"Don't blow it this time, boy!" I yelled. "A big important dead journalist has better things to do than save your sorry ass twice a month!"

I felt kind of bad about depriving Limbaugh of what was possibly his last cache of mood elevators, so I decided to help him with that Boston Market side dish problem. I decided to give him a recipe for the finest macaroni and cheese a man can make without following in the weaving footsteps of Alice B. Toklas.

It follows below. After a baking dish full of this stuff, he would probably consider narcotics quite tame.

A few key things to remember:

1. The more cream you use, the more decadent it gets. You can use three cups of cream, you can use three cups of milk, or you can settle anywhere along the spectrum connecting those extremes. I like one cup of cream and two cups of milk.

2. You have to melt the cheese *slowly* and thoroughly. Melting the cheese too fast, getting it too hot, and/or baking it too long makes it stringy. Velveeta doesn't have this problem, but then again, it's not cheese. Any more than methadone is fine Mexican smack.

3. You do not have to use cheddar.

Beyond that, students, improvise to your heart's content. The Good Doctor grants license.

½ pound elbow macaroni
9 tablespoons butter
3 tablespoons flour
2 cups milk
1 cup heavy cream
3 egg yolks
½ teaspoon salt
2 teaspoons pepper
20+ ounces sharp cheddar (shredded is easiest to work
with)
½ cup bread crumbs

Preheat the oven to 350°F. Boil the macaroni and butter it with 3 tablespoons of the butter. You want it firm, like the upper slope of a Brazilian Carnaval dancer's breasts. Cook the flour in

3 tablespoons of the butter and then add the 2 cups of milk and get it near boiling. Put the cream and egg yolks in a bowl and mix thoroughly.

Move the milk mixture to a big microwavable bowl and add the cream and egg yolks, salt, and pepper. Using a mixer, beat until smooth. Then microwave until nearly boiling. Throw in 9 ounces of the cheese and use the mixer until the cheese melts. I believe this is where Alice would add the vital herb.

Maybe you're a misguided mutant who thinks only sissies buy shredded cheese. Spend half an hour trying to grate your own cheddar and then tell me that. I don't care if it costs ten dollars a pound. I'm buying shredded. When it comes to hedonism, don't be afraid to spend. You'll get a lot more out of life. And you'll inhale a lot less mannitol.

What you want to end up with is a thick, cheesy, smooth roux. You don't want to heat the cheese too fast. The microwave is safer than the stove because it heats gradually. If you think it's taking too long, consider stirring a few Seconals into your planter's punch.

Pour the roux into a 2-quart or larger Pyrex dish. Add the macaroni, stir, and bake for 20 minutes.

Melt the remaining 3 tablespoons of butter and toss the bread crumbs in it. If you want to add snob appeal, use upscale bread crumbs or make your own crumbs from a stale baguette. Alton Brown—that strange, wonderful boy—recommends panko bread crumbs, which are special crumbs used by sushi chefs. Who are often trained in the method of extracting just enough toxin from a fugu to get you through a Howard Dean briefing without twitching. Add some pepper. Mix in 3 ounces of the cheese.

After 20 minutes, take the dish out and cover the top of the macaroni with the bread crumb and cheese mixture. Then put it in for 10 more minutes.

Add chunks of bacon if you want. Try double Gloucester

instead of cheddar. Whatever makes you happy. Remember, all food is experimental. Just like the .44 reloads I use to discourage autograph hounds.

I still feel something is missing. A certain adrenal twang.

Time to pay another visit to Hitchens.

CHAPTER 21
TWICE-FRIED FRIES COOKED IN BEEF FAT

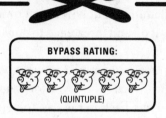

BYPASS RATING:

(QUINTUPLE)

NOTE: THOMPSON DID such a fine job, I decided to let another celebrity handle the fries.

Hi, folks. Chris Walken here. I know Steve Graham from a little misunderstanding we had a while back. He was impersonating me on the Internet.

Don't get me wrong. It was funny. Christopher Walken is a man who loves a good joke. Even at his own expense. I will chuckle heartily along with the crowd, and rarely—*rarely*—will I feel moved to use the icepick. However, there is a fair chance that the joker will receive a judicious backhand.

It's not an emotional backhand. I don't use my rings. It's almost what I would call an *administrative* backhand. Purely to make sure everyone remembers there are limits to Christopher Walken's patience. I deplore excessive violence. It musses one's hair and rumples one's suit. I am satisfied with a look of contrition and perhaps, from one corner of the mouth, a slight trickle of blood.

Anyway, Steve had this website, and he was writing as me, and it was remarkable stuff. He claimed he was having a gay fling with the Burger King. You know the guy. White stockings. Plastic head. Steve claimed he woke up in bed with this—excuse the term—fegeleh next to him, grinning from ear to ear and waving a gigantic meat sandwich. Steve said he was not gay, but that he did what he had to do. To get the. You know. Sandwich. And as me, he wrote something about how I went over to his house and told him to knock it off and threatened to dunk the Burger King's head in a Fryolator.

The Fryolator thing, honestly, I thought was a nice touch. I had no problem with that. The Fryolator is a wonderful tool of persuasion. I used one back in the day, to persuade Travolta to decline the role of Sergeant Toomey in *Biloxi Blues*.

I was already irked that he got *Saturday Night Fever*. That role called for a hoofer, and Travolta is no hoofer. Christopher Walken is a hoofer. I got it all. Jazz dancing. Tap. Ballet. Salsa. What does Travolta know from dancing? What? Did he dance in *Welcome Back, Kotter*? Was there a scene where he shuffles into the classroom and dips Arnold Horshack? Because if so, I did not see that episode.

And I had a Betamax.

Mr. Woodman . . . now *there* was a natural dancer. The taut, wiry physique . . . the sinuous catlike grace . . . unmistakable. There was a man I would have perceived as a threat.

His parents were acrobats back in the Yiddish theater. His mom used to hang by her knees with her hands cuffed and eat hamantashen off her own belly. Artists, those people. Giants. But Travolta? A lurching, closeted cult freak, sublimating his forbidden urges by flying around in a jet with a suggestively shaped fuselage. A nothing. Nada. Niente.

Get out, Kelly, while you still can. You're a beautiful woman. You should not spend yourself on this . . . this potbellied fenocch'.

I am a married man, and a married man who cheats is no man at all, but I have single friends who would appreciate your beauty. Not actors. But well off. Mostly in construction. And waste management. Friends of the opera. I think you understand.

I did not mind the Fryolator thing, because it felt right. Realistic. Edgy. Gritty, if you will. What I minded was the suggestion that I would involve myself in a grotesque, tawdry relationship between a fat middle-aged lawyer and a polyvalent sideshow freak with a fiberglass face. It was not *seemly*. It could cost me respect. And in my world, respect is the only currency. Well, respect and kneecaps. I have a special fondness for kneecaps.

I went over to Steve's in the wee hours of the morning and, not wishing to be loud and boorish, I sat on the edge of his bed and gently pushed the barrel of a .45 up his nose and waited until he awoke.

Nice bed. Tempur-Pedic. Swedish. Foam. They really work. You can set a glass of wine on the corner while on the other side, your boys work a stoolie over with cable ties and a red-hot grapefruit spoon. And it will not even rock. Regardless of the kicking and flailing. Doesn't help with the screaming, though. You can still hear that fine.

I have one, too. Fortunately, I did not have to pay for it. It fell off a truck. And later the truck fell into a phosphate pit. Tricky business, truck driving. You never know when you're going to slide off the road and into an abandoned pit full of submerged cars. Especially when you're a Boy Scout hardhead and won't let your new friend Chris draw water from the well.

So Steve wakes up, and I ask him if he slept well. Because personally, on a Tempur-Pedic, I go out like a light. I mean *out*. One minute, I'm worrying about deliveries and gratuities and where to buy a ton of lime on a cash-and-a-handshake basis, and the next, it's 1965 again, and I'm in the wedding scene in *Fiddler*, dancing with a bottle glued to my hat. Only Tevye is a giant orange lizard with purple fangs, and all the Cossacks look like Ruth Westheimer.

Dreams. Go figure.

Steve says he guesses he slept okay, and he asks if maybe there is something he can do for me. Sharp kid, Steve. Nothing escapes him. I tell him to get me a Campari and soda, and he says it might be easier if he didn't have a gun up his nose.

Soon we're in Steve's living room, and I'm sipping my Campari—which is a little strong, but I say nothing, because Christopher Walken is a gracious guest—while a couple of my boys hold Steve's head under the water of his fifty-gallon fish tank.

Steve has tetras. Tetras and those other little—what do you call them?—dwarf cichlids. Little pansy fish that don't even fight. I realize it is a matter of taste, but me, I always went for the heavy artillery. Oscars. Piranha. Small sharks. Some people feed their carnivorous fish goldfish. I fed mine Yorkies.

I cannot abide a small defiant dog that looks like a Slinky.

I give him a few minutes of that—in, out, gasp for breath, in, out, gasp for breath—while I check out his CD collection. I'm an LP man myself. Gotta have vinyl. Gotta. But he has some good stuff there. Hot Fives and Sevens, remastered. Sweet. Needs a little Bobby Vinton, of course, but maybe his tastes haven't matured to the extent where he can fully appreciate the subtleties of "My Little Neon Rose."

I have a rule. If I see streaks of undissolved syrup in my Bosco, I got to snap somebody's pinky toe.

When the time is right, I have my boys pull his head out and sit him on the sofa and get him a towel and some Bosco. He has Bosco in his cupboard. I respect that. That bought him some points. I'm a Bosco man myself. Some guys like Ovaltine. That's okay, I guess. I shot a guy in the face for drinking Ovaltine. Once. But I was young. Full of hormones. Exuberant. I would never do that now. Today I would be satisfied with slamming his head on the counter a couple times.

So I sit next to Steve and put my arm around him, and I ask if the Bosco is to his liking. And of course, it is. I showed my boys the right way to mix it. None of that business with the dark smear around the bottom of the glass, with spoon marks in it. The key to a good Bosco is thoroughness. The *key,* amigo.

I have a rule. If I see streaks of undissolved syrup in my Bosco, I got to snap somebody's pinky toe. I don't care whose. Finding the culpable toe is not my department. They can draw straws if they want. But somebody's toe is going to snap. When they hear that snapping sound, it really drives the message home. Call it a mnemonic device. Snap two or three pinky toes at one shot, and you'll be drinking well-mixed Bosco for a good five years before you have to snap another one.

"Steve," I said, "it's not that I don't like your work. Truly, I am nothing if not a patron of the arts. Especially my first true love, which is the dance. I think you know my history." And I got up and gave him my best Bill "Bojangles" Robinson. Lovely man, Bojangles. Got that monicker because he ate a lot of fried chicken. I prefer Popeyes. But let's not reopen that can of Pandora's worms.

I had my tap shoes on. Sometimes I wear them when I'm on a job. Because I am not a thug. I do not simply physically abuse and intimidate. I certainly *do* those things. With vigor and relish. But I also strive to educate. So if, while I'm ramming your hand down a garbage disposal and asking you about a missed loan payment, I take a break to give you a little Donald O'Connor or even Ray Bolger, it can only be considered time well spent.

My boys applauded, and they looked at Steve, and he jumped a little and started applauding, too, and then I sat down next to him again. "Steve," I said, "I need you to lay off the Burger King pederasty jokes. I mean, if you want to put *yourself* in those stories, that's fine, because—I can't lie—it's highly plausible. But as for me, I would appreciate being left out. Do you think you can do that for me, Steve? Do you think you can reach down into your heart and find it in yourself to do this tiny favor for your uncle Chris? So he doesn't have to come here again and bring his table saw?"

Yes, he could do that. Definitely. We had an understanding. I knew we would. I had a feeling about this kid. Weird, definitely. Perhaps in need of some sort of counseling. And a vasectomy. But fundamentally solid. Once you got his attention and made him understand your needs.

I felt bad about ruining his sleep, so I told him that while we were talking about Fryolators, I would give him a great treasure. A recipe for perfect fries.

Fries are important. Because the art of making fries has been lost. Like tap or the correct way of attaching concrete to a former employee's feet. Back in the day, they used to fry them in beef fat. From like, a cow. You could buy yourself a fifty-pound block of beef tallow, or wait for one to fall off a truck, and you could melt it down and heat it in a big pot, and you were in business.

Don't knock beef fat. Show respect for the old ways, my friend. Beef fat was highly thought of back in my time. One of my best pals was a guy we called Manny Suet Hair. I mean Jersey City Manny Suet Hair, not that other guy. Not Passaic Manny Suet Hair. Not Jersey City Manny Red Pants. Different guy. Had an extra toe, which he used to rub at the crap table for luck. Called it his lucky devil toe.

Personally, I thought it was crass. But that's me. I am a throwback to more elegant times, when a man of substance knew better than to take off his special shoe and hang his deformed feet over the rail at a crap table.

Whenever some beef fat fell off a truck, Manny went and got a little taste, and he put it in the cabinet under his bathroom sink.

Used it to slick his hair back. That's how respected beef fat was at one time in this country.

Dogs loved that guy. Adored him.

Unfortunately, I had to drop him out of a window. We were at a meeting, about a thing, and this putz had the stones to call Fred Astaire a *culattone*, which is a very vulgar term describing a certain sexual proclivity. He called Astaire a *culattone*, simply because the man could dance and had a flair for accessorizing. Shortly thereafter I found myself dangling him from a ninth-story window by his scarf. "You listen to me, you little *strunz*. Fred Astaire was no *culattone*. I once saw him hitch-kick a guy's brains out, ba-*bing*, because the guy made fun of his paisley spats. When you can do *that*, then you can call Fred Astaire a *culattone*, you jamook!"

Then his scarf gave way and he started to fall. I grabbed for him, but all I could get was a handful of hair, and, you know. Beef fat. Slippery.

So you get yourself some fat. How? I don't care how. What am I? The beef fat delivery guy? A *man* finds his *own* beef fat. Personally, before I reached a status where people respected me enough to bring me beef fat without my having to ask, I went to the store and I asked the guy at the butcher window to save it for me. They give it away. Like, *free.* You don't even have to threaten their families.

Morons.

You get your fat, and you put it in a big pot, and you put it in the oven at 250°F for like a day. Then you throw out the lumps that remain. Now you have fat. You want *Don't get me started on big, flat fries that fry up all mushy on the inside. Do not take me down that road, because I will not be responsible if I lose my composure and end up stapling you to a garage door.*

a half gallon, minimum. Anything less is small-time. Although you can cut it with corn oil when you get desperate. Just don't put corn oil in your hair. Because you will smell like a bucket of buttered popcorn. And people will call you something like Manny Movie Popcorn Head.

I would not fool with less than half a gallon of fat. More fat means bigger batches of fries. And leave half the fryer empty. Because when you dump the fries in the hot fat, it will boil over. Like Joe Pesci when a waiter brings him eggplant parmigiana instead of veal.

Okay, so you get yourself some russet potatoes, and you take most of the peel off. I leave a little on, for color. Then you cut them in strips no bigger than a quarter inch on a side. Don't get me started on big, flat fries that fry up all mushy on the inside. Do not take me down that road, because I will not be responsible if I lose my composure and end up stapling you to a garage door.

How do you make the strips? You can use a knife, but personally, I prefer the mandoline. It has a thing on it to hold the potato, and you slide it over the blades, and presto, strips. The mandoline has other uses, but why bring those up when we are having such a pleasant chat?

Now you must wash the fries. You put them in a big bowl and add cold water and let them stand a bit. Do this three times, if you must. Do it until gooey starch stops accumulating at the bottom. Because the starch will make the fries stick together, and it will stick to the pot and burn, then when you serve the fries, your guests will laugh, and somebody's hand will have to go down the garbage disposal. To restore decorum. And that is a downer for your guests and also not good for your pipes.

You heat your fat to 250°F, and you dry your fries and throw them in. "What?" you are asking yourself, "Has Christopher Walken lost his *mind?* Frying fries at two hundred fifty degrees? Perhaps he is getting soft. Perhaps this is the time for an ambitious young Turk to make his move."

Do not make this mistake, friend. That line of thinking leads to one place. The landfill. Or, if I am truly annoyed, several landfills. I am not suggesting you fry at 250°F. I am suggesting you *blanch* at 250. For 7 minutes. Then you pull the fries and drain them and put them in the fridge until they get cold.

While the fries are in the fridge, something happens to them. What, I do not know. If you have to know what happens to the fries, you may as well go suck on a pistol, because you are not going to find out here. I am not a potato . . . *scientist*. I do not have a degree in advanced nuclear potato physics. I act. I dance. On the side, I dabble in this and that. I do not have time to delve into the dark mysteries of the potato. All I know is, you have to cool your fries. Accept it. Or else doubt my word and then find yourself taking a long ride in the trunk of my Town Car.

So your fries are cold. Now what? Now, finally, you may fry them. Heat your oil to 350°F and fry your fries for 7 minutes. Keep the batches fairly small, so they brown good. If you pile them all in there and they don't brown good and then you blame Christopher Walken for your ineptitude, well . . . you may find out the other thing a mandoline is good for.

When your fries are good and brown, you pull them and drain them and salt them down and eat them. Good, right? The best you ever had? Of course the best you ever had. I knew this would be the case. I have a certain prescience about things like this. It almost scares me.

Now I must add a few bits of information. First, if you are truly serious about frying, you may wish to buy a dedicated fryer. I know of an inexpensive one. It is made by a company called Bravetti. Guinea outfit. Runs around a C-note. Second, you may wish to use something other than cow fat. Maybe you like cows. Maybe you live in the suburbs and you had a pet cow when you were a kid. How do I know? What I do know is this: many people swear by duck fat. And you can actually buy it, if you look around on the Web. Or goose fat. Same thing, right? It quacks. It has a beak. No difference.

If you like ducks, too, I can be of no help to you. I am a man of considerable knowledge, but there is a limit to what I know. I know I like fries. I know I like kneecaps. If I need more knowledge than that, I will find someone who has it and extract it at the point of a cattle prod.

This recipe is the recipe I gave Steve. It is my gift to you. I expect nothing in return. And when I say "I expect nothing in return," I mean, "I make no crass demands, but I expect you to do what is right." Like say mailing your uncle Chris a C-note whenever you make these fries. I think that would be appropriate.

And don't let me hear you talking crap about Astaire.

CHAPTER 22
PERFECT 10-MINUTE STREET PIZZA

BYPASS RATING:

(TRIPLE)

I HATE TO INTERRUPT a humorous book with a chapter about something as serious and important as pizza, but I'm going to do it anyway, because I feel strongly about it and I have no common sense.

Your homemade pizza sucks, right? Of course it does. Mine did, too, for years. It was so bad, I quit making it. The crust was like sponge cake. The sauce was orange. The cheese threw off grease and water. Sound familiar? Probably.

I have great news. Now, thanks to me and my obsessive personality and my twisted friend Mike, you can make the best New York street-style pizza you have ever eaten—including pizza you've paid for—with under *Ten minutes* of prep work. I don't mean cooking or letting the yeast rise. Those things take time. But the actual kneading and rolling and applying sauce and toppings . . . ten minutes. Tops. And best of all, you can use a food processor.

Mike is my only remaining childhood friend. The others were all dorks. I got in touch with him recently, and it turned out he had matured into a capable and possibly dangerous cook. He had all sorts of horrifying recipes. One was for pizza.

I had quit trying to make pizza, but like all normal people, I still craved it every second of my waking life. So I listened while Mike gave me his recipe, which he squeezed out of an Italian employee of his whose family owned a pizzeria.

The problem with getting recipes from Mike is that he's an artistic cook, like I used to be before I started writing cookbooks. He says "about" a lot. "About a cup." "About a pound." He never measures. I tried to get his recipe written down, but it didn't work for me, because he was guessing at the amounts he used, and he was way off.

But he gave me a lot of important information. For one thing, he told me how he combines a pizza stone and a screen to get a perfect crust every time. That, all by itself, is gold. A stone is a pain to use by itself. Using only a screen can give you crappy results. Combine the two, and you have pizza crust by the throat.

I'm going to try to get Mike to put his recipe in a future book, but you won't see it here. Sorry about that. He didn't hand me a finished recipe, but like Paul Henreid in *Casablanca*, he at least got me off my fatass and back in the fight.

I'll tell you what drove me to perfect my own recipe. Hate. Hate for everyone who succeeds at something and pretends to tell others how to succeed then holds something back.

You know what I'm talking about. I'll give you an example. Ever seen a grotesque, veiny, pimply bodybuilder tell a talk-show host all he does is work out thirty minutes a day? Ever bought their moronic, nonworking products and used them faithfully, only to find that little girls continued kicking sand in your face because you still had twelve-inch biceps?

Bodybuilders get big because they take drugs. End of story. There are a few freaks on the planet whose bizarre gorilla genes enable them to become huge without steroids, but the simple truth is, an average guy who does nothing but work out will never look like Arnold Schwarzenegger. When Arnie competed, he had more horse hormones in him than a processing vat at a dog food factory.

Oh, he still promoted workout products for money. He took his big drug-swollen arms and held up stupid toys like the Bullworker and posed for ad photos. But without the drugs, he would still be a moderately muscular guy with man-boobs, handing out towels in a gym in Austria. (I *think* it was the Bullworker, anyway.)

Fine president a guy like that would make. Journalists would ask, "How are we going to solve the problem of international terrorism?" And he'd say, "De Bullwookah vill ztop tewwowism een jost zix shoht weeks!"

Call me crazy, but here's how I see it. Full of crap at twenty-five, full of crap at sixty.

Life is full of cheats and hacks and cabals and cliques, and most of the time, they will go over you like a steamroller, and you will never re-

It is virtually impossible to make real pizzeria pizza using the garbage they sell in the sauce aisles of grocery stores.

alize you didn't have a chance. That's how pizza is, believe it or not. It is virtually impossible to make real pizzeria pizza using the garbage they sell in the sauce aisles of grocery stores. Don't ever buy it again. I don't care what your fat friends who think they can cook tell you. Pizza is a maze, and I am the rat that found the cheese. You listen to me from now on.

First thing: real pizzerias use sauce made in a small region of California. Only a couple of companies make it. They have technology you can never hope to recreate in your kitchen. Their plants are among the tomato fields. They take freshly picked, completely ripe tomatoes, process them immediately, and put them in gallon cans. The tomatoes are only cooked once. The puke they sell in grocery stores is cooked at least twice, and it wasn't that great to start with. It can never—*never*—be tarted up until it tastes like California sauce.

I know it sounds crazy, saying New York pizza is made with California sauce. But I know what I'm talking about. Buy this stuff, even if you have to have it shipped. Without it, you will forever wander in darkness. You may be able to make a fine gourmet-snobby sauce with fresh tomatoes, but street pizza sauce? Highly doubtful.

Here's the second thing you need to know. Grocery cheese is crap, too. Most of the shredded stuff they sell in bags cooks up like vinyl. The cheese they sell in solid bricks is full of water, and in the oven, the water comes out and ruins your pie. Your best hope, in a grocery, is the mozzarella and provolone they sell at the deli counter. You may be able to get whole-milk low-moisture cheese there. But your best bet is to buy cheese from a food service company that sells to restaurants.

Third thing: pizza flour is a myth. You can make staggeringly good pizza with any all-purpose flour, regardless of whether it's high or low in gluten or made from "hard wheat" or blessed by the pope before it leaves Italy. Believe it.

You can buy special pizza flour. It's called 00 flour, and the snobbiest brand is Caputo. The "00" refers to the grind; this stuff is ground so small it barely exists. I've tried it, and I was disappointed. Sometimes it was okay. Sometimes the pizza came out so delicate that when I chewed, my face couldn't really establish a relationship with it. And that's good, because 00 flour is expensive as hell. It makes a good pizza, and you may prefer it. But you may prefer the stuff you buy for pennies a pound.

Pizzerias all over America make delicious pies with normal flour. Some people claim you can fake pizza flour by combining cake flour with all-purpose in a 1:3 ratio. However they are wrong. I've tried it. You get a hard crust you might like, but it's nothing like 00.

My pizza is already so sublime, I can't be bothered with stupid foodie flour. But buy it, if you really must have the king manhood-compensating pizza of all time.

Fourth: you don't need a pizza oven. If your oven goes to 550, you're fine. Maybe a special pizza oven is better—you can buy countertop ovens that go to 650—but you're not going to be disappointed with 550.

Fifth: you need pizza screens and a stone. You can get a stone at any mall, and the screens are available online at places like Instawares.

Before you listen to your fat ignorant buddies who disagree with me, let me point out that I grew up in the north end of Miami, which

Don't let some Papa John's–eating boob from Grand Rapids tell you I'm talking through my hat. I know good pizza.

was full of Italians, and we had great New York–style pizza there. I also went to college in New York, and I had pizza all over the city. Don't let some Papa John's–eating boob from Grand Rapids tell you I'm talking through my hat. I know good pizza.

Here's what I'm going to do. I'm going to tell you how to make a perfect pizza crust using a food processor, with a regular blade, in about two minutes. I'm going to tell you what ingredients you can use and how they'll affect the crust. I'm going to tell you how to roll it and bake it. I'm going to tell you what brands of sauce and cheese to buy. I'll give you a recipe that is excellent, but which might not suit your tastes. But by telling you what the ingredients do, I'll give you the information you need to tailor the pie to suit you. Your job is to supply patience and practice. And a big sloppy gut.

Buy yourself a stone. Decide what size pie you have to have, and size the stone accordingly. I get by with a 15-by-18 stone. If I want a sixteen-inch pie, I lay a wad of foil under the edge of the crust that hangs off the stone, to keep it from flopping and burning. Some people buy eighteen-inch-square unglazed quarry tiles from Home Depot and Lowe's.

Buy yourself at least one screen. It's nice if the screen is bigger than the pie. Gives you room for mistakes.

Get round pizza pans to serve the pies on; it's nice if they're bigger than the pizzas. Get pan grippers, if your pans work with them. They make life easier, although pliers are actually better for yanking hot screens out of the oven. A simple wheel cutter will work great; just make sure it's a big four-inch wheel that turns well. I like the Good Grips brand. Finally, you'll need a peel. You can get them online. Don't buy wood. They're dirty and they don't work well. Buy thin aluminum.

If you like Sicilian, buy rectangular pans.

Okay, you have everything you need. Now it's time to cook. We'll start with the crust. I'll give you a recipe for a thin fourteen-inch crust with a lip. You can scale it up for other sizes.

This is for pizza *today*, like an hour from now. I almost never save dough in the fridge or freezer until the next day, but you can do it. Dough changes when you store it; you might try it to see if you like it better. (This may be easier if you use 2 cups of flour and scale the other stuff accordingly.)

CRUST

4 ounces water

2 teaspoons sugar

1 teaspoon dry yeast

1½ cups flour (high-gluten King Arthur, if you like it chewy, but any all-purpose will do)

½ tablespoon gluten (if you *really* like it chewy—won't make it tough)

1 teaspoon salt

½ teaspoon pepper

1–2 tablespoons olive oil (leave it out if you like your crust hard—oil doesn't seem to work well with low-gluten flour)

Let me give you the facts about flour. Gluten makes dough chewy, and in my experience, it seems to hold moisture. If that turns you on, you need high-gluten flour or you need to buy gluten and add it. Or both. The King Arthur company makes great high-gluten flour, but any bread flour or hard wheat flour should be fine. Check the protein amount on the side of a five-pound bag. High-gluten flour has at least four grams in the little table.

You may like a crisper, lighter-tasting crust. If so, use regular all-purpose flour suitable for biscuits. Gold Medal is fine.

You should be able to buy gluten powder at hippie organic "natural foods" grocery stores. You can have a lot of fun putting varying amounts in your dough to see what it does. Seems like too much gluten makes dough taste watery.

King Arthur also makes a great blend especially for pizza, but you can only buy it online.

Oil makes the crust heavier and more flavorful, and it makes it tear easier and crunch less. So it takes the leathery quality out of crust. If you like leathery crust with a crunchy rim, leave the oil out. If you like a light crust, leave it out. You don't need a drop of oil to make a perfect and authentic pie.

I put pepper in the dough because it wakes up the flavor of the crust, and somehow, a small amount doesn't taste like pepper. This is an ancient idea. The black specks you see in many pizza crusts are dots of pepper. Or filth that fell out of the cook's chest hair, or cigarette ashes. Anyway, you can leave it out.

Salt slows down the yeast, but a good pizza needs a lot of salt. More than you probably realize. Even the cheese has salt in it. Ever wake up in the middle of the night after having a pizza, dying for a drink of water? Now you know why.

The sugar feeds the yeast and makes the crust taste better. Putting small amounts of sugar in food makes it taste better without making it seem sweet.

I use Red Star fast-acting dry yeast. I can promise you it will work. I'm sure your favorite brand will work, too.

Okay, now you know what the ingredients are and what they do. It's time to make a pie, try it, decide what you don't like about it, and start making changes. Your first pie will be thin, without too much sauce, and it will have a light crust that isn't tough.

Start by getting the yeast ready. Put the 4 ounces of water in a bowl or something. Dissolve the teaspoon of sugar in it. Make sure the water is not hot if you're using a food processor. The processor will heat the dough, so it should be fairly cool (100°F or less) when you put it in. You don't want the heat to cook your yeast. If you knead by hand, warm the water before adding yeast. A 110°F should be fine. In any case, stir in the yeast until it's completely wet. Wait until the yeast starts to foam up. That proves it's not dead. May take 10 or 15 minutes.

Use plain old all-purpose flour with a "3" in the "protein" box on the side of a five-pound bag. If all you have is high-gluten flour, use that. Not a big deal. Put the flour in the bowl of a big, sturdy food processor and add the other remaining dry ingredients. Blend briefly, using the regular blade. If you use oil, add it next and blend until mixed in. I suggest you not use oil this time, because this is a baseline pie.

Start a timer running where you can see it. Start the food processor. Add the yeast mixture slowly, until the flour clumps up so most of it is in one big mass. Look at the timer when this happens, note the time, and keep processing for a full minute. Open the processor and check the dough. If it's too sticky to handle, throw in two or three tablespoons of flour and blend for maybe 3 seconds. That will make it less tacky, although it may break it up so you have to mash it back together. You want the dough dry enough to roll but wet enough so it stretches without too much trouble. It's nearly impossible to measure flour accurately, so don't be afraid to adjust.

You may have heard of the windowpane test, which tells you if dough is ready to use. I don't do it, and my pizza is fine.

Remove the dough and form it into a ball. You can knead it a couple of times to make it pretty. Just fold it in half and moosh it together until it looks nice.

If you really hate oil in your dough, you can use flour to keep it from sticking while it rises. Put the dough in a small covered dish—I like disposable food containers—after dusting the bottom of the dish with flour. The best way to spread flour evenly is to put it in a strainer and shake it. Put the dough on the flour and dust the top of it and close the dish. If the flour bugs you, I suppose you could line the bowl with no-stick foil.

If a little oil doesn't scare you, grease the dish and the underside of the lid lightly and dump the dough in and cover it. If you love oil, put a couple of tablespoons in and roll the dough in it and then cover it. For this pie, I suggest a very light film of oil on the bowl and lid.

The dough will take 30 to 60 minutes to rise, depending on the breaks. You want it to at least double in volume. A little bigger may actually be better.

Start the oven heating at least 30 minutes before you bake. Set it at 550°F. If your oven goes higher, great. Do 650. Put the stone as low in the oven as you can. If your crust gets too dark, move the stone up next time.

Now, let me give you some tomato knowledge. There are two companies that make decent sauce. One is called Escalon, and the other is Stanislaus Foods. Escalon's prepared sauce (really a sauce base) is called Bontá. It contains nothing except tomatoes and basil. Maybe some salt. Stanislaus makes all sorts of products. They have oven-ready sauce with various things in it, but I use their Bontá-like "scratch-ready" sauce, which contains only tomatoes, basil, salt, and citric acid. These companies also make tomato puree and so on, which you might want to check out once you master the basics.

I've used mainly Stanislaus products. I can buy them locally at a place called Gordon Food Service. The cans are huge, but they cost four to five bucks each, so it doesn't matter. You can make approximately five million pies with one can. All the sauces I've used contain basil. They make no-basil versions, so know what you're buying.

Stanislaus makes a sauce called Full Red. It's supposed to have the freshest flavor of all their sauces. It's not as thick as the others. The flavor is a little less intense. It's excellent. You have to dilute it with water. I'd start at 3:1, sauce:water, and go from there.

Saporito is another product they make. I like it more than Full Red. It's extremely thick and powerful. I dilute it 2:1.

Super Dolce is the best Stanislaus sauce I've tried. It has a fruitier taste, and it somehow tastes more grown up. Seems to have more of a pear-tomato flavor. Dilute it 2:1 if you use it in your first pie.

Bontá pizza sauce is excellent, too. Tied for first place in my heart. I dilute it 3:1. It has a less obtrusive, subtler taste. Some people claim it's better because it has no citric acid. Whatever. You cannot go wrong with any of the sauces I have named. And don't be fooled; you can't tell much by tasting it right out of the can. If you want to judge a sauce, you have to make a pizza.

You don't have to add a damn thing to these sauces. The first pizza sauce on earth was just tomato chunks and basil leaves. But for the hell of it, let's start with a couple of small changes. They improve the sauce slightly.

SAUCE
4 ounces Stanislaus Super Dolce or Saporito pizza sauce
2 ounces water

OR

4½ ounces Stanislaus Full Red or Bontá pizza sauce
1½ ounces water

Now, add a tablespoon or two of olive oil, half a teaspoon of dry oregano, and half a teaspoon of garlic powder. I use powder because it's what sidewalk pizzerias use, but obviously, you can use fresh garlic. Believe it or not, you can make a great pizza with no garlic at all. Stir your sauce until everything is mixed. You may also want to try adding a teaspoon of sugar. You can substitute butter for the olive oil.

Mike taught me something shocking. Pizza sauce is better if you increase the acidity. By adding vinegar. You can get by with just canned sauce and water, but this is what I really like:

3 ounces (by weight) Super Dolce sauce
1 tablespoon white vinegar
1 tablespoon balsamic vinegar
½ teaspoon sugar
¼ teaspoon pepper
½–1 teaspoon pressed garlic
½ teaspoon dry oregano
1–2 tablespoons olive oil
Enough water to make it speadable

If you ever get desperate for pizza and can't find good sauce, you can get by with tomato paste. Believe it or not, commercial sauce is more like paste than crushed tomatoes or puree. This recipe will give you an okay sauce you can live with in an emergency. Just mix it up.

DESPERATION SAUCE
1 (6-ounce) can tomato paste
4½ ounces water
1 teaspoon garlic powder
1 teaspoon dry basil or 3 teaspoons minced fresh basil
2 tablespoons olive oil
1 teaspoon sugar to simulate quality tomatoes

When you get to be a big, confident pizza chef, you may want to use red wine in your sauce instead of water. I use plain old Carlo Rossi Paisano.

Stanislaus and Escalon make a wide variety of products, including canned tomatoes. Once you feel like you understand basic sauce, you can start adding tomato chunks and so on. Check their websites for recipes.

You're going to need cheese. The most highly regarded source of pizzeria cheese is a company called Grande. You can buy their cheese online at a place called Vern's. Google it. I love a 50/50 mozzarella/provolone blend, and they just happen to make one. They also make 100 percent whole-milk low-moisture mozzarella, which is a bear to find in a grocery store.

I used to think all prepackaged store cheese was garbage, but I made an acceptable pie with Sargento shredded low-moisture whole-milk mozzarella. So I guess some brands are okay.

Shredding your own cheese will probably give slightly better results, because pre-shredded cheese has cellulose powder in it. But even with the cellulose, your pizza will be better than anything you can buy.

Gordon Food Service happens to sell excellent pre-shredded cheese. There's a rumor that it's actually repackaged Grande cheese. I dunno.

I've gotten good results with sliced Boar's Head whole-milk low-moisture mozzarella from my grocer's deli. You can also use scamorza cheese, if you can find it.

Here's how it works. Mozzarella is buttery and bland and not as chewy as provolone. Provolone (which is always made with whole milk) is a little tougher and more flavorful. Scamorza is even more buttery-tasting than mozzarella. There are other cheeses out there that give good results, but you should start with something you're absolutely sure of. So get yourself some mozzarella or a blend, and make sure the quality is there, and make sure it's low moisture.

Part-skim cheese is chewier but burns in a hurry. You can get away with it in this recipe, because at 550°F the pie only cooks seven minutes. Whole-milk cheese tastes richer and burns less but throws off more grease.

You should add a small amount—about half a cup, loosely packed—of grated hard cheese to your mix. Grana Padano is good, but you could use parmesan or romano. Grated cheese will add flavor to the pie and create the illusion that the sauce is full of mysterious seasonings. This is a good part of the recipe to screw with when you're trying to improve your pizza.

Okay, put a layer of flour on your rolling surface and flop the dough onto it. Dust the dough with flour, if needed. Start rolling. Use a pin no longer than ten inches, so you'll be able to keep it in the center of the crust as it grows and form a lip at the edge. Rolling dough takes practice; I can't help you with that. Try to get a fourteen-inch circle out of it. It's okay to lift the dough and throw more flour under it when it sticks. If you turn the dough over while you roll it, you'll have a pizza with flour on the outer rim. If you like that, it's not a problem.

Don't flip out if you don't get perfect circles. Remember, when you lay your dough out on the screen, you can cheat and force it to be circular.

When I use oil to keep a no-oil crust from sticking to the bowl, I like to flop the dough out so it sits on the side that touched the oil. I want the upper side of the crust to be completely free of oil so it will be crisp.

Tossing the dough will give you a crust with no flour on it, because you're up in the air all the time, and you don't need to use lots of flour to keep it from sticking. I am told it will also bubble more. If you toss the dough, you may want to buy a docker, which is a tiny rolling pin with spikes that poke holes in the dough and prevent bubbling. If you use a docker, make sure you do it before the pie goes on the screen, because otherwise it will unite the dough and screen permanently. I toss dough a lot, and find a docker unnecesary.

When the dough looks like a pizza, put it on the screen and spread it out. Be careful not to put pressure on it, because that makes it stick. Never wash your screen unless you have to. Oil will bake onto it and make it stick less.

Your first pie won't have much sauce on it. Try not to use the whole 6 ounces. Using a soft spatula, spread it around until the pie is red, but don't make a big, thick, cakey layer of sauce. Leave no more than half an inch of the rim bare. If you're a clod and wuss who lacks the testosterone to eat the bare crust, and you cry for Mommy to take it away, and you call it something unbelievably stupid like "pizza bones," you can apply sauce pretty much all the way to the edge.

You only need enough sauce to turn the pie red. If you go easy on the sauce the first time, you can use more the second time and get a better idea of how much suits you. If you use too much sauce and end up with a bad pie, you may not realize the sauce was the problem. You really should start out with less sauce, so you know what a decent pizza tastes like.

This is a good time to apply grated cheese, because the red background shows you where it landed. You want enough to make the pie more white than red. Not a big thick layer, but basicaly white.

Put the main cheese on the pie; use 12–16 ounces by weight. It's hard to overdo the cheese, although some people barely use any. Spread it well, as close to the edge as you can get it. Sprinkle a teaspoon or two of decent-quality oregano, such as McCormick, on it (avoid cheap brands because they will ruin the pie). Apply a little salt. You're done.

We're not using toppings on the first pie. If we were, you would spread half the cheese on the pie, then apply toppings, and then finish the cheese. Having some cheese on top of the toppings makes them dry out less and stick better. And don't overdo the toppings. They go further than you think.

Center the pie (not just the screen) on the stone. Bake for 4 minutes. Open the oven. Lift the pie off the screen with the peel. If it's stuck, give up and leave it there. If not, using the pan gripper or pliers, grip the screen by the sturdy edge only and pull it out. Put it on the rack above the pizza, because otherwise flour dust will fall off of it and onto your floor. Using the peel, center the pie on the stone again. Close the door and bake for 3 more minutes.

Look at the pie. If the edge is getting brown and it looks done, take it out and put it on a pizza pan. Some people like to put paper plates on the pan to absorb oil when the pizza is sliced. Up to you. You can slice the pizza right away. I like twelve slices instead of eight. Less fighting over slices, and it's easier to hold in your hand.

This bitch is going to be really hot for at least five minutes. It's not like a tepid congealed pie that sat in the backseat of an old Jetta while a driver from Uzbekistan tried to find your house.

I like big wheel cutters, but a rocking blade can be better if you have lots of toppings.

This bitch is going to be really hot for at least five minutes. It's not like a tepid congealed pie that sat in the backseat of an old Jetta while a driver from Uzbekistan tried to find your house. Let it cool a little before you try to eat it.

Now, ask yourself what needs to be changed. Want a crust that's less leathery? Add oil next time. Want it chewy? Add gluten. More flavor in the cheese? More provolone and hard cheese. More buttery flavor? Pure mozzarella or scamorza.

By all means, play with the sauce. You know that if you screw up, you have a safe recipe to come back to.

When you start using toppings, don't use huge chunks. Always slice your toppings thin. Believe it or not, the best topping I've ever had was a few pieces of cooked shrimp cut in slices ⅛ inch thick. It you like Italian sausage, you can slice it thin if you cook it first. You should never put raw meat on a pizza anyway. It throws off grease like you would not believe. You can bake it, fry it, or nuke it first. A covered Pyrex dish makes a great container for nuking meat for pizza. A Cuisinart with a slicing blade slices firm toppings very nicely.

If you like Sicilian, use more dough and bake in an oiled pan on the rack with no stone in the oven. You may want to stretch the dough by hand. It's a bitch, rolling a rectangle. A seasoned or Teflon pan should not stick, but you can make sure by sprinkling the pan with semolina, Cream of Wheat, or corn meal before adding the dough.

Here is my final advice. Check out the forum at www.pizzamaking.com. It's packed with great information. As well as crap only an idiot would believe. Be selective. Also, take a look at www.pennmac.com. You can buy Bontá sauce there, as well as other pizza goodies.

Okay, that's it. I have stolen fire from Mount Olympus and handed it to you on a greasy aluminum platter. You are *free* from the tyranny of pizza shop owners. Want pizza at 4 a.m.? Now you can have it. Pizza for breakfast? Pizza during a football game, when everyone else has to wait two hours for delivery? It's yours, baby. And it will be the best pizza in your whole town. And don't stop here. Experiment with homegrown tomatoes and different cheeses and so on. This is just a beginning.

Garlic Rolls

Garlic rolls are easier than you would think. And if you do it right, you can make them arrive at about the same time as the pizza.

It's simple. Make two batches of dough instead of one. You might leave the pepper out of the batch you use for the rolls. Up to you. I use two tablespoons of oil in the roll dough, for flavor.

Let both batches rise. Roll the garlic roll dough out maybe ¼ inch thick. Cut it in pieces around ⅝ inch wide and 6 inches long. Take each slice, tie it in a knot, and put it on a pizza screen with the ends of the knot on the bottom. Let the rolls recover from the rolling and abuse while you roll and decorate the pizza.

When you put your pizza on the stone in the bottom of the oven, put the rolls on a rack higher up. When you open the door after 4 minutes to remove the pizza screen from beneath the pie, your rolls will probably be done. I don't have to tell you how rolls look when it's time to take them out.

Throw the rolls in a bowl and add sauce. Here's what I use.

¼ cup olive oil
3 or more cloves crushed garlic
2 tablespoons (measure packed down) or more fresh parsley
Salt

Put the oil and garlic in a nukable container and cook it. Enough to fry the garlic a little and kill the raw taste. Shred the parsley into the oil. Pour the mixture over the rolls, salt them well, and toss. I also like to add a huge quantity of grated cheese. You can use butter if you like it better than olive oil. Or combine butter and oil.

You should probably use high-gluten flour for rolls. I add extra gluten.

Okay, you are now the pizza king of your entire geographic region. Seriously.

CHAPTER 23
PEACH COBBLER

BYPASS RATING:

(DOUBLE)

LET ME BEGIN with a crude stolen joke.

> *"Did you hear about the nude man who just ran through town?"*
> *"No."*
> *"He ran by the butcher's. He ran by the baker's. They caught him by the cobblers."*

That's an English joke. I think I originally read it in one of those English veterinarian ficto-bios from the seventies. *All Creatures Toothless and Flatulent.* Something like that.

If the joke offends you, blame the English. They're not too swift with a toothbrush, but they know their lowbrow humor. Shakespeare is 90 percent genitalia jokes. I learned that in college. It's one of those things that make me feel good about spending sixty grand on a degree.

I'm a huge cobbler fan, because cobbler has all the attractive attributes of pie, only it's much bigger. How much can a pie weigh? Two and a half pounds, max? A cobbler can go twenty, easy.

My grandmother in Kentucky used to make cobbler all the time. Blackberry cobbler. Kentucky is a weird place. If you live in Kentucky and keep your weeds down and look after your yard, what do you get? Nothing. If you lie back on your big ass and let nature take its course, what do you get? Blackberry briars, laden with fruit, as far as the eye can see. And a welfare check.

The blackberry is the strongest laxative known to medical science. Well, the strongest natural laxative. On the list of all known laxatives, it falls in the somewhere between Liquid-Plumr and C-4.

There's a lesson in that for all of us.

The blackberry is the strongest laxative known to medical science. Well, the strongest *natural* laxative. On the list of all known laxatives, it falls in the space between Liquid-Plumr and C-4.

It makes sense to use blackberries in dessert, the final course, because after eating them, you can't really hang around the table. Although if you wanted to get away from my grandmother's table, you had to jump while she wasn't looking or wait until every scrap of food had been eaten. Along with some of the flatware.

ME:

Well, that was good. Excuse me for a minute.

GRANNY:

Where you going?

ME:

I'll be back.

GRANNY:

Eat that dumpling.

ME:

When I get back.

GRANNY:

Eat that chicken leg.

ME:

In a minute.

GRANNY:

Finish that cobbler.

ME:

For the love of *God,* let me go.

GRANNY:

See if you can fit a whole turnip in your mouth.

I guess you can make cobbler out of anything. Apples are popular. For this book, I picked peaches. Don't ask me why. It's an artistic decision. Why did Rubens paint fat chicks?

Maybe because they worked for food.

Technically, "cobbler" means a giant pie with a biscuity top and no bottom crust. Whatever. I had no idea the definition was that restrictive and oppressive when I created my recipe. I make mine with pie crust, when I feel like it, and I always have crust on the bottom. Dinner is dinner. It's not a food-science seminar. If it's good, it must be right. Right? Right.

I decided to go with a raised biscuit crust for the cobbler. It's ridiculously easy.

FILLING
64 ounces peaches, sliced to pie-size chunks
1½ cups brown sugar
2 tablespoons vanilla extract
¼ teaspoon ground nutmeg (half that much if nutmeg isn't your thing)
4 tablespoons butter

Are you ready? Are you ready for the Herculean task of making the filling? Here it goes. Plop the above stuff into a big microwave-safe bowl, mix, and microwave. Maybe 4 minutes, twice, with some stirring in between. Pretty easy, huh? You want this stuff to be hot and about half cooked when you add it to the cobbler. If you don't cook it a little in advance, it won't be done after you bake it, and then what do you have? Raw peaches and sugar inside a giant biscuit. Which isn't so bad.

Cook's Illustrated says you should remove the red parts from the peaches. I'm too lazy.

CRUST
6 cups self-rising flour
$^3/_8$ cup sugar
1 teaspoon salt
$^3/_8$ cup bacon grease
$^3/_8$ cup butter ($^3/_4$ stick)
1½ cups milk

Okay, you are going to love me for this. I worked you so hard on the brownies (I assume you skipped ahead and made them already). When you see how easy this is, you're going to get down on your fat, scabby knees and thank me.

Preheat the oven to 400°F. Dump the flour in a bowl. Add the dry ingredients. Combine the bacon grease and butter, add it to the flour, and cut it in until you get tiny little crumbs. Then add the milk and mix it up. You're making biscuit dough, more or less. The butter is for flavor. The bacon grease makes it lighter and a little tastier.

Roll this stuff out ⅜ inch thick. Thinner is acceptable. Thicker will cause a problem. When it rises, the peaches will be pushed out over the sides of the pan, and you'll end up with a huge cara-melized peach sculpture on the bottom of your oven.

A small amount of skill comes into play when you put this in the baking dish. You want a Pyrex dish, 9-by-13. Line the inside of it with dough, and use a sharp knife to cut the dough off at the rim of the dish. It shouldn't stick, so don't worry about spraying with PAM or other foul vegetable-based secretions.

Pour the peach mixture in. Now, cut yourself some nice strips of dough and lay them across the top. You don't have to cover it. As long as you cover about half of the dish, you're okay.

Brush the exposed dough with melted butter and sprinkle it with sugar. You can sprinkle a little cinnamon on it, too, for looks, but go easy with it.

Bake for 45 minutes. Let it cool for 20 before cutting it. Don't worry. The filling will still be roughly as hot as the surface of the sun. At noon, even.

I just love this stuff. Bury it in vanilla or peach ice cream and plow in. So good, and so lethal. The whole thing probably has as many calories as three pizzas, but calories aren't the whole picture. Look at the added white sugar. The totally gratuitous bacon grease. The extra salt. Sometimes when I think about unhealthy ingredients, I feel the way Sam Peckinpah must have felt about stage blood.

The crust works with any fruit filling. For that matter, you can put the peach filling in a pie. Or you pour it on the kitchen floor, lie down on it, and make filling angels.

What do I care what you do with it? Like I keep saying, I already have your money.

CHAPTER 24
ICE CREAM LASAGNA

BYPASS RATING:

(TRIPLE)

I HATE CELEBRITY CHEFS. You know why? Because they're lazy sacks of crap.

I don't have to tell you what happens when you watch celebrity chefs. You turn on the tube. You watch them cook. You watch their audience of Pavlovian drones moan in ecstasy when they taste the food. You write down the recipes. You try them yourself. You do everything they did on TV. And the food tastes like used cat litter.

Why? Because the recipes are awful. TV chefs have to come up with new stuff every day or at least every week, and they're so busy pimping their books and their TV-dinner-quality chain restaurants and their floundering sitcoms, they can't be bothered writing recipes that taste good. Instead, they pack their studio audiences with mindless monkeys who

They pack their studio audiences with mindless monkeys who would clap for snot on toast, and then they cook garbage and pass it around for guaranteed approval.

would clap for snot on toast, and then they cook garbage and pass it around for guaranteed approval.

Let's talk Emeril. The Cajun chef from Louisiana. Oops, he's not from Louisiana. Or a Cajun. He's a Yankee from Massachusetts, and he's *Portuguese and Italian.* Okay, let's not hold that against him. He cooked at the Commander's Palace, so he ought to know a couple of things, right?

I dunno 'bout that.

I found his recipe for béarnaise sauce on the Internet, on the Food Network site. I was in a hurry, and I needed béarnaise sauce, and I thought, Surely this guy can be trusted with glorified mayonnaise. Then I made it. It was like tartar sauce mixed with Absorbine Jr.

All right, anyone can have an off day. Maybe a disgruntled intern deliberately added an extra pint of white vinegar to the recipe, because he passed Emeril in the hall at the Food Network and couldn't get a high five. Maybe I missed something in the directions. Okay, one bad recipe doesn't prove anything.

Then I saw him on the tube last week.

Emeril had just made lasagna. I didn't see that part, because I don't watch food shows. They cut into my little-person-porn time. But I was flipping channels, and there he was, talking about lasagna. It doesn't have to be savory, he says. It can be sweet. He'll demonstrate, he says.

He takes out—as God is my witness—two crackers. They're some sort of sweet wafer-type thing. They look like giant wontons. He goes into the fridge and grabs some pistachio ice cream, which he admits is several days old. And pistachio is crap, regardless. He plops a cracker down on a plate, he prys out a lump of ice cream, and he drops it on the cracker, breaking it. "*Oooooooooooh,*" go the drones, like they've been stranded at sea for a year, eating rats and drinking fish blood. "*Oooooooooooh,*" two crackers and a wad of green ice. Honey, go get the camcorder. This is history in the making.

I am convinced his audience has been lobotomized and trained to cheer, using special seats that deliver scorching shocks to their genitals.

He drops the other cracker on top. *"Oooooooooooooh,"* that was brilliant! They didn't see *that* coming! I suppose they thought he was going to pour gravy on it. My guess is, none of these people were taking the day off from NASA.

I know you're already on the verge of orgasm, but hold on. There's more. He took a shaker full of confectioner's sugar, he held it up over his head, and he shook it onto the ice cream and crackers, yelling, *"BAM! BAM! BAM! BAM! BAM!"*

All I can say is, I hope the seats in that studio were covered with plastic, because the Emeril Monkey Squad flat went into orbit. *Sugar on a dessert! Oh, God! Who would have thought of that but Emeril? It's genius! And most of it hit the plate!*

And what's with that "BAM!" business? It's like something Dustin Hoffman would have done in *Rain Man*. "BAM, I'm definitely not wearing my underwear." "BAM, I only fly Quantas." "BAM, severely injured by Mario Batali . . ."

Now, you *know* the ice cream thing tasted like crap. Old ice cream between two sugar crackers? What's next, Benadryl? Boiled hot dogs on folded white bread? But if you had gone into the studio and bitched in front of the audience, they would have burned you for a witch, in Emeril's warming drawer.

Dude, you make like, what, nine million dollars a week? You were a professional chef for years? And you have the *gall* to throw ice cream on a cracker and call it "dessert lasagna"? Are you *high?*

I am not a professional chef. I make significantly less than nine million dollars a week. I have no training, and I cook on a crappy electric stove with an oven light that doesn't work. But I thought about the concept of ice cream lasagna for approximately eight seconds, and I came up with something so sweet and sinful it will make your pancreas leap out of your body and run screaming into the night. Okay, not eight seconds. More like a minute and ten seconds.

Is it fair for me to criticize Espadrille? No, of course not. He's a busy guy, managing three hundred Emeril restaurants, five Emeril theme parks, two Emeril nursing homes, the Emeril museum, the United Church of Emeril, the Emeril Symphony Orchestra, and his own line of edible Emeril lingerie. If he had a minute and ten seconds, I'm sure he could wipe the floor with me.

And what's with that "Essence of Emeril" he sells? First of all, it has an unwholesome sound, like they're wringing out his sweaty toques and bottling it. Second, you know you're a lousy cook when your entire cooking style can be crammed into one tiny jar of cruddy dried spices. I guess I'm complex; sometimes I use four different seasonings in one week. Colonel Sanders used eleven. He must be a god.

The idea of ice cream lasagna is incredibly stupid on its face. But let's ignore that. Let's pretend it's a legitimate food concept. Okay, Elavil used two crackers and a wad of stale ice cream. What should we use? How about—instead of something dry and unbelievably boring—something like a brownie? But that would be too easy; you're not paying me money to rehash junk I already make. Okay, let's make it a blondie. With chocolate chips and pecans. We'll bake it into a sheet, and we'll stack the sheets in a pan, and between the sheets we'll put . . . coconut ice cream. An original recipe. I mean, ordinarily, I'd do like the professionals and just use whatever I happened to have *moldering in the refrigerator,* but I'm just an amateur, so cut me some slack.

What will we put on top of it? Chocolate sauce! Good idea, but again, too easy. I had a *full minute and ten seconds*, remember? Let's use all of it. Think, Steve, think. I thought real hard with my tiny little non-millionaire-chef brain, and all I could come up with was *caramel sauce made from scratch*.

God, I hate celebrity chefs.

I scribbled out the recipes, and I made them all and threw them together, and it was absolutely excellent and—dare I say it—even better than dried-out pistachio ice cream between two moldy cookies Emeril found in the pocket of his sweatpants.

This stuff is *really* good. But I warn you, it's incredibly rich. You might want to consider taking about a cup of the brown sugar out of the blondie recipe.

Or not. Pig.

ICE CREAM
1½ cups milk
1½ cups cream (I use whipping cream)
½ cup coconut flakes, packed before measuring
¼ cup sugar
1 teaspoon vanilla
1 small (about 7 ounce) can Coco Lopez
4 eggs
½ teaspoon salt

Here's the instructions: make ice cream. If you don't know how to make ice cream, do this:

1. Go to the store.
2. Buy an ice cream maker.
3. Open the box.
4. Look for a pamphlet labeled "Instructions."
5. Do what it says.

You mix the ingredients with a mixer, you dump them in the machine, and eventually, you get ice cream. Now, this is a big-ass recipe. If you're using a quart-and-a-half machine with a tub you stick in the freezer, it may not freeze a recipe this big. I suggest giving it a head start by chilling the mixed ingredients in the freezer until they start to freeze. Or use two bowls, one after the other.

BLONDIE
- 1½ sticks butter
- 4 eggs
- 1½ teaspoons vanilla extract
- 1 teaspoon salt
- 2½ cups brown sugar
- 1 cup all-purpose flour
- 6 ounces dark chocolate chips or chunks
- 1 cup chopped pecans

Preheat the oven to 400°F. Melt the butter and let it cool a bit so it won't cook the eggs when it hits them. Or just let it soften at room temperature, if you have more patience than I do. Dump the eggs, vanilla, salt, butter, and brown sugar in a bowl. Beat with a mixer on "high." Give it several minutes of beating. Make it nice and smooth and gooey. Then mix in the flour. Next, fold in the chocolate chips and pecans.

Now, you have to pour out a thin layer of this stuff—as thin as you can get it, which isn't very thin—and bake for 10 minutes or until it starts to brown. How you're going to do that . . . that's *your* problem. You want a piece of blondie the length and width of a 9-by-13 Pyrex pan. You can spread it on a Silpat mat and bake it. Make a rectangle of batter about 7 by 10 inches in size, and it will be bigger than 9 by 13 when it cooks. Chill it in a freezer, flop it off of the Silpat onto a sheet of wax paper, use a pizza cutter to trim it to size, and put it back in the freezer to keep it from falling apart while you cook the next one. Maybe you have a better way of doing it. Some people prefer to use parchment paper.

You want to accumulate three sheets of blondie. I suggest you freeze them all before using them in the dessert, because if you put ice cream on a warm sheet of blondie, it will start to melt.

Drop the first sheet of blondie in the pan. Add half the ice cream. Spread it out as level as you can. Repeat with the second sheet and second half of the ice cream. Put the third sheet on top, as a lid. Freeze.

If you tear up the sheets, relax. You can put them back together, like a jigsaw puzzle. It will taste the same as if it were pretty.

CARAMEL SAUCE
¼ cup water
¾ cup sugar
½ cup heavy cream
1 tablespoon butter
½ teaspoon salt

Put the water and sugar in a saucepan and put it on high heat. You won't have to stir it. The sugar will dissolve when the mixture gets hot enough. Let it boil until it turns about the color of tortoise-shell eyeglass frames.

Remove it from the heat immediately. Drizzle the cream in very, very slowly while stirring with a whisk. When it's all mixed in, add the butter. Whisk until it's melted.

Return it to the stove and reduce it over medium heat. Stir constantly. This will take maybe 10 minutes. Test it by dropping a little on a cool plate. When it's thick enough to make you happy, take it off the stove.

Making this stuff is an art. If you make the caramel too dark, it will be a little bitter and not sweet enough. If you make it too light, you end up with sugar sauce. Don't be afraid to practice.

If it comes out too dark, you can add sugar to it to think it out. Also, you may want to try it with ¼ teaspoon of salt before adding the rest.

When the dessert is ready to serve, take a very sharp, sturdy knife and cut it into squares. Pry one out and put it on a dish. Drizzle a teaspoon or two of the sauce on it. If you prefer chocolate sauce, use that.

This stuff is so rich you may hallucinate, so watch it.

Now, if you (like me) think ice cream lasagna is a moronic notion, do this instead: make ice cream sandwiches. Use two layers of blondie instead of three, and slice the sandwiches out of the finished slab of dessert. You can dribble a little sauce on top of the ice cream before you lay the top piece of blondie on it.

There. That was real hard, wasn't it? I can certainly understand why TV chefs rely on crackers and leftover ice cream.

Now, try it. While I go run after my pancreas.

CHAPTER 25

YEAST-RAISED FRIED DOUGHNUTS IN COCONUT/ BANANA SAUCE

BYPASS RATING:

(QUADRUPLE)

NOTE: To cover the doughnut recipe, I chose a third celebrity chef. Give it up for my man Al Franken. This is an actual transcript of a tape he sent me. No, really.

Hi, everyone. It's me, Al. I probably sound a little gloomy. Do I? I'm sure I do. I'm sure I do. It's just that we're in what, the seventh year of the Bush administration? And Bush still hasn't been impeached. And Dick Cheney isn't in jail. Even though he shoots guys in the face. And Air America quit payin' me, because it turned out the only people who listened to my show were my mom and my little conservative Christian friend, Gary Bauer.

I never felt welcome there. Okay? There, I said it. Gary said to let it go and be like Jesus. But I can't help it. I never felt welcome.

My interns were mean to me. Can you believe that? Interns. They ought to be grateful I went down to juvie and gave 'em a job.

I tried to get on their good side. I really did. I'd come in every day, and I'd offer 'em some of the peanut butter fudge Gary made for me, and I'd go, "Hey, Leaf. Hey, Anoop. What up, my homeys?" So they'd know I was "down." I can say that. I'm not too old to say that. I was "down by law." I almost went to Woodstock. But my friends said there was no room on the bus. Although it looked half empty to me.

I felt like I was connecting with 'em, but then I'd go to the restroom to splash water on my face before the show, and I'd come back and the "On Air" light would go on, and I'd take my seat, and there I'd be. Sittin' in peanut butter fudge.

I told on 'em. I went to my boss and I'd go, "Hey, Scott. Hey. I know you're walkin' to your stretch Prius, but I have to tell you somethin'." And he'd agree to listen, although he didn't always slow down. I'd go, "Scott, my darn interns are so mean to me. Look at my pants. Look, okay? Just turn this way for a second and look. I know they're washable, 'cause they're hemp. But this isn't right. And Gary worked all mornin' on that fudge. He even made little icing crosses."

I told him it was okay that they weren't payin' me. Because it was for the cause. Speak truth to power, y'know? It was okay that they weren't payin' me, but it seemed like every day I sat on a different snack food, and darn it, I was startin' to get tired of it.

It hurt. Okay? 'Cause it was just like when I was a kid, and I couldn't get on the band bus after the games 'cause the other guys took me to the girls' locker room and glued me to a toilet seat. I swear, they did that once a week. Ha ha. Real funny. My mom started makin' me carry a screwdriver to take the seat off so I could go home.

Tom Cruise isn't really gay. I told him Tom had a baby and even tried to eat the afterbirth.

I hope Bill O'Reilly doesn't hear about that. Oh, God. I can just hear him now. "Stuart Smalley got glued to a toilet seat. Stuart Smalley sits in peanut butter fudge. Stuart Smalley is a fudge-sittin' toilet seat popinjay."

I don't know what I'd do without Gary. He's so goshdarned nice to me. He goes too far sometimes, I know. On slow days he calls my show so I'll have someone to talk to. He pretends to be someone else, but I can tell it's him, 'cause he always says the same thing. He says God sent us al Qaeda because of Tom Cruise. No matter how many times I tell him Tom Cruise isn't really gay. I told him Tom had a baby and even tried to eat the afterbirth.

I don't know why no one listens. I guess America doesn't want to listen to good radio. I guess they'd rather listen to O'Reilly, lyin' big fat lies out of his big fat lyin' liar face.

I talked to Anoop and Leaf. I told them I wanted to have a meeting with them in the intern office. I said I wanted to rap about some heavy stuff, so I would appreciate it if they would meet me in their crib so I could lay the 911 on 'em.

I went in there and sat down, and they seemed real nice. They were quiet, and they listened, and they even offered me gum. I told 'em I didn't want to come off like a big paternalistic Eurocentric white male bloviator. Like O'Reilly. I said I knew they were just showin' that they were important and valid, too, and that that was . . . okay. But it wasn't cool that I kept sittin' in fudge and Rice Krispie treats. And they needed to knock that stuff off.

They asked if they could go out in the hall and talk about it, and I said sure, and that that was awesome and totally radical. And after about forty minutes I tried to get up and go check on 'em, and that's when I realized I was glued to the chair. And it turned out that gum was Feenamint.

I had to run down the hall in my underpants, and I ran right past Joni Mitchell, who was there for an interview about cold fusion. I had a manila envelope on my head, but I couldn't see where I was goin' and I ran into a pillar and I fell down and the envelope came off.

I got in the men's room and I called the receptionist and said I needed her to contact Gary and have him get me more pants. She said pants were sexist and symbolized rape. I explained that they were made from hemp, but she said that didn't make any difference. So I had to ride the subway in a prairie skirt. And a guy pinched me. Really hard.

You know what? I tried to help. I tried to give real Americans—the patriotic 90 percent of America that realizes that terrorism is caused by war toys and Nativity displays—a voice on the air. And they turned me down. They turned me down, and I sat in fudge, and I didn't get paid, and then Joni Mitchell saw me in my underpants. So to heck with it. I'm sorry. To *heck* with it. That's how mad I am. H-E-C-K.

Oh, God. I shouldn't have said that about Nativity displays. Now Gary's gonna be all pissy.

I'm gonna go be a senator now, but before I go, I have one more thing to talk about. It's about the fudge. Gary makes really good fudge, and he's a good friend. But I have to be honest. If I had to pick my favorite snack food to sit on during my show, it would have to be homemade doughnuts. Especially the filled ones, because it feels cool when stuff squirts out of 'em.

Here's a doughnut recipe Steve made up. You could probably make it with no-gluten millet flour and sugar from union-chopped cane if you wanted, but this is how he wrote it. He uses stuff that's probably—I don't know—probably made in sweatshops by little brown kids wearin' chains made by Halliburton.

You could eat these with rum raisin ice cream. Just make sure the raisins aren't from grapes picked by scab labor.

Pour a 14-ounce can of Coco Lopez into a saucepan and add a big shot of banana liqueur. Sometimes Gary and I drink banana liqueur when we watch *The View*. It's really good with peanut butter fudge. Anyway, you add the liqueur and boil the mixture until it's thick. Like Halliburton crude oil on the neck of a poor helpless mom penguin.

You can add a teaspoon of vanilla extract if you want, although most of the money from vanilla goes to Malaysian right-wing vanilla barons put in power by the Reagan administration. If you can live with yourself—if starving vanilla workers living in labor camps where they can't get partial-birth abortions are just, you know, okay with you—then go ahead and use it. Throw in a pinch of salt.

1 cup evaporated or scalded milk from oppressed cows
1 packet dolphin-safe yeast
2½ cups *white bourgeois* cake flour
¾ cup potato starch (cornstarch or flour if you can't get it)
³⁄₈ cup white sugar subsidized by Republicans
1 tablespoon salt
4 tablespoons lard or coconut oil or cruelty-free butter
1 teaspoon vanilla extract grown on land that used to be
   rain forest

If you're using regular milk, scald it. I don't know why. Steve said to do it, although he also made fun of stem cells and called them "the new duct tape." Otherwise, just put the milk in a cup or somethin' and stir in the yeast.

Don't add the yeast until the milk has cooled to where it's merely warm. If it's too hot, the yeast feels pain. I learned that from Cameron Diaz. And then you get nasty letters on recycled paper, from People for the Ethical Treatment of Fungus. Give the yeast a few minutes to activate.

Put the flour and starch and sugar and salt in a Cuisinart. Which is a great product. Because it's French. Blend in the lard or oil or whatever. Add vanilla to the milk mixture and add it to the dry stuff slowly while processing. When the dough forms a ball, you can quit pouring. Then give it another 30 seconds. If the dough is too sticky to handle, add more flour. But don't waste it, because every day, America loses a thousand acres of precious wheat forest.

The lard bothers me. Those poor helpless pigs. Sometimes I sit in the kitchen and cry for them. But I can't get Gary to throw out his blue Hush Puppies. You know what? You know what? Forget the lard. I know this is Steve's book and I'm supposed to do what he says, but the thought of those sad little lonely pigs . . .

Just use coconut oil, okay? It tastes better than lard. Just replace all the lard in the recipe with coconut oil. Get a good kind that smells good. I like Nutiva brand. No one will know. I won't tell, and Gary won't tell. You can also use butter, if you don't want your doughnuts to smell like a coconut.

If you knead by hand, knead until it's all mixed in. Maybe 5 minutes. About as long as it takes O'Reilly to tell sixty or seventy big fat right-wing lies and say "Barack *Hussein* Obama."

In case you haven't done this before, you butter your hands and push the heel of one hand into the dough until it flattens, fold the flattened dough over, and repeat. While I do this, I like to sing Guatemalan work songs or sometimes "Look for the Union Label."

I know butter comes from oppressed cows, but hear me out. I buy butter from Gaia Farms Wiccan dairies, and they get the cream out of the cow in a humane manner. It's kind of interesting. They do this thing . . . they convince the cow that it's sort of a . . . sort of a sex act. So the cow actually enjoys it. And that's . . . okay.

Now you have to cut the dough and let it rise. I spray a cookie sheet lightly with PAM, which Steve doesn't like, and I roll the dough out about three-eighths of an inch thick. Then Gary cuts the doughnuts with a cutter and puts 'em on the sheet with plastic over them. Or you can lay 'em on non-stick foil. Let the dough at least double in size.

PAM really keeps things from stickin'. At Air America, I used to put it on the toilet seats.

If you let the doughnuts get big and airy, they'll be light, which is nice. If you don't let 'em rise very much, they'll be more dense. Which is also nice. 'Cause I believe in doughnut diversity.

The starch makes the doughnuts soft 'n' mushy, like Bill O'Reilly's brain. So if you like 'em chewy, use more flour. If you want 'em really tough, like Nancy Pelosi, you can use flour with a lot of gluten.

Put your fryin' grease—whatever you decide on—in a deep saucepan. You want it at least 1½ inches deep. Steve uses lard. Because he doesn't care about the little lard pigs, raised in tiny wire cages and forced to listen to Kathy Lee Gifford CDs all day. But you know what? You can substitute coconut oil, just like you did in the dough. That's what I do.

Get your oil or lard to deep-frying heat, around 350 to 375°F. Drop the doughnuts in one at a time, fryin' 'em first on one side and then the other. You don't need to get 'em dark; that makes 'em hard. Like Newt Gingrich's heart. As they come out, put 'em in a large bowl containin' several thicknesses of paper towel. You can fry the holes, too. They're good for people who can't open their jaw all the way 'cause they're differently abled.

When you have the doughnuts fried, you just dip 'em in the Coco Lopez glaze and eat 'em. Sometimes Gary sneaks in and steals one and eats it before I glaze 'em, and I tell him Jesus sees him, but he eats it anyway and then prays for forgiveness.

I have to go now. I'm unpackin' the stuff Anoop and Leaf sent from my old office at Air America. My belongings, like my *Mother Jones* desk calendar and the sock Castro wore when he spoke to the UN. Usually it's easy to unpack stuff like that. But for some reason my stuff seems to be stuck to the box.

> *This is Steve again. As soon as I sent that chapter to my publisher, Bill O'Reilly's attorney called me and threatened to sue me for tortious bloviation. Luckily, I was able to buy O'Reilly off by allowing him to pen the rest of the chapter.*

The subject of today's Talking Points Memo? Stuart Smalley, who says I'm a big fat lying liar. Not only is that reediculous and not pithy; it's libel. Accordingly, I've instructed my attorneys to sue Mr. Smalley down to a small, smoldering, penniless stain on the sidewalk. While I'm at it, I'm also suing his parents for conceiving him. Fox legal analyst Andrew Napolitano says that's stupid. I'm suing him, too.

Talking Points is not a mean guy. But I will not stand for a popinjay like Napolitano, trying to tell me I can't sue Stuart Smalley's bloviating parents. If you disagree, I'll give you the last word. Then I'll sue *you.*

Talking Points doesn't deserve to be treated like this. Talking Points is the highest-paid, highest-rated cable news host in the history of this universe or, I might add, any universe that could possibly be imagined. You can read more about how highly rated Talking Points is in the premium area at www.billoreilly.com. It only cost seventy-five dollars a week, and you get a free sweatband, and soon I'll have a twenty-four-hour-a-day roving Factorcam so you can see me bashing liberal pinheads not just here, but in stores and restaurants and even while I sleep.

Many people talk in their sleep. Only Talking Points has also trained himself to interrupt.

Don't get the idea that Steve and I are friends. The guy's a popinjay. Only a popinjay makes unfilled doughnuts. Steve's doughnuts are as empty as Stuart Smalley's head. Talking Points invited Steve to come on the Factor and defend himself while I talk over him, but he refuses to come, because he's not a stand-up guy. Also, he claims the post office never delivered my letter, which was addressed to "Popinjay, Coral Gables, Florida."

Talking Points is fed up with guys like Steve, who make fun of me and claim I make women call me "Talking Points" in bed. So to teach Steve a lesson, I'm going to show that Talking Points is a better cook than Steve, by showing you how to make filled doughnuts. Honest, no-spin blue-collar doughnuts, like the ones we used to eat when I was a kid back in Levittown. In the dirt.

You start with the doughnut dough Stuart Smalley told you about. I recommend you use butter in the dough for this kind of doughnut. I don't care if some popinjay dairy cow gets its feelings hurt by the milking machine. Back in Levittown, tough street kids like me wore a milking machine all day, just for kicks.

Then instead of cutting doughnuts out of the dough, you cut three-inch circles. And you let them rise until they're big and pillowy, like a backstabbing associate producer's breasts, who Talking Points did not harass or grope in any way, regardless of having paid a gargantuan settlement to her and her pecksniffian popinjay attorneys.

Then you fry the doughnuts as described above, only once they're done, you make filling and shoot it into them. You poke a hole at one end of each doughnut with a really skinny knife and you sweep it back and forth in there to make a pocket, and then you shoot filling in there with a horse hypodermic with the needle removed.

Most far-left mainstream journalists have no idea what's in

a good doughnut filling, but Talking Points has uncovered the answer.

FILLING
6 large egg yolks plus 1 egg
¾ cup sugar
3 tablespoons cornstarch
3 tablespoons all-purpose flour
3 cups heavy cream
3 tablespoons butter
3 teaspoons vanilla extract
¼ teaspoon salt

Mix the egg yolks, the egg, and 2 tablespoons of the sugar. Add the starch and flour and whisk until blended in. Put the cream and remaining sugar in a microwave-safe container and heat it until the cream starts to steam. Pour yourself a Scotch and go answer some viewer e-mail. But only if it's pithy.

Pour half of the heated cream into the egg mixture while whisking. Get it nice and smooth. You want it loose, like Stuart Smalley's knees after he receives a summons from my lawyers.

Now, here you have to be a stand-up guy and weigh some risks. You can either pour all the cream and the egg mixture and the butter into a saucepan and heat just until boiling—whisking the whole time—or you can put them in a microwavable bowl and heat them. The saucepan is safer, because the heating will be slower and more uniform, and you won't have to worry about over-boiling. Talking Points prefers the microwave because it's faster and easier.

Disclaimer: Talking Points' boss, Neil Cavuto, owns stock in General Electric, which manufactures fine microwave ovens. Which Talking Points would never endorse on the air, even though they're really nice and can be also used for heating flavored massage oil in the green room.

Remove from heat and stir in the vanilla. Talking Points likes to add it last because he has a theory that the flavor evaporates if you boil it.

Talking Points can also help you with chocolate sauce, although he considered hiding the recipe in the premium area at www.billoreilly.com.

CHOCOLATE SAUCE
2 ounces unsweetened chocolate
⅓ cup water
2–3 teaspoons cornstarch
1 cup sugar
3 tablespoons butter
½ teaspoon vanilla extract
¼ teaspoon almond extract
Dash salt

Melt the chocolate in the water in a saucepan over low heat, or in a double boiler, or in the microwave. Talking Points recommends stirring it with a fork, because sauce will stick to a spoon or spatula when you take it out.

Add the cornstarch, sugar, and salt and heat the mixture again. Stir until everything dissolves. Add the butter and stir until it blends into the mixture. Stir in the vanilla and almond extracts.

Fry the doughnuts. Fill the doughnuts. Dip the doughnuts. It's as easy as falling off a log or suing Stuart Smalley until he has to sell his home and go live in a cardboard box with the other homeless lugubrious popinjays.

In conclusion, Steve is an insect, Smalley is a fudge-sitting jerk, and Talking Points is rapidly achieving deity status. Right now you can join the premium area at www.billoreilly.com by paying Talking Points a few dollars. But eventually the price will be a human sacrifice.

Dine well.

And that's the memo.

CHAPTER 26

COCONUT FLAN

BYPASS RATING:

(TRIPLE)

I HAVE A FRIEND named Karyn. I met her in law school.

Karyn is not the sort of person other women like a whole lot. She's thin and athletic and hot, and she stays that way by sticking to a strict diet of everything she can get her hands on. The people at her job gave her a nice nickname because she went to the food area every day and brought back plates and arranged them around the top of her desk. They call her Buffet. As for exercise, she only moves when reaching for food or her next cigarette. And the only place she ever gains weight is in her boobs. Which are tremendous.

Flan makes Karyn happy, and when Karyn is happy, she does a special dance. And the dance has a lot of bounces in it.

A long time ago, Karyn decided she liked the coconut flan at a local restaurant. Being Karyn, she bought an entire flan the size of a birthday cake. And she paid the individual serving price, so she was out about forty bucks. I believe she spent the weekend in bed with it with the phone unplugged, watching *Buffy the Vampire Slayer.* I'm sorry if that sounds like a joke. Because it isn't.

I decided to save Karyn some money. I sat down with a pen and pad and scribbled down a recipe for coconut flan, relying on good fortune and The Force to guide me. And I cooked it, and it made the restaurant flan—which was very good—taste like sweetened snot.

I don't see Karyn as much as I used to, because she moved to LA. But whenever I'm out there, I try to drop by and make flan for her. Because flan makes Karyn happy, and when Karyn is happy, she does a special dance. And the dance has a lot of bounces in it. And I like making Karyn look for special pans and things to use, because she has to bend down and search under the counter, and her low-cut jeans barely cover her rear end even when she's standing up straight. RE me and Karyn's rear end . . . not a lot of mystery left.

Believe me when I say this dish is good. I know flan. I live in Miami, after all. I've fed this to countless Cubans. I've had them moan and whine about how their abuelas make the best flan in the world, and then they try my flan and their eyes glaze over and they start to shake. What do you think of abuela's flan *now*, pendejos? That's right. Abuela got P3NED.

If the CIA had been smart, they would have fed this stuff to Castro instead of poisoning his cigars.

I got lucky. I admit it. I didn't deserve success like this. So what? Screw you. Don't eat it. You're only hurting yourself.

As for health concerns, look at what's in it. Seven egg yolks. A 1,300-calorie can of condensed milk. Coconut, which comes from one of the few plants that produce lard. And a layer of burnt sugar on the top. If the CIA had been smart, they would have fed this stuff to Castro instead of poisoning his cigars.

1 can Eagle Brand or other sweetened condensed milk
½ can Coco Lopez (about 6 ounces)
½ cup half and half
1 teaspoon vanilla extract
¼ teaspoon salt
3 eggs
4 yolks
⅓ small package Baker's shredded coconut (I tried the
other brands)

You want to end up with a layer of caramel on the top of this thing. But you can't really spread burnt sugar. So what do you do? You put caramel in the bottom of a dish, bake the flan in it, and then turn it upside down when you're done. The flan flops out with the caramel on top.

Get yourself a Pyrex dish about eight inches in diameter. You'll also need a saucepan that can tolerate really high heat. Put about eight heaping tablespoons of good old white sugar in the pan. Add about two tablespoons of water. Put the pan on high heat and bring the resulting syrup to a boil.

Generally, in the kitchen, you're trying *not* to burn things. Here, it's the exact opposite, so once it starts smoking, you may feel an irrational urge to yank the pan off the stove. But don't. Keep heating it after it starts boiling, occasionally swirling the syrup to keep it from burning unevenly. Sooner or later, it's going to start to turn brown. And when it does, you keep up the swirling, or you end up with syrup that's burned in some places and not in others.

It's very tricky to judge the darkness of the syrup. What you want in the Pyrex dish is a substance about the color of tortoise shell sunglass frames. In the pan, it's going to look darker than it really is. You can always try this a couple of times before you actually make the flan. Too dark is better than too light.

Pour it all into the dish, swirl it to make sure it coats the bottom, and let the dish cool.

Preheat the oven to 350°F. Empty the can of milk into a big bowl. Add enough Coco Lopez (half a can, or one small can) to bring the total amount up to 16 ounces. You have to be careful with Coco Lopez. It has a lot of smooth, silky, delicious fat in it, and sometimes it solidifies, so when you pour it out, you get the water and the sugar, but no fat. You can prevent this by setting the can in a pot of hot water long enough to melt the fat. Or you can just be a man and cut the top of the damn can off.

Add the half and half, so you end up with 2½ cups of stuff. Add the vanilla extract, the salt, the eggs and yolks, and beat the mixture until smooth. Some people strain out the little white goobers that come with the egg yolks. Whatever. I've never been able to find one in the finished product.

Place a large, flat dish in the preheated oven and fill it with boiling water. Give it time to reach a stable temperature. Put the Pyrex dish inside it. Pour the mixture into the Pyrex dish. Lower the temperature to 325°F. The water should be about as high as the level of the flan mixture.

Now, *men* . . . I know you think this business with the water is a stupid, pointless thing to do. The oven is hot, you want the flan hot, so the water is just in the way. No, sorry, it doesn't work that way. The water is *crucial*. It keeps the flan from boiling. If it boils, you end up with something like a plastic sponge.

Sprinkle shredded coconut on top of the mixture, so that you end up with enough to make a thin layer (a little less than a quarter inch) when the flan is cooked. Try to spread it around. It will eventually float to the top. Bake for 1 hour. Switch oven to low broil to brown the coconut layer to taste. This works best if you have the flan on a low rack; on the upper racks, it browns unevenly. If it's far enough from the heating element, you can use the higher broil setting. It helps to shine a flashlight on the flan while it browns; the red light from the heating element is deceptive.

Here's the hard part. It's difficult to tell when this stuff is done. The recipe I just gave you is tried and true, but I can't take all the skill out of it and make it pure monkey-see-monkey-do. You should be able to put a knife into the center of this thing when it's done and pull it out nearly clean. If it's cooked just right, tasting it will make your knees buckle. If it's overdone, it will merely be great. Underdone? Coconut soup.

After it's done, you have to chill it. This will take hours, but if you don't get it cold, you'll never get it out of the dish.

Once it's cold, run a butter knife around the edge and separate the flan from the wall of the dish. Then put a big plate on top of it and turn it over, fast. The flan should come loose and plop onto the dish in a minute or so.

You're going to end up with a layer of caramel stuck to the dish. If you want, you can add a tiny amount of water, microwave the dish, dissolve the caramel, and pour it on the flan. You want a thick syrup. Thicker than pancake syrup, thinner than molasses. You pour this over the flan slices as you serve them.

This unbelievable recipe yields something like 3,100 calories, or maybe 400 calories per slice. If that's not enough, you can always have two. Fat greedy bastard.

CHAPTER 27

540-CALORIE BROWNIES

BYPASS RATING:

(DOUBLE)

LONG AGO, IN A GALAXY FAR, far away, I was a big fat loser who couldn't bake decent brownies. It ought to be the easiest thing in the world. Brownies have about three ingredients, and you don't have to make icing. But I was hopeless. I tried recipe after recipe, and what did I get? Cake.

Brownies are not cake. Cake is made with self-rising flour. When you heat self-rising flour, it gives off gas. Much as I myself would. The gas makes bubbles, which get permanently baked into the batter, and the first thing you know, you have a light fluffy cake about as dense as a sponge.

A brownie is not supposed to be like that. A brownie is a chocolate brick.

I tried mixes. How hard can it be to make a good brownie mix? Chocolate, sugar, flour . . . that about covers it. But they all suck. Duncan Hines, Ghirardelli . . . they all gave me a weak chocolate taste and lots of off-flavors from vegetable oil.

When I was in law school, I found myself a prizewinning brownie recipe. It was in a book of recipes by some broad who claimed to be the queen of fattening desserts. I gave it a try. What a disappointment.

First of all, it wasn't sweet enough. This lady is European, and you know how Europeans are about sugar. Maybe it's because they're so used to being overrun by other Europeans and thrown in camps where they have to season their food with dirt, but you just can't get them to use the damn sugar. Have you ever tried whipped cream made by a European? It's like unflavored yogurt. Barely sweet at all. A waste of time. Worse than their toilet paper.

On top of that, the brownies were dry. Again, perhaps this is related to Europe's long, proud history of poverty and misery, but she went *way* too easy on the butter. I guess that in Europe butter has traditionally been saved for hair grooming and bribing feudal lords not to rape your daughters, but times have changed. Hey, Europeans! It's time to wake up and live like prosperous, deodorant-using Americans who can afford to use butter as landfill.

Hey, Europeans! It's time to wake up and live like prosperous, deodorant-using Americans who can afford to use butter as landfill.

Socialism. Don't get me started.

Finally, she used the wrong nuts, and not nearly enough chocolate. Brownies should be *brown,* not kind of a dark reddish tan. We're making dessert, not adobe.

Thankfully, the recipe was basically sound, and it gave me a foundation on which to build. And build I did. New nuts. More butter. More *everything.* I ended up with pecan brownies so rich and sweet and delicious, they rank second only to a medical degree on the list of tools useful for getting into women's pants. Third, if you count sedatives.

Yet I was not satisfied. "Chocolate and pecans?" I scoffed, gesturing broadly and spilling my martini on the dashboard. "What kind of weakass deal is *that*? I can beat that with one oven mitt tied behind my back." And I did.

Here is the horror I came up with: chocolate brownies with pecans, dark chocolate chips, and a layer of *butter-soaked coconut flakes* in the middle. Sit back and think about that. I did a calculation, and these things weigh in at a heart-stopping, pancreas-popping *five hundred and forty calories each!*

I started making these things and passing them around at law school, to get comments from the women. Who cares what the men thought? What do men have to offer? Friendship? What good is that? You can't *spank* your friends. You can't tie them up with silk scarves and blindfold them and torture them with tiny, soft paintbrushes dipped in hot grapeseed oil. Well. These days, a lot of guys can. But I can't.

To this day, when I meet women I knew in law school, they want to know when I'm making them brownies. I never have the nerve to ask the obvious question in return, i.e., "When do I get to chain you to my bedposts?"

To this day, when I meet women I knew in law school, they want to know when I'm making them brownies. I never have the nerve to ask the obvious question in return, i.e., "When do I get to chain you to my bedposts?" But I think if I did, a lot of them would say something like, "How about Tuesday?" Because I have a monopoly. There is no other source for brownies like these. I am the OPEC of five-hundred-and-forty-calorie brownies.

How lucky you are to have this book. This is the one recipe I refused to part with until it got published. You don't understand what I'm giving up. All the girls I know who still pretend to find me marginally attractive will now buy this book, run right home, and take me off their speed dial.

2 sticks butter
5½ squares unsweetened chocolate
4 eggs
2½ cups sugar
1 teaspoon vanilla extract
¼ teaspoon almond extract
2 teaspoons instant coffee
½ teaspoon salt
1 cup all-purpose flour
**1 small package Baker's flaked coconut + 1 tablespoon
  sugar**
2 cups pecan pieces
1 (6-ounce) bag Nestlé bittersweet chocolate morsels

All right. This is not going to be easy. A lot of you, frankly, will be too inept to make these brownies. But give it a shot anyway, because you can always give up and eat the batter with a spoon.

Preheat the oven to 400°F. Line a 9-by-13 Pyrex dish with no-stick foil, with the no-stick side up. If you can't find this stuff, you can spray the dish with PAM and then spray the inside of the foil with PAM, but it doesn't work as well.

Put 1½ sticks of the butter in a microwavable container. Add the unsweetened chocolate. Heat carefully until the butter melts and the mixture is hot enough to melt the chocolate. Set aside while the chocolate melts.

Place the eggs in a large bowl. Begin beating them with a mixer. Once they're blended pretty well, drop in 1 cup of the sugar. Beat until it's mixed in well. Repeat. Do this until you have 2½ cups of sugar in there, and run the mixer at high speed for at least 5 minutes.

While the egg mixture is mixing, add the vanilla extract, almond extract, coffee, and salt. You may want to use Sanka to avoid getting wired. If you don't have instant, you can use half a teaspoon of ground coffee.

Using a fork or whisk or something, stir the butter and chocolate mixture until you're positive the chocolate is completely melted. Then pour it into the egg mixture and blend it in.

Add the flour. Blend.

Melt the remaining half stick of butter in a bowl and add the coconut and the tablespoon of sugar. Mix well.

Now it's going to start getting tricky.

Pour the pecans out into the Pyrex dish. Spread them out on the foil as well as you can. Pour *no more than half* of the chocolate, egg, and flour mixture over them, spreading it around as well as possible. Take a small fork and mix the nuts and chocolate mixture to make sure the nuts are covered and the mixture is level and reaches the sides of the dish.

Drop the coconut flakes by spoonfuls onto the mixture. This is not easy to do correctly. You're going to be surprised how quickly you run out of coconut. When you get it all spooned out, distribute it evenly. If you can.

That was hard, wasn't it? Well, it gets worse.

Add the chips to the remaining chocolate mixture. Mix them in. Drop the mixture by spoonfuls on top of the coconut. You have to make sure it covers all of the coconut and reaches to the sides of the dish. It will spread itself out a little in the oven, but you can't start with big holes with coconut showing through. You might try squeezing it out of a pastry bag. I'm too lazy.

I think doubling the coconut layer would be fun.

Bake for 25 minutes. If you like your brownies gooey, take them out and then get them into a refrigerator as soon as you can. If you like them firmer, turn off the heat, let them sit in the oven for 5 more minutes, and *then* let them cool and refrigerate them.

These things are just about impossible to handle without

tearing them up. You have to chill them—freezing is best—until they're cold all the way through. Then you pull up on the foil until it comes loose from the Pyrex. It shouldn't stick. It's easier if you do it one corner at a time.

When the brownies are loose, turn the dish upside-down on a cutting board and let them drop out. Now you have to peel off the foil. If you used non-stick foil, the brownies should pop right out in one big flat mass. If not, you may have to spend half an hour peeling the foil off.

Once the foil is off, slice the brownies once the short way, right across the middle. Believe me, you don't want to do it the other way first. Then cut each half in half, perpendicular to the first cut. Then cut each quarter in half, also perpendicular to the first cut. This will give you eight long strips, each of which can be cut into three or four brownies. They slice much better if you keep them upside-down.

The knife is going to try to stick to the brownies. You can spray it with PAM, but it won't work. The only answer is to get a clean cloth really wet and completely clean the knife after every cut. A coping saw would be the perfect tool to cut these things, but I'm going to go out on a limb and assume you don't keep one in the kitchen.

Okay, sit down, put your head between your knees, and take deep breaths. You made it. Or not.

Let me offer hope to those of you who ended up with a man-agled brown lump with bits of burned coconut sticking out the sides. You don't have to use coconut. You don't have to use chips or nuts. You can just make the batter and dump it into the dish by itself.

If you leave out the coconut layer, you can make one homogeneous bowl of batter containing *all* the ingredients (nuts, chips, lime jelly beans, whatever), and just flump it into the dish and shove it in the oven. You don't even have to spread it very well.

The heat will make it level itself as long as it's not too far off to start with.

By the way, there's no law that says you can't mix the coconut into the batter.

These things are fantastic with ice cream, especially if you leave out the coconut. You put a brownie in a bowl, microwave it for maybe 45 seconds, and then put the ice cream on top. And you can make your own hot fudge with Eagle Brand milk and unsweetened chocolate, pour it on top, and cover the whole mess with crushed almonds and whipped cream.

Ladies, if you just can't seem to get these right, do not give up hope. Send me a photo of you in a bikini.

Whatever you do, don't put almonds or walnuts in the brownies themselves. Almonds will stink when they get hot, and walnuts are bitter.

Ladies, if you just can't seem to get these right, do not give up hope. Send me a photo of you in a bikini. I still have those soft little paintbrushes and a whole drawer full of silk scarves.

CHAPTER 28

CHOCOLATE CHIP COOKIE DOUGH HOT FUDGE DESSERT/PMS REMEDY

BYPASS RATING:

(QUINTUPLE)

WHEN DID WOMEN get to be such pigs? I mean, we all knew they were secretly pigs, breaking wind loudly when they think no one can hear and muttering among themselves about how George Bush's flight suit shows off his package, but when did they become so open about it? We men always knew they were just like us, but who wants to be reminded?

At the moment, I'm thinking more about their impressively pig-like dietary behavior and not so much about the many, many other ways in which they have come to resemble God's tastiest creature. Over the last twenty years or so, women have turned into voracious eating machines that consume everything in their paths.

Sort of like that tremendous thing on the original *Star Trek* that floated around eating planets while looking like a giant spliff.

SPOCK:

Captain, we have the creature on screen.

KIRK:

(*looking*) What the f—

SPOCK:

Sir?

KIRK:

Looks like a giant spliff. Scan this system for enormous Jamaicans.

SPOCK:

It appears to be headed for our colony on Viagra 6.

KIRK:

Do we know anybody on Viagra 6?

SPOCK:

Well, you have two brothers who live there.

KIRK:

Figures. I have a brother on every planet. It's the twenty-third century and my idiot parents still use the rhythm method.

SPOCK:

Shall we try to stop it?

KIRK:

Hold it. My girdle is pinching. (*adjusting*) Okay, Mr. Sulu, hit it with the tractor beam.

SULU:

Sir?

KIRK:

Let's see how it likes being pelted with tractors. (*Spock whispering to him*) Really? Belay that.

SPOCK:

We could send an away team.

KIRK:

Right. Go find a black ensign in a red shirt.

ENSIGN FITTY CENT:

Peace out, Crackers! (*running off the set to call his agent*)

KIRK:

Do we have any Mexicans?

SPOCK:

If there were only some way to satisfy its hunger while we devise a plan . . .

KIRK:

Do we have any Mexicans?

SPOCK:

Only during picking season.

MCCOY:

We're all going to die!

KIRK:

I was waiting for that.

SPOCK:

Doctor, try to calm yourself.

MCCOY:

We're all going to die, and all you care about is calming ourselves! You green-blooded, inhuman . . . (*Spock heel-kicking him sharply in the groin*)

MCCOY:

(*talking from below the frame*) Mmmf.

KIRK:

What happened to the nerve pinch?

SPOCK:

I like to mix it up. Captain, look . . . on the creature's under-side . . . aren't those . . .

KIRK:

Boobies! We're saved!

SPOCK:

Sir?

KIRK:

Quick, get to the galley and synthesize a hundred-foot-high tub of Ben & Jerry's! Any flavor will do. They're all packed with chocolate.

SPOCK:

Excellent plan, sir.

KIRK:

Meanwhile, let's distract it. Open a hailing frequency and send it some episodes of *Gilmore Girls,*

SPOCK:

I sincerely hope it's PMSing. Chocolate is most effective at that time.

ALL MALE BRIDGE PERSONNEL:

EWWWWWW.

Anyway, as I have surely said elsewhere in the book, women will eat almost anything if it has chocolate in it, and I have also learned that they like buying tubes of cookie dough and eating them with a spoon. You can even buy ice cream with bad-tasting imitation cookie dough lumps in it. Naturally, thinking about that set the little wheels in motion, and I came up with a dessert so nasty, so vile, so re-voltingly decadent that if it ever becomes legal to trap women for their hides, this will be the bait of choice.

I came up with a dessert so nasty, so vile, so revoltingly decadent that if it ever becomes legal to trap women for their hides, this will be the bait of choice.

Here's what you want to do. I know you won't believe it, but trust me. First you make cookie dough. I took an ordinary recipe for cookies and jazzed it up a bit so it would taste especially good raw as well as cooked. Then you bake cookies. *But wait! There's more!* You take half of the dough and chill it in the freezer until it gets fairly stiff.

You still with me? Okay, you got your cookies. You got your dough. Now you need hot fudge. As luck would have it, I have a simple recipe for really thick, gooey hot fudge (see page). So, you get cranking on that while the cookies are in the oven and the dough is chilling.

Now, to make matters worse, you make homemade ice cream. You remember homemade ice cream, don't you? Remember, your dad made it twice when you were a kid and then put the machine in the garage and never touched it again? It was great, wasn't it? Too bad he was so lazy. You remember; he sat on the back steps next to a bag of rock salt, cranking the handle for about a year, while ashes from his Pall Mall flittered down into the cream. It's much easier to make now, so don't be afraid. Tell your dad you made it, but don't give him any until he does all his chores.

Time for the final insult: whipped cream. This one is fast and easy. Dump a pint of heavy cream in a bowl, add a teaspoon of vanilla extract and sugar to taste, and beat until it turns into whipped cream. Pinch of salt, maybe.

By now, the ice cream and cookies should be done.

You have to work fast, while the hot stuff is hot and the cold stuff is cold. Put two scoops of cookie dough in a bowl. Add two scoops of ice cream. Jam warm cookies into the ice cream, edgewise. Throw on the whipped cream. Pour hot fudge around the base.

If you can eat more than four spoonfuls of this stuff, you are certifiably mental. But it's really, really good. Just make sure you don't have anything important to do later in the day.

COOKIE
½ cup butter
1 egg
1 teaspoon vanilla extract
½ cup sugar
½ cup brown sugar
1 teaspoon baking powder
1 cup all-purpose flour
6 ounces bittersweet or semisweet chocolate, in pieces
    small enough for cookies
½ cup crushed pecans, optional

Preheat the oven to 375°F. Beat wet ingredients together until fluffy. Add sugar, brown sugar, baking powder, and flour and blend in. Fold in chocolate and nuts. Drop onto cookie sheet with teaspoon, 2 inches apart. Bake 12 minutes. Allow to cool until firm. They should be thin.

ICE CREAM
2 pints half and half
2 eggs
1 cup sugar

2 teaspoons vanilla extract or ritzy foodie equivalent
¼ teaspoon salt

If you don't know how to make ice cream, I can't help you. I mean, you blend this stuff, stick it in an ice cream machine and press the button. Does that help?

No reason you can't use Häagen-Dazs.

HOT FUDGE
1 can Eagle Brand milk
1½ ounces unsweetened chocolate
½ teaspoon vanilla extract

Put these things in a microwave-safe thing and heat—carefully—until it all melts. Stir once in a while. The chocolate will take a long time to melt, so just get the mixture really hot and take it out of the oven and wait. You don't want to heat the whole thing until the chocolate gives way, because the rest of the fudge will turn into charcoal.

You're all set. Call me from intensive care and tell me how it worked out.

CHAPTER 29

BLUEBERRY BUTTER CHEESECAKE

BYPASS RATING:

(QUADRUPLE)

I'M SO LAZY I got another celebrity to write a recipe for me. Sorry if the references are a little dated. Blame my publisher. When you're as obscure as I am, the lead time on your books is equal to the half-life of carbon-14.

Hi, folks! Tom Cruise here!* I was really happy when Steve called me and let me know he wanted me to write something for his book. I got on the couch and jumped up and down, and then I pulled down my pants and started singing "Old Time Rock & Roll," and then Katie reminded me that there were painters working on the new nursery. So I pulled my pants back up and put my Ugg boots back on.

But I was still really happy. You're always happy when you're a Scientologist. Because if you're not, we *take you down and make you wish you had never been born.* That's how we roll. We're here to spread joy and peace and enlightenment, and if you get in our

Disclaimer: Not really written by the totally heterosexual Tom Cruise.

way, we will sue the bejeezus out of you and destroy everything in your life that gives you pleasure, and if you try to hide under a rock, we will just sue the rock.

That was a joke. You know my famous sense of humor. Like when the South Park guys made fun of me, and I thought it was so funny, I played a little joke on *them*! I called Viacom and said they could take my publicity tour for *Mission Impossible 3* and *ram it right up their bottoms if they ever ran that episode again.* And Comedy Central pulled the episode, and I was like, "Hey, Matt and Trey: *Gotcha!*"

Man, that was a funny joke. It would be even funnier if I could get them fired. That would be great. If they lost their houses and cars and their wives left them and no one in Hollywood ever talked to them again and they died shivering in a ditch . . . that would be the *bomb*.

Matt and Trey didn't think it was funny. I had my people call their people and offer them a free Scientology massage, but I haven't heard back from them yet. Maybe they're scared of the straps. Which are for their own safety.

Anyway, as you may know, I'm planning to eat my baby's placenta. Because placenta is beautiful and natural and nutritious. Animals eat their placenta all the time. They also lick their rectums, so that must also be beautiful and natural and nutritious, too. But I don't know for sure, because my neck is too short.

Anyway, as you may know, I'm planning to eat my baby's placenta. Because placenta is beautiful and natural and nutritious. Animals eat their placenta all the time. They also lick their rectums, so that must also be beautiful and natural and nutritious, too. But I don't know for sure, because my neck is too short.

Steve wanted me to write a few delicious placenta recipes, and I'm happy to oblige. Here are a few of my favorites.

PLACENTA OMELET

This is a good one. It's full of protein. And stuff.

1 large placenta
1 tablespoon butter
2 eggs
¼ cup diced shallots
1 teaspoon cumin
1 cup goat cheese
Salt and pepper, to taste

It's better for you if you use three eggs and throw out the yolks, but I figured you backward non-Hollywood people wouldn't understand. Have you read the research? I've read the research. I'm so educated, it's amazing that I didn't graduate from high school.

Take the placenta to the sink. Scrape off the dried blood and goo. Save it in a bowl to make sauce. Melt the butter in an omelet pan on medium heat. Whisk the eggs until light and fluffy. Add the shallots. Pour into omelet pan and cook until it starts to set up. Then add the placenta, shallots, cumin, cheese, salt, and pepper, and fold the omelet.

To make the sauce, heat some butter in a saute pan and fry 2 tablespoons of soy flour until it starts to brown. Pour in the blood and mucus and stir well. Add a pinch of saffron and a splash of half and half. Add crushed garlic and a little gingerroot and remove from heat.

This stuff is *so great*. I gave some to Oprah, and she said it was out of this world. Then I told her what was in it and she blew lunch on my kitchen island. Then Stedman tried to hit me with his man-purse, but he missed and got Oprah's special friend Gayle instead, and Oprah made him go sit in the car.

PLACENTA CROQUE MONSIEUR
2 slices bread
1 slice cheese
1 generous portion fresh placenta
Fresh dill

I learned to make these in France, where Johnny Depp lives. *People* magazine says he's the Sexiest Man Alive. Sure, it's easy to be the Sexiest Man Alive when nobody is making South Park cartoons where you refuse to come out of the closet.

Butter the bread and put the cheese and placenta inside. Press a sprig of dill into the outside of each slice. Put in a buttered sandwich press and heat for 5 minutes or until brown.

Some people like their placenta cooked rare or medium. I advise against it. You should always eat your placenta well done, because you can get whatever gross diseases the placenta donor had. Right in your mouth, so you can't do closeups. The exception is placenta seviche. Use plenty of lime juice.

Here's one more recipe.

BLUEBERRY-BANANA PLACENTA SMOOTHIE
½ cup fresh blueberries
2 bananas
2 cups skim milk
1 large placenta
1 large tube Neosporin
Dash Zovirax

Place ingredients in a blender and grind to a smooth consistency. Chill and drink. In a smoothie, you really need a nice raw placenta, so add the Neosporin and Zovirax just in case. Otherwise you might eat a live germ or a herpes sore or something.

Ordinarily, I don't like drugs, but man, nothing sucks as bad as herpes on the inside of your mouth. Anyway, it's not mind-altering, mental-case drugs, like the ones Brooke Shields took when she went crazy after having her baby. Sick psycho Amazon. She thinks she's so cool just because she's TALL. I wouldn't eat her placenta if she *paid* me.

I'll bet she screamed bloody murder while she was giving birth. Scientologist women give birth silently. Sometimes they forget and they let out a yell. Then the husband has to smack them.

I'm so excited about being a celebrity chef. Are you guys excited? I'm excited. I think I'm going to jump on the couch again! Here I *goooooooooo!!!!!* My pants are down, just like in *Risky Business*, but instead of "Old Time Rock & Roll," I think I'll sing "Cabaret." For some reason, I just love Liza Minnelli.

No, I won't. I'm getting down. I have more stuff to say, and you won't hear it if I'm jumping on the couch singing show tunes. I know you hate it when I pull my pants up. I hate it, too, and so does Katie. Her feng shui aromatherapist says old sperm need more oxygen.

I told her Scientology aromatherapy was better. She goes, "How do they do it?" And I go, "They put a bunch of money in a big pile, and you smell it!" And she goes, "Whose money do they put in the pile?" And I go, "Yours!" And she goes, "Do they let you take the money back when you're done?" And I go, "Not so far." And then she made me promise from now on to use singles instead of fifties. But the guys at the Temple say fifties work a lot better.

Anyway, anyway, anyway . . . I solved the energy crisis! *Tom Cruise* solved the energy crisis! Geez! *Geez!* I wish L. Ron was here to see this. His pants would be down, too!

I was sitting here the other day having a placenta sundae with cradle-cap sauce, when it hit me: we're wasting valuable power! *Placenta* power! All over the world, women are throwing out chewy, delicious placentas, when each one contains enough power to push a small car over a hundred yards!

I got on the phone to the Scientology center here in LA, and I asked if there were any engineers down there who could help me. Like maybe the guys who invented the E-Meter. Although I hear they quit Scientology after they used the E-Meter design as the basis for the Fisher Price phone.

Unfortunately, John Travolta answered my call, and we got in a big argument. He said that if Maverick had a fight with Vincent from *Pulp Fiction,* he'd get his ass kicked even though Vincent probably fought like a girl and pulled hair, and I said "no way," because Maverick was a buff jet fighter pilot and Vincent was a fat slob hit man addicted to mind-altering drugs just like Brooke Shields.

Vincent would be lying on the couch doing drugs, and he'd be on the phone, going, "Oh, I really like the *heroin* you sold me, Brooke," and Maverick would zoom in on his F-14 and drop a laser bomb right down his chimney! *shhhppkowwwwwww!!!!!!*

He thought he won the argument, but he didn't, but I made him put somebody else on the line, and I asked if they had any engineers, and they sent the guys who designed the special forklift we use to put people's life savings into the Scientology vault. And we had some placenta fajitas with fetus picadillo, and we got to work.

He was going to punish them. By making them watch Battlefield Earth.

Actually, they got to work, and I took off my pants and went sliding around on the wood floors in my socks! I wonder if we could turn all our highways into wood. Then we could *slide* to work with our pants off, singing "Cabaret."

For a while they complained that they couldn't make a car run on placenta, but then I reminded them that L. Ron was watching them from heaven, and He was making a list and checking it twice, and if they didn't make the car work, he was going to punish them. By making them watch *Battlefield Earth.*

Ha ha ha ha ha ha ha ha! I was kidding. That movie *sucked,* though, didn't it? Your movie *sucked,* Travolta! "Oooh, look, I'm a big blue alien, and I'm *Vinnie Barbarino!*" You *loser!* You looked like a giant Viagra.

Mr. "I'm so Cool." Mr. "I have a jet airliner in my backyard." Hey, *a—hole,* my F-14 could fly *Rings* around your little airliner. Your little . . . little *bus* with *wings.* "Oooh, look at me, I have a flying *bus!* Look, Kelly Preston, who isn't even that hot anymore, I'm Ralph *Kramden!*" Does your bus have missiles? Crap no it doesn't. It has a drink cart, that's all. See if the stewardess will give you an extra bag of peanuts while I shoot my Sidewinders up your fat junkie loser rear end!

By the way, your wife is old and mine's not.

The engineers finally realized they were letting L Ron down, and I guess they really, *really* didn't want to watch *Battlefield Earth,* because they made the car work. We got the car to run, after going through a whole bag of placentas I found in the gutter behind Planned Parenthood.

So I got behind the wheel, and I took it around the block, and then I pulled down my pants and ran around with my arms in the air, because I was so happy I had solved the world's energy problem.

I guess the engineers are out of Dutch. I told them that if they were bad engineers, when Christmas came, L. Ron wouldn't fly to their houses on His sleigh to put *War of the Worlds* DVDs in their stockings. I think that scared them.

Anyway, world, here is my present to you, world. The placenta-powered *Prius.* It smells when it runs, and it only goes nine miles an hour, and every twenty minutes you have to clean out the placenta combustion chamber with a coat hanger, but we have to make sacrifices if we want to beat our oil addiction. We're like Brooke Shields, people. And the Middle East is a big jug of Paxil.

I practice what I preach. I use my Placenta Prius all the time, unless I'm in a real hurry. Then I ride in my twenty-seat jet-powered stretch Hummer Maybach limo with the hot tub and pool table in the back.

Mainly I use the Prius to go to the end of the driveway so I can check my mail. Unless the engine stops. Then I make my servants carry me.

The engineers told me the Placenta Priuses would cost a lot. I asked how much, and they said probably eighty or ninety thousand dollars. I wanted a second opinion, so I called Dustin Hoffman. And he said, "About a hunnerd dollars." And he's really smart. If Brooke Shields dropped all her pills at once, before they hit the ground, he could count them.

Even if they cost ninety thousand dollars, no biggie, right? You just go to Japan and make a ten-second Hello Kitty! commercial. I made one where they made me wear a Hello Kitty! suit, without pants, and dance to a David Hasselhoff song. Hey, I don't care. As long as no one sees it over here.

Okay, I have to go now. Katie is having labor pains, and she just made a moaning noise, so I have to give her a lecture.

Don't tell Travolta. That fat slob. He hates me because I made Operating Thetan III before he did. They even let me stroke the Orbs of Truth.

Okay, I have to go now. Katie is having labor pains, and she just made a moaning noise, so I have to give her a lecture.

I wish I could invite you to the house after this is over. We're using amniotic fluid to make margaritas.

Oh, wait. I was supposed to give you Steve's fattening recipe for blueberry cheesecake. It looks pretty good, but I think it would be even better with a little placenta.

CRUST

2 ½ cups Keebler graham cracker crumbs
½ cup sugar
²/₃ cup butter, softened or melted

This is two times the regular old recipe on a graham cracker crumb box, except Steve uses butter instead of margarine. If you don't like a thick crust, adjust it until it makes you happy, just like I adjust the shims in my shoes until I'm as tall as my leading ladies. It will pack down while it cooks.

Mix the crumbs, sugar, and butter in a bowl. Make sure they're mixed thoroughly. Pretend the mixing spoon is Maverick's Tomcat jet in an inverted flat spin.

Spray the inside of a clean 10-inch springform pan with PAM. Dump the mixture in the pan and press it down into a level disk that covers the bottom. Freeze for 10 minutes so it will be stiff when you pour the batter on it. Like a placenta chilled for slicing into carpaccio.

CHEESECAKE

4 warm packages cream cheese (*not* Neufchatel)
8 ounces minced placenta (optional)
½ cup sour cream
½ stick butter from cows that have been E-Metered
4 eggs
1 teaspoon vanilla extract
½ teaspoon almond extract
3 tablespoons lemon juice

¼ teaspoon lemon zest, grated (optional)
1¾ cups sugar

Preheat the oven to 350°F, or have your personal assistant make someone do it. Make sure your cheese, sour cream, and butter are warm and soft. You can do this by putting them on the counter and having your assistant text you when they're ready. Put them in a bowl and use a mixer to break them up. Add eggs and beat them in. Add the remaining ingredients and beat until smooth. If necessary, use a spatula to remove lumps from the walls of the bowl so they can be beaten into the batter.

If you beat it too much, the top will crack when you bake it. But it will still be great. The topping will hide it.

When the batter is completely smooth, pour it on top of the Graham crust and level it. Place in the oven on a rack, with something on the next rack down to catch leaked batter. Now you have some time to go E-meter yourself and see if any body thetans flew into you while you were mixing the batter. Don't bend over when you open the oven door, because body thetans always go in that way. That's why I had the Scientology R&D guys make me briefs with a Kevlar crotch.

After 15 minutes, reduce the heat to 250°F. Cook for 90 minutes. Remove and chill until you're sure the cake is cold all the way through. Remove the springform pan and put the blueberry topping on top of the cake.

Cheesecake expands when you cook it. So you need to leave some headroom in the pan. At least a third of the pan's total height. I hate that word. "Height."

TOPPING
¾ cup sugar
3 tablespoons cornstarch

¼ cup water
4 cups blueberries
1 tablespoon lemon juice
Smidge of placenta

I warn you in advance, this is just enough stuff to cover the top of the cake. If you want to go full-throttle, increase the amounts of everything. Make your personal shopper take an extra trip to Ralph's.

Combine sugar, starch, water, and 2 cups of the blueberries in a saucepan. Mash berries while they cook. They should be broken but not pureed. Cook over medium heat until the berries are cooked completely and all the available juice is extracted.

Heat 1 cup of water in the microwave for 1½ minutes. Rest a large strainer on top of the pan. Using a large slotted spoon, gather all the solids in the mixture and put them in the strainer. Add a little of the heated water to the solids and mix so the water rinses out the remaining juice. Repeat until the water is gone. Remove the strainer and dump the solids, the way I dumped Mimi Rogers when she turned forty-four, I said, "It's okay that you're tall, but you can't also be old."

Place the mixture on the stove on medium-low heat and cook, stirring, until the rinse water evaporates. It should bubble a little, and the cornstarch should turn clear.

Remove the mixture from the stove. When you're ready to use it, stir in the lemon juice and add the remaining 2 cups of blueberries.

Now, here's the hard part. If you want to get through this, the spirit of L. Ron has to be with you. Chill it for an entire *day.* And chill the filling overnight, too, before you mix and apply it. Don't ask me why—maybe L. Ron knows—but overnight, the flavor multiplies by ten. The crust kind of bonds with the pan, but you can make your valet and your downstairs maid team up to get it loose. I guess you could hold a piece of string between your hands and pull it really tight and sort of saw the crust loose. I would ask the Scientology engineers, but they're at the Temple putting gold leaf on L. Ron's favorite truss.

If you don't care what your food looks like because you have to eat in a hurry and then get to the annual Scientology Jamboree in Clearwater, use a 2-quart Pyrex dish. Spray it with PAM first. Chill the cake thoroughly after you cook it. Then turn it upside-down on a platter and wait for the cake to drop out. Most of the time, it'll fall out in one nice piece.

One way to make sure it falls out is to coat the bottom of the Pyrex with a layer of caramelized sugar before you cook the cake. Just heat about half a cup of sugar and a couple of tablespoons of water on high until it turns dark brown, then pour it into the Pyrex and make sure the bottom is coated. Turn it upside-down and let the excess drip out.

Of course, that gives you caramel cheesecake. So the blueberries won't really work.

I know you will like this cheesecake. If you don't, you must be as crazy as Brooke Shields.

CHAPTER 30
CHEESE BAKLAVA

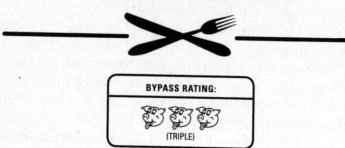

BYPASS RATING:

(TRIPLE)

DID YOU HEAR about the Greek bank robber? The cops identified him when the baklava fell off his face.

Well, I thought it was funny.

I don't know if baklava is a Greek dish. They sell it in Greek restaurants, but those places also sell cheeseburgers. They really do. It's not just a *Saturday Night Live* thing. Due to a currency ratio anomaly, a person who earns minimum wage in a diner can go home to Greece for nine months of the year, live in a castle, and own slaves. And any idiot can learn to flip a cheeseburger. So virtually every diner in the universe is run by Greeks.

I visited Greece on the way home from doing four months on a kibbutz. At that time, the beef supply in Israel was like the hairless female shin supply at Smith College. They had cows there, but they were dairy cattle. You only got to eat one if it was struck by lightning or stepped on a landmine. And dairy cattle are built like Elle MacPherson. All bones and udders. There's a thin layer of meat between the skin and bones, like a giant cow-shaped Steak-Um. It's as tough as a Kevlar vest but doesn't taste quite as good. But when I was there, a cheeseburger sold for around ninety-three dollars.

When I left Israel, I was ready for some meat. I dropped my luggage at the Thisseus youth hostel in Athens and hit the pavement running. Believe it or not, Athens turned out to be full of diners, just like the ones I knew from my college days in New York. Only it was possible to eat at these diners without having a bum come to the window by your table and stimulate himself at your food. I guess I don't have to tell you I lived in New York before Giuliani showed up.

I went into the first diner I saw and ordered two cheeseburgers and a side of fries. It cost something like three and a half cents. I'm not sure why I ever came home.

Athens was full of weird little dudes who stood on street corners saying hi to Americans. One day I decided to say hi back instead of diving for cover.

I told you, I used to live in New York.

The guy said his name was Bill. Probably short for "Billocrates" or something. And he practically pleaded with me to go see his bar. At that time, I had insane dreams about being a writer, and I was always on the lookout for adventure, so I let him take me there.

Right away I knew what this was. They were going to drug me and sell my kidneys to some jerkweed in Singapore.

This place was creepy. It was a converted storefront, with the windows totally blacked out. The air conditioning was set at the temperature where helium freezes. There was a big fat Greek Luca Brasi–looking guy at the bar and *no customers.*

Right away I knew what this was. They were going to drug me and sell my kidneys to some jerkweed in Singapore. But I ordered a Coke.

Bill ran and got a girl for me to talk to. I think she was on a shelf under the bar. "Nice American girl," he said. Exactly what I came to Greece for. The girl climbed on the stool next to me and started asking me the kind of questions you ask someone when you're trying to get him to stick around long enough to buy a time-share. And this girl was hot. Clingy knit dress. Cute little boobs with no sign of a bra. Dazzling smile. Something was wrong. Good-looking women don't just *talk* to me. I mean, sure, sometimes, if they're asking directions or I'm standing on their dogs' leashes. But other than that? No way.

I was polite and all that, but all the time I was sitting there, I kept thinking about how much I enjoyed relieving myself, and how much I would miss it if my kidneys were in Singapore, peeing for some stranger. I paid for my Coke and ran like hell.

Actually, I had her figured for a whore or a white slave. Whatever she was, she gave me the willies. Now, if they had put a fat whiny girl next to me and she had ignored me completely, I would have felt right at home.

I did say I went to college in New York, right?

Anyway, like I said, I'm not sure baklava is Greek. It's always on the menu at Arab joints. Maybe the quasi-Arab Turks forced the Greeks to eat it back when they ruled half the world. No, if that were true, the Greeks would make it and then stand in a circle spitting on it.

But I like baklava. It's loaded with flour and sugar and honey and butter. It's like eating a honey and butter sandwich. It's practically Elvis food. But I got to thinking about it the other day, and I realized I could make it far, far worse. What this stuff needed was a layer of cheesecake batter.

So I installed one. And I changed the walnuts to pecans,

because walnuts are bitter. And it was pretty glorious. Elvis would be proud. Baklava by itself is kind of monotonous, but the cheesecake makes it much more interesting and considerably more dangerous.

It's incredibly easy to make, and once you get the hang of it, you can put anything you want in it. Dried apricots. Raisins. Raisinets. Goobers. Sno-Caps. Jujubes.

I have to learn to go easy on the beer when I write.

2 sticks butter
2 packages cream cheese
3 eggs
1½ cups sugar
¼ teaspoon salt plus dash
½ teaspoon cinnamon, plus extra for sprinkling
½ pound phyllo sheets cut to 9-by-13
2 cups chopped pecans
Whole cloves
¾ cup honey
1 tablespoon lemon juice
½ cup water

Melt the butter in the microwave. Put the cream cheese in a bowl and let it soften. Add the eggs and ¼ cup of the sugar and the dash of salt and beat until smooth. Mix ½ cup of the sugar with half a teaspoon of the cinnamon. Preheat your oven to 350°F.

Butter the bottom of a 9-by-13 Pyrex baking dish. Place a sheet of phyllo in the dish. Butter it heavily with a pastry brush. Add another sheet and repeat the butter thing. Do this until you have 6 sheets in the dish. Spread half of the pecans on top of the top sheet. Sprinkle half of the sugar/cinnamon mixture over the pecans.

Put 6 more sheets of phyllo on top of the pecans, buttering in between.

Sprinkle the top sheet lightly with cinnamon. Pour the cheese batter onto the phyllo and spread it out. You may not need all of it; use your own judgment. Sprinkle the cheese batter lightly with cinnamon.

Put 6 sheets of phyllo on top of the cheese batter, just the way you did the first 6. Then add the rest of the nut mixture. Add the rest of the cinnamon/sugar mixture. Put 6 more sheets on top of the nuts, buttering as before.

This part is kind of tricky. Get a very sharp knife and cut the baklava into 2-inch squares. Phyllo does not slice easily, so it will try to bunch up. It's best to punch downward through the top of the baklava with the point of the knife, over and over, moving across the baklava until you have a continuous cut. And you can place a finger on the phyllo on either side of the knife to hold it apart and keep it from being displaced when the knife goes in.

Put one whole clove in the center of each square. Sprinkle the top of the baklava lightly with cinnamon. Bake for 40 minutes at 350°F. If needed, turn the heat up to 375 and bake until nicely browned. I'm afraid my oven blew up while I was trying to nail this down, so do your best.

You should have ¾ of a cup of sugar left. Put it in a saucepan with the honey (I recommend orange blossom honey), ¼ teaspoon salt, lemon juice, and water. Boil for about 20 minutes or until as thick as pancake syrup.

When the baklava comes out, pour all the syrup into it, covering it as evenly as you can. Let the baklava cool thoroughly before you eat it.

That's it. It's really good, and it's really easy. Come up with your own variations. This stuff has endless potential.

CHAPTER 31

RED LAGER AND ROOM-TEMPERATURE-BREWED ALE

BYPASS RATING:

(DOUBLE)

WOW, HOW a homebrewer's horizons recede.

When I started homebrewing, I spent maybe two hundred bucks on equipment, and over a hundred of that went on one item: the brew kettle. I figured that would hold me.

That was five years ago. Here is a partial list of the crap I have bought since then.

1. Two chest freezers with external controls to keep them at beer temperature
2. Two beer towers with two faucets each
3. Two CO_2 tanks for dispensing draft beer
4. Two CO_2 regulators
5. Two nitrogen tanks
6. One nitrogen regulator

7. Approximately one ton of tubing and beer plumbing parts
8. Eight Cornelius kegs
9. One Tap-A-Draft portable beer dispensing system
10. An extra temperature control for my spare fridge
11. A second carboy
12. One two-liter growler
13. A billion 12-ounce bottles—some *used*

Clearly, I have lost my mind and should be kept in an airline pet carrier and have my money managed by a committee.

The worst thing about it is that I've become unbelievably spoiled. There is almost no commercially produced beer I look forward to drinking, because even my worst beer is better than nearly anything I can find in a store. I don't *mind* choking down a Warsteiner or a bottle of Chimay, but when I do, I feel put upon.

You think I'm bragging. I am. But it's true. And if you learn to make beer, your beer will be better than store beer, too. Unless you're totally hopeless.

Let me present two of my favorite recipes.

I was going to start with stout. I get so tired of candyass losers who are afraid of it. "Ooh, Steve, it looks like motor oil. Ooh, Steve, it looks so strong. Ooh, Steve, hold me. I'm scared."

If that sounds like you, you need to make a quick visit to your urologist and have yourself inspected to make sure you're really male. You disgust me. It's just *beer*, you sack of progesterone. It's not going to leap out of the glass and give you a wedgie in front of the girls' gym class.

Look, it may surprise you to learn this, but most stout is pretty light. The color is dark, but it's not thick, gooey beer. And it's not always high in alcohol. Mine is, of course. Girly man. But Guinness isn't. As a matter of fact, Guinness is fairly low in calories. So don't worry; you'll still be able to fit in that little black dress.

Anyway, I was going to start with stout, but I decided to give you a couple of recipes of which I am somewhat prouder. I have five or six recipes I absolutely love, and it's killing me to do triage, but this book weighs like three pounds already, and my publisher doesn't want people to confuse me with Norman Mailer. Although I guess in order for that to happen, I'd have to publish immense boring books *and* get innocent people killed.

I'll give you the first recipe I came up with that really blew what passes for my mind. It's so good, I hate to drink it because I can't bear the thought of running out.

When I was in college, I used to love German amber beers with lots of caramel flavor. Like Altenmunster. But they're hard to find in Miami. I decided to try to make something similar, with all-American ingredients. I used 2-row to add color, and I used Bavarian lager yeast, but for a twist, I picked some fairly wicked American hops.

I missed the target completely. I was shooting for a caramel-tasting beer with spicy hops. What I got was a hundred percent better. This stuff has a citrusy aroma you can pick up from across the room. It's slightly sweet but very bitter (~45 IBU). The flavor is powerful *My beer is nothing like that. It's like nothing you're ever tasted. And it's 5.5 percent alcohol, which is nice.* and complex, but it's so smooth you can drink it all day. It was my first lager, and it's the best one I've made yet.

Don't get the wrong idea, if you've had reddish beers before and you didn't like them. Don't even mention Killian's. Near as I can tell, it's your basic Budmilcoors, with orange dye added. My beer is nothing like that. It's like nothing you've ever tasted. And it's 5.5 percent alcohol, which is nice.

9.5 pounds 2-row pale ale malt (Maris Otter is fine)
1.5 pounds Crystal malt 60L
1.25 pounds Munich malt
White Labs WLP830 German lager yeast
1 ounce Nugget hops (boil 60 minutes)
0.75 ounce Crystal hops (boil 45 minutes)
1½ teaspoons Irish moss
1.25 ounces Crystal hops (steep 10 minutes)

This is for 6 gallons. Mash at 130 for half an hour, with about 4½ gallons of water. Then crank it to 150 and hold it for an hour. Mash out at 168. I don't remember where those first two steps came from. I think I stole them from another recipe.

You're going to boil it for a total of 60 minutes. Start with 1 ounce of Nugget hops. Half an hour later, add a half ounce of the Crystal hops. Ten minutes before the end of the boil, add 1½ teaspoons of Irish moss. After the boil, steep 1.25 ounces of Crystal.

Ferment for one month at 50°F, and secondary for one week at 50°F. Now, that's if you want to be safe. In truth, this stuff may finish primary fermentation in a week.

The word "lager" is a verb. It means to store the beer while various nasty yeast by-products disappear. This improves the taste. But don't be misled. You can drink a lager as soon as you keg it. It may not be as good as it could be, but it will still beat the hell out of Bud.

You may want to do a diacetyl rest between the primary and secondary. That means you raise the temperature of the primary to 56°F for a day or two, so the yeast will eat whatever buttery-tasting diacetyl they've produced. But it's my understanding that the yeast I used isn't likely to produce a diacetyl flavor at 50°F. I had no problems with it. You may want to play it safe.

Store this stuff at 38°F and don't let a lot of people know you have it. Once they find out, you'll have to make it twice a month to keep up with demand.

I'll give you another recipe. You'll love me for this one, because you can brew it in your living room, at 75°F. Supposedly there is a chance you'll get heavier alcohols at that temperature, and they cause hangovers. I haven't had a problem with that, but then I don't drink ten beers at a sitting, either. You can always drop down to 68°F. The great thing about brewing at room temperature is that it's easy for guys whose wives refuse to let them buy fermenting fridges.

As before, I'll give you the amounts for 6 gallons; that gives you some extra beer you can afford to lose if you screw something up.

9.0 pounds Maris Otter or other 2-row ale malt
1.0 pounds 10L Crystal malt
1.25 ounces Columbus hops, first-wort or at beginning of
**   60-minute boil**
1.0 ounce Crystal hops, 15 minutes before end of boil
1.0 ounce Crystal hops, after boil (steep 10 minutes)
0.25 pounds cane sugar
White Labs WLP500 Trappist ale yeast
Irish moss

This beer is ridiculous. I wanted to make something sort of like Flying Dog Snake Dog Ale, but I ended up with something I like a lot better. It's a little heavier (shoot for 1.056–1.060 original gravity), and it's complex as hell. Slightly sweet from the Crystal, but loaded with hop bitterness and aroma. Try it. Just try it. I suggest you use oxygen and a big yeast starter and mash at 152, because this beer likes to get stuck at 1.020. Be careful, though, because the oxygen may make it ferment so fast it blows out on the floor.

The sugar is there purely to increase the alcohol content. Remove it if you want.

If you think it's too sweet, cut the Crystal malt in half next time.

I adore this beer. The Crystal malt makes the high bitterness (~60 IBU) completely painless. It goes great with big deli sandwiches. Or cigars. Or nothing.

I truly believe you will enjoy these beers. And remember, the point is not to get drunk. The point is to savor the complexities and nuances.

If you *do* happen to get drunk . . . well. That's just the price you have to pay.

CHAPTER 32

FIVE GREASY PIECES

IT HAS BEEN SUGGESTED to me that in addition to creating real recipes for actual food, I might also want to add a few items for frat boys, men over the age of sixty, women under the age of forty, and other people who make up the sad segment of the population known as the Cooking Impaired.

Fine. Why not? Not everyone has the finely tuned motor skills required to open a can or flip an egg. Might as well throw in a few quick recipes for the TV dinner crowd.

Let me admit I was never a frat boy. My lengthy college career started at Columbia University, a wimpy Northeastern school where belonging to a frat was about as cool as having your mom drive you to class. But that didn't keep me from being a drunken pig with the social skills of an Abu Ghraib guard.

Any party where the beer was free and there were more than three women (who weren't dancing with each other and wearing overalls) was considered exceptional.

My friends and I threw the best dorm parties that fine institution had to offer. That isn't saying much. Any party where the beer was free and there were more than three women (who weren't dancing with each other and wearing overalls) was considered exceptional. But we did okay. We usually had four kegs of imported beer, plus all sorts of booze and a table buried in fattening snacks. And while the women were nothing to write home about, and they whined a lot about Oxfam and Amnesty International and other crap in which we had zero interest, we did manage to convince them to come.

The most depraved party we ever threw involved several cases of booze we stole from the dean's office. There was a bartending class on campus, and I found out where the educational materials were kept. My friends and I cleaned them out, went to the liquor store, and exchanged the whole load for vodka. Then we filled a fourteen-gallon Civil Defense can (don't ask) with fruit punch and poured the vodka in. And we had a toga party.

We were not frat boys, but we were still awfully gross. At the end of the night, I saw my friend Greg relieving himself in the direction of a window. And I said, "Greg, that window is closed." And he said, *"I know."*

Anyway, I can tell you about a few quick, easy things you can fix that are good, but not great. The appeal of these recipes is the speed. So don't go waving my book around to your effete foodie pals, saying, "Look what this guy thinks is good food." This is desperation food, for people living at the ragged edge of sanity.

I may as well start with something from college. It isn't my recipe. My buddy Dave taught it to me. I shared an apartment with four guys, and we took turns cooking, and one of the things we liked best was Dave's WASP chicken.

"The WASP" was our name for Dave, who was a Brooks-Brothers-wearing preppy from Delaware. Dave was not known for his cooking skills, but somewhere he found himself a recipe that made us happy, and I guess we had it once a week. Here goes.

2 eggs
Salt and pepper, to taste
2 pounds boneless chicken breast cut in small chunks
Corn oil for frying
Four Seasons bread crumbs with Italian seasoning
Italian dressing

This is going to sound really stupid, but try it. Beat the eggs. Salt and pepper the chicken. Let the chicken sit a bit to absorb the salt.

Heat half an inch of corn oil in a big skillet. Shoot for 350°F. Dip the chicken bits in the egg, roll them in the crumbs, and fry, turning once. Get them reasonably brown, and drain them over paper towels.

Here is the weird part. Serve with Italian dressing. I am completely serious. You pile these on your plate and squirt them with dressing and eat them. I know how crazy that sounds. But they're good.

Dave also served Stove Top stuffing on the side, which he referred to as "Stove Plop." I think you just mix it with hot water. Check the package. And don't knock it until you've tried it. Real stuffing takes work. Don't turn up your nose at easy stuffing that is merely not too bad.

If you want a relatively tasty meal you can fix in half an hour, this will do the trick. But if you tell anyone you heard about it from me, I will have no choice but to kill you.

Moving on from my college days, here is a shameful recipe that tastes better than it has any right to. I have probably eaten this a thousand times in my life, five hundred of them *after* I knew how to cook real food.

½ stick butter
½ pound dry pasta, like spaghetti
Salt
Garlic or garlic powder
Parmesan cheese

Cut the butter in slices. Cook the pasta according to the directions on the package, and be sure to put plenty of salt in the water. Drain it but do *not* rinse it. I have never understood why people rinse pasta. Throw the butter in the pot, dump the pasta on top, add garlic to taste, and mix it up so it doesn't clump. Now add as much grated cheese as you can get it to absorb.

An odd thing about this recipe is that garlic powder and cruddy canned cheese seem to work better than real ingredients.

It's somewhat gross, but you'll like it. I know how you are. You'll end up with buttery pasta gummed up with cheese. It sticks to a fork like you wouldn't believe, making it easy to eat in a rapid and efficient fashion. What could be easier?

I still eat that sometimes. I'm so ashamed.

Here's kind of a stupid one. It may sound obvious, but it isn't. It's very simple, but people ruin simple food every day. If you do it my way, you are guaranteed to get a fantastic result. It's a recipe for cheeseburgers.

½ pound hamburger or ground chuck
Salt
Pepper
Garlic or garlic powder

I assume you have cheese and some sort of bun and can figure out how to work them. I like the big Pepperidge Farm "sandwich" buns with sesame seeds. Their hamburger buns are tiny, but the ones labeled "sandwich" are actually big enough to use without having doubts about your sexuality.

You need a grill. I use gas, but charcoal will obviously work. Get it very hot before you put the meat on. If you fry it, don't use a stainless skillet. For some reason it never tastes right. Cast iron is best, but even Teflon is better than bare stainless.

Dump the burger on a plate. Salt it down pretty heavily. Hit it with the pepper and garlic. Fresh garlic is considerably better in burgers, but garlic powder is fine. Now, mix it all in and form a patty around ½-inch thick.

I realize this is not the kind of exciting information you expect to receive when you pay good cash for a cookbook, but it's more important than you would think. Try it before you start to bitch. Mixing the seasoning into a burger instead of sprinkling it on the outside makes a world of difference. This is why preformed meat patties are worthless.

On a really hot grill, you'll give this about 4 minutes on a side. Less, if you want it pink inside. Toast the inside of the bun while you're at it. I give them about 45 seconds. Then I turn them and let the heat get to the outside, too. Apply cheese and whatever else, and you're all set. Butter the bun, if you're man enough.

If you want to get weirder without really learning to cook, check the side of a package of dried onion soup. There will probably be a recipe for burgers using the mix as seasoning. If not, it's real complicated. Summon your mental powers and see if you can handle it. Here goes: mix dry soup into burger and cook. Just try to get the proportions right.

Have you ever gotten a wild hair on a Sunday afternoon and made a sudden decision to have homemade cookies? But you knew you were too stupid to make them? Let me help you out with that.

Cookies are ridiculously easy to make. No one seems to realize that. Not even lonely chicks with big fat butts and sweatpants who eat cookie dough with their fingers four nights a week. Let me show you. Just try it, for God's sake. If if doesn't work, you can still eat the dough.

> **½ stick butter**
> **1 cup light brown sugar, packed tightly**
> **1 egg**
> **1 teaspoon vanilla extract**
> **½ teaspoon baking soda**
> **½ teaspoon salt**
> **½ teaspoon baking powder**
> **Pinch ground nutmeg (less than ½ teaspoon)**
> **1 cup all-purpose flour**
> **1 ¼ cups old-fashioned (not "quick") oats**
> **½ cup golden raisins (brown ones are okay)**

It's so simple. Preheat the oven to 350°F. Whew, that was hard. You poor thing. Now get out a cookie sheet. I like the hollow ones that don't burn the cookies. Spray it with PAM or something similar.

Soften or melt the butter. Mix everything but the flour, oats, and raisins thoroughly with a fork. You don't even need a mixer. I swear. Dump in the remaining ingredients and mix well.

If that's too hard for you, you need to be fed with a tube. That's the whole job. Can you handle that, or should we hire a team of monkeys to squeeze your belly and help you breathe?

Plop a generous tablespoon of dough onto the cookie sheet. Plop another one 2 inches away. Keep going until you cover the sheet. Bake the cookies for around 12 minutes. Oh, the toil. How will you survive?

You can scrape these off the hot sheet with a greased metal spatula and drop them on a sheet of foil. That will cool them in a hurry and clear the sheet so you can bake the rest of the dough.

That's all. You dirtied one bowl and maybe a Pyrex cup, plus a spatula, a fork, and a cookie sheet. And now you have a pile of really excellent hot cookies. Surely that was worth it.

Add other ingredients if you want. You can use almonds or pecans or chocolate chips. Take out the nutmeg if necessary. If you hate oatmeal, make it up with flour. Just add enough to get a good dough-like consistency.

I know you think you can just buy a roll of dough and cook it. Don't do it, my friend. That stuff has no butter in it, and it tastes fishy and stale. If you make my recipe beside that garbage, you will throw the commercial stuff in the yard and beg the Lord and the ghost of James Beard to forgive you for cooking it.

If you liked the gummy pasta, and I know you did, you will enjoy the following treat, the preparation of which requires the mental acuity of a goose. Bacon-grease popcorn. I learned this from my aunt Jean, who was an excellent cook and not one bit scared of pork fat.

8 tablespoons bacon grease
½ cup popcorn
Salt
Cheese

If you already know how to make popcorn, swell. Do it. If not, put a medium-size or bigger saucepan on medium heat with the grease. Make sure you have a lid. When the grease is hot, toss in the popcorn. You can do yourself a big favor by buying expensive white popcorn, like White Cat Corn, but Orville Redenbacher's is edible.

When the corn starts popping, put the lid on, and leave it slightly ajar to let steam out. I've always wanted to drill a few holes in a pot lid and use the pot exclusively for popcorn, but I'm too lazy. Shake the pan once in a while, and when the corn slows down to where you can count three between pops, empty it into a big bowl. Salt it. If you're hardcore, buy salt flour, which is salt ground into a dust that won't bounce off popcorn. Maybe you can make it yourself in a coffee grinder.

Unfortunately, the cheese has a way of falling off the popcorn and into your couch cushions. Deal with it.

Now, here is the fun part. Dump grated cheese on it. You can use canned Parmesan, which is fine. Or you can grate really sharp cheddar onto it. You don't have to mix it in much; it will cascade down into the corn as you eat.

If you look around on the web, you can actually buy powdered cheese. This stuff is dry and fine and really coats the corn. You can put the corn in a paper bag with it and shake and get it spread out really well. Whatever turns you on.

This will be exponentially better than lameass cheese-free popcorn cooked in fishy-tasting vegetable oil. Unfortunately, the cheese has a way of falling off the popcorn and into your couch cushions. Deal with it.

Bacon grease *generally* goes well with corn. You can put it in the foil with ears of corn when you roast them. Or if you're ever forced to eat canned corn, you can stir a tablespoon of grease into it before you heat it.

Okay, losers. That's five things you can throw together in a hurry to keep you from dying. If stoves and spoons and spatulas scare you, start with this chapter and then try to secrete a little testosterone and move on to the harder recipes.

In the meantime, try to learn the difference between a dorm window and a urinal.

CONCLUSION

That about covers it. I hope you enjoyed it, and that the food does not kill you, and that you were not offended badly enough to file a lawsuit. Thanks for reading my book.

If you took even one word of what I wrote seriously and you want to send me an e-mail telling me how much you hate me, feel free. You can find me at www.stevehgraham.com. Just remember, I may use your delusional rant in my next book, and for every nasty e-mail I receive, I plan to eat one serving of factory veal while wearing my favorite harp seal diaper.

INDEX